A Dartmouth Reader

A Dartmouth Reader

Edited by Francis Brown

HANOVER · NEW HAMPSHIRE
Dartmouth Publications 1969

Grateful acknowledgment is made of contributions from *An Astronomer's Life* by Edwin C. Frost © 1933. By permission of Houghton Mifflin Company; from *Penn State Yankee* by Fred Lewis Pattee through the courtesy of the Penn State Collection, Pattee Library, The Pennsylvania State University, University Park, Pa.; from *Such Is Life* by William W. Grant, permission by William W. Grant Jr.; "A Hero's Uniform" by John R. Scotford Jr. First published as a "Yesterday" in *Sports Illustrated*, November 14, 1966, under the title "The Dream Book—Spalding 1966 Edition" Copyright © 1966 Time Inc.; from *Fresh Waters* by Edward Weeks © 1968; "The End of the Quest" is reprinted with the permission of Charles Scribner's Sons from *My Quest for Freedom*, pages 215-259, by John Moffatt Mecklin. Copyright 1945 John Moffatt Mecklin; from *The Wayward Pressman* © 1945, 1946, 1947 by A. J. Liebling. Reprinted by permission of the Author's Estate and its agent, James Brown Associates, Inc.; from *No Lamb for Slaughter* © 1963 by Edward Lamb; Foreword by Budd Schulberg. From *The Golden Book on Writing* by David Lambuth Copyright © 1964 by The Viking Press, Inc. All rights reserved. Reprinted by permission of The Viking Press, Inc.; "Lew Stilwell." Copyright © 1969 by Richard Barber; "Hopkins of Dartmouth" by Stearns Morse. Reprinted from *The American Scholar*, Volume 36, Number 1, Winter, 1966-1967. Copyright © 1966 by the United Chapters of Phi Beta Kappa. By permission of the publisher; from *Return to Cassino* © 1964 by Harold L. Bond; from *No Place to Hide* © 1948 by David Bradley; "How We Climbed Everest" by Barry C. Bishop. Copyright © 1963 by the *National Geographic Society*; from *Mission in Torment* © 1965 by John Martin Mecklin; from *The Plastic Age*, copyright 1924 by Percy Marks. Copyright renewed 1957. By permission of the Century Co., affiliate of Meredith Press; from *The Professor's Wife* by Bravig Imbs. Copyright 1928 by the Dial Press; from *The Dartmouth Murders* by Clifford B. Orr. All rights reserved. Reprinted by permission of Holt, Rinehart and Winston, Inc.; from *The Disenchanted*. Copyright 1950 by Budd Schulberg; from *Complete Poems of Robert Frost*. Copyright 1916, 1923, 1930, 1939 by Holt, Rinehart and Winston, Inc. Copyright 1936, 1942, 1944, 1951, © 1958 by Robert Frost. Copyright © 1964, 1967, 1970 by Lesley Frost Ballantine. Reprinted by permission of Holt, Rinehart and Winston, Inc.; and from the *Dartmouth Alumni Magazine*.

COPYRIGHT © 1969 BY TRUSTEES OF DARTMOUTH COLLEGE
LIBRARY OF CONGRESS CATALOG CARD NO. 79-108876

CONTENTS

FOREWORD 9

IN THE BEGINNING

Founding the College, ELEAZAR WHEELOCK 15
A Letter From John Ledyard 25
Commencement, 1774, JEREMY BELKNAP 27
A Student in the Wilderness, JOSEPH VAILL 33
On the Demolition of Dartmouth College, PHILIP FRENEAU .. 40

ON THE CAMPUS

Outrage and Riot, AMOS KENDALL 45
A Cycle of Webster Letters 50
The Coming of the Civil War, EDWARD TUCK 54
In President Bartlett's Time, EDWIN B. FROST 63
Country Schoolmaster, FRED LEWIS PATTEE 69
No Room at the Inn, WILLIAM W. GRANT 74
As the Century Turned, DOUGLAS VANDERHOOF 82
A Return to Hanover, BEN AMES WILLIAMS 94
The Diary of a Freshman, DEXTER MARTIN 102
The Camel, EDWARD M. HOLMES 106
You Can't Go Back Again—
But in a Way You Can, WILLIAM ROTCH 110

VISITORS

An Anti-Slavery Apostle, PARKER PILLSBURY   115
Choate's Eulogy of Webster, HENRY J. RAYMOND   121
Wendell Phillips' Visit to Hanover, SAMUEL R. BOND   132
As a Strong Bird on Pinions Free, WALT WHITMAN   137
A Letter to Pete Doyle, WALT WHITMAN   141

EXTRA-CURRICULAR

Wearers of the Green, WILLIAM BYRON FORBUSH   145
The First (and Only) College Balloon Race, JOHN PEARSON   152
Cattle Boat, CHARLES HAYWOOD   158
A Hero's Uniform, JOHN R. SCOTFORD, JR.   173
The Presidents in the Grant, EDWARD WEEKS   180

TRIBUTES

The End of the Quest, JOHN MOFFATT MECKLIN   189
John Moffatt Mecklin, A. J. LIEBLING   200
Campus Liberal, EDWARD LAMB   206
David Lambuth, BUDD SCHULBERG   212
Lew Stilwell, RICHARD BARBER   215
Hopkins of Dartmouth, STEARNS MORSE   219

ROUND THE GIRDLED EARTH

The Death of Captain Cook, JOHN LEDYARD   233
Desert March, WILLIAM EATON   240
In Flanders Fields, ALEXANDER J. M. TUCK   251
The Liberation of Rome, HAROLD L. BOND   258

Able Day, DAVID BRADLEY 266
How We Climbed Everest, BARRY C. BISHOP 273
Vietnam, JOHN MARTIN MECKLIN 281

THE VOICE OF A NATIVE

North of Boston, PARKER MERROW 289

SOME FICTION

The Plastic Age, PERCY MARKS 299
The Professor's Wife, BRAVIG IMBS 306
The Dartmouth Murders, CLIFFORD B. ORR 313
The Disenchanted, BUDD SCHULBERG 321

COMMENCEMENT 1955

A Graduation Address, ROBERT FROST 329

FOREWORD

THE VARIETIES of the Dartmouth experience have been so rich that no book can do more than suggest the richness and variety accumulated in the two centuries of the College. *A Dartmouth Reader* does just that, drawing upon the materials of history, and most frequently personal history, for the episodes and adventures that have been a part of the Dartmouth story and that of Dartmouth men since Eleazar Wheelock went into the wilderness.

A reader is for reading, and that is the purpose of *A Dartmouth Reader*. It can be opened at random. It can be savored in bits and pieces, and perhaps it is better that way. Chronological order, though followed in the sub-divisions as a matter of convenience, has not the significance that belongs to formal history and the sub-divisions themselves serve only as framework. In the *Reader* are blended the light and the serious, the enlightening and the entertaining, and though the old nostalgia blooms, it does not, I hope, overwhelm.

Many hands were involved in the making of this book after Richard Morin, then the College Librarian and chairman of the College's Bicentennial Publications Committee, persuaded me during a New York luncheon that the undertaking was worth while. His interest and effort on its behalf were untiring. Edward Connery Lathem, now the Librarian of Dartmouth and a good friend, placed the facilities of the College Libraries at my disposal, made suggestions, supplied often needed encouragement. Moreover, his many contributions to the *Alumni Magazine* and elsewhere of obscure chapters of Dartmouth were tailor-made for the kind of book that began to take shape. I would have missed Philip Freneau's poem, for example, had not Edward Lathem been there before, and I have lifted bodily such *Alumni*

Magazine entries of his as Edward Webster's letters and those of Edward Tuck. Kenneth C. Cramer, the College Archivist, and Miss Jane Martin, Assistant to the Librarian, helped me. So did many another with ideas and clues and presentations.

I have a particular obligation to Professor-Emeritus Stearns Morse and his wife, Helen, who did the greater part of the research for the *Reader*, seeking out likely material in the many volumes of the *Alumni Magazine*, ransacking files of undergraduate publications long forgotten, running down books by and about Dartmouth men and about the College. Their ingathering was wise and catholic—and invaluable.

The time came, of course, when I had to fish or cut bait. I had a mass of material, and some of it from my own research, and I felt like the old preacher who, in announcing the hymn, said let's sing all twelve verses, they're all too good to omit any one. But twelve verses are too many, and I know that a principal hazard of research is unwillingness to discard facts and figures and episodes that interest, but have small pertinence to the business at hand. There is also an ever-present danger in the lure of byways that, however attractive, lead nowhere.

I kept returning, for instance, to the fascinating *Sketches of the Alumni of Dartmouth College* by George T. Chapman 1804, published in 1867. Often the sketches contain amusing anecdotes and revealing characterizations, and the facts of these Dartmouth lives are almost a social history of the time. Did not some of all this belong in the *Reader*? Was there not some way that I could work in a mention of Samuel Taggart 1774, who, Chapman said, was "absent-minded and eccentrick, caught flies in prayers at the College Chapel, and being reproved for inattention, vindicated himself by repeating all that had been said in the devotion"? He became a minister of the Gospel and a member of Congress where he tangled with the acid-tongued John Randolph.

What could be done about John Humphrey Noyes 1830, founder of the Oneida Community? Chapman seems to have had mixed feelings about Noyes, describing him as having "become a Perfectionist and Communist pronouncing marriage a fraud. With these ultraisms, he founded a new sect at Oneida Creek 4 miles south of Oneida depot, N.Y. . . . The situation is said to be very beautiful and the estate, 600 acres in extent, is admirably cultivated, having a population of 200."

Chapman lists 3550 graduates from 1771 to 1867, among whom were 15 Senators, 61 Representatives, 14 Governors, 25 Presidents of Colleges. Was there no place for any of them: Philander Chase 1796, Bishop of Ohio and founder of Kenyon College (he reminded Chapman of the founder of Dartmouth); Thaddeus Stevens 1814, a principal architect of Reconstruction; or Salmon P. Chase 1826, Lincoln's Secretary of the Treasury and Chief Justice of the United States? And what about James W. Grimes 1836, Governor of Iowa, United States Senator, who ruined himself and his career by casting the deciding vote against the impeachment of Andrew Johnson?

And could there not be a corner for such an anecdote as that pertaining to General William T. Sherman, who having been caught in a deluge at the Centennial Commencement of 1869 and having had to listen to interminable speeches, is supposed to have remarked that war is hell but there is no hell like a Dartmouth Commencement?

Eventually the answer in every instance had to be a reluctant no. These men just did not fit the emerging pattern of the *Reader*; they belonged in another book as did a distressing amount of the research. It was not easy to rule for the story of one man against that of another. It was not easy to select one episode instead of another, to decide what was relevant for a broad, on-going collection that would illuminate the Dartmouth experience. If the decisions had not been made there would have been no book.

I have learned a lot of Dartmouth history in the editing of the *Reader* and I have come to know many a long-gone Dartmouth man I would otherwise not have known. There has been a sense of living with the Dartmouth generations. I hope that this book will give those who come to it some of the pleasure that its making has given me.

FRANCIS BROWN 1925

Again among the hills!
   The shaggy hills!
The clear arousing air comes like a call
Of bugle notes across the pines, and thrills
My heart as if a hero had just spoken.
Again among the hills!
The jubilant unbroken
Long dreaming of the hills!
Far off, Ascutney smiles as one at peace;
And over all
The golden sunlight pours, and fills
The hollow of the earth, like a God's joy.
Again among the hills!
The tranquil hills
That took me as a boy
And filled my spirit with the silences!

O indolent, far-reaching hills, that lie
Secure in your own strength, and take your ease
Like careless giants 'neath the summer sky—
What is it to you, O hills,
That anxious men should take thought for the morrow?
What has your might to do with thought or sorrow
Or cark and cumber of conflicting wills?
Lone Pine, that thron'st thyself upon the height,
Aloof and kingly, overlooking all,
Yet uncompanioned, with the Day and Night
For pageant and the winds for festival!
I was thy minion once, and now renew
Mine ancient fealty—
To that which shaped me still remaining true,
And through allegiance only growing free.

So with no foreign nor oblivious heart,
Dartmouth, I seek once more thy granite seat; . . .

                —from "Comrades"
                Richard Hovey 1885

IN THE BEGINNING

Founding the College
ELEAZAR WHEELOCK

≫ To promote his Indian Charity School at Lebanon, Connecticut, Eleazar Wheelock published in March 1763, a pamphlet, *A plain and faithfull Narrative*, in which he told of the school, its purpose and progress and need for support. There were nine of these *Narratives*, from 1763 to 1775, and it is from the last three of these that the following excerpts are taken. In them Wheelock wrote not only a personal history of the early Dartmouth, which grew out of the Charity School, but revealed his skill as a shaper of appeals for funds.

FROM THE NARRATIVE OF 1771

MY NEXT OBJECT was now to obtain such an incorporation as would effectually secure the generous donations made to this school, to the only use and design of them, and as would also be reputable for youth who may receive an education here, with a view to their public service in the churches of Christ, and accordingly I imployed a proper agent to solicit his Excellency *Governor* [John] *Wentworth*, whom God has raised up to serve the interests of the great Redeemer in his province [of New Hampshire]; and who appears to be unwearied in doing good, and by him have obtained a generous charter, by the name of DARTMOUTH COLLEGE, endowed with all the powers, and privileges of a university ... though the school itself remains under the same jurisdiction and patronage as before.

But as neither the honorable trust in England, nor the charter had fixed upon the particular town or spot [in New Hampshire] on which the buildings should be erected.

Wherefore to compleat the matter as soon as the ways, and streams would allow, I took the Rev. Mr. Pomeroy [his brother-in-law] and Esq; Gilbert, (a gentleman of known ability for such a purpose,) with me to examine thoroughly, and compare the several places proposed within the limits prescribed, for fifty or sixty miles on, or near said

[Connecticut] river; and to hear all the reasons, and arguments that could be offered in favour of each of them, in which service we faithfully spent eight weeks. And in consequence of our report, and representation of facts, the trustees unanimously agreed that the south-westerly corner of Hanover, adjoining upon Lebanon [N.H.,] was the place above any other to fix it in; and that for many reasons, viz. 'Tis most central on the river—and most convenient for transportation up and down the river—as near as any to the Indians—convenient communication with Crown-Point on Lake Champlain—and with Canada, being less than sixty miles to the former, and one hundred and forty to the latter, and water carriage to each, excepting about thirty miles, (as they say) and will be on the road which must soon be opened from Portsmouth to Crown-Point—and within a mile of the only convenient place for a bridge across said river. The situation is on a beautiful plain, the soil fertile and easy of cultivation. The tract on which the college is fixed, lying mostly in one body, and convenient for improvement, in the towns of Hanover and Lebanon, contains upwards of three thousand acres.

After I had finished this tour, and made a short stay at home [Lebanon, Conn.] to settle some affairs; I returned again to the wilderness to make provision for the removal and settlement of my family and school there before winter. I arrived in August, and found matters in such a situation as at once convinced me of the necessity of being myself upon the spot. And as there was no house conveniently near, I made a hutt of loggs about eighteen feet square, without stone, brick, glass or nail, and with 30, 40, and sometimes 50 labourers, appointed to their respective departments, I betook myself to a campaign. I set some to digging a well, and others to build a house for myself and family, of 40 by 32 feet, and one story high, and others to build a house for my students of 80 by 32, and two stories high. They had so near finished my house, that by advice of principal workmen, I sent for my family and students, but when they had dug one well of 63 feet, and another of 40, and found no prospect of water, and I had found it therefore necessary to remove the buildings, I sent to stop my family, and try'd for water in six several places, between 40 and 70 rods, and found supply for both buildings—I took my house down and removed it about 70 rods. The message I sent to my family proved not seasonable to prevent their setting out—they arrived with near thirty students. I housed my stuff, with my wife, and the females of my family in my hutt—my sons and students made booths & beds of hemlock boughs, and in this situation we continued about a month, till the 29th day of October, when I removed with my family into my house. And though the season had been cold, with storms of rain and snow—two saw-mills failed, on which I had chief dependance for boards, &c. and a series of other trying disappointments, yet by the pure mercy of God, the scene changed for the better in every respect—the weather uncommonly favourable—new resources for the supply of boards, &c. till my house was made warm, and comfortable—a school-house built, and so many rooms in the college made quite comfortable, as were sufficient for the students which were with me; in which they find the pleasure, and profit of such a solitude; and since the settlement of the affair all, without exception, are sufficiently ingaged in their studies.

But that which crowns all, is, the manifest tokens of the gracious presence of God by a spirit of conviction and consolation. For no sooner were these outward troubles removed, but there were evident impressions upon the minds of my family and school, which soon became universal, insomuch that scarcely one remained who did not feel a greater or less degree of it, till the whole lump seemed to be leavened by it, and love, peace, joy, satisfaction and contentment reigned through the whole.

The 23d day of January was kept as a day of solemn fasting and prayer, on which I gathered a church in this college, and school, which consisted of twenty-seven members, and three added since; on which occasion they solemnly renewed their oath of allegiance to Christ, and intire devotedness of body and soul, and all endowments of both, without reserve to God, for time and eternity.—And a solemn and joyful day it was, for they rejoyced, (many of them at least) at the oath, as having sworn with the whole heart. The Lord make us steadfast in his covenant, and enable us by his grace, on which alone we depend, to perform unto him our vows, and never more suffer among us an evil heart of unbelief in departing from God, nor any root of bitterness, resulting from it, to spring up in this seminary....

FROM THE NARRATIVE OF 1773

A LITTLE MORE than three Years ago, there was nothing to be seen here but a horrid Wilderness, now there are eleven comfortable Dwelling-Houses (besides the large one I built for my Students, and other necessary Buildings, as Barns, Malt House, Brew-House, Shops, &c.) and some of them reputable ones, built by Tradesmen, and such as have settled in some Connection with, and have been admitted for the Benefit of this School, and the most of them near finished, and all expect to be habitable and comfortable before Winter, and all within Sixty Rods of the College—By this Means the Necessities of this School have been relieved in Part as to Room for my Students—Yet the present Necessity of another and larger Building appears to be such, that the growth of this Seminary must necessarily be stinted without it. This Necessity I have represented to my honored Patrons in England, and doubt not they will recommend the charitable Design as they shall think adviseable. I also recommended it to the honorable Corporation of this College at their Meeting last May; in consequence of which they applied to the honorable General Assembly of this Province (who were then sitting) for their Encouragement and Assistance; who generously granted £500 Lawful Money out of the Province Treasury to begin with. Whereupon the Trustees taking into their Consideration, how graciously God had opened the Hearts of his People on both Sides the Water, to contribute so liberally to support and build up this Institution, and that through his Blessing their reasonable Expectations have been so fully answered in the Progress and Success of it hitherto, as that none have Occasion to regret their Expence, or indulge the least uneasy Reflection on Account of their past Liberality towards it; but on the other Hand the Prospect of the extensive Utility of it, to the great and pious Ends proposed by the Benefactors, is so fair and promising, as may justly inspire a Confidence that God will not forsake it, but on the other Hand, will yet open the Hearts of such as he has honored with Ability to contribute Supplies for this Necessity also. Whereupon they unanimously came to the Conclusion that, suspending all other Methods, it be first attempted by a Subscription.

I am not yet able very precisely to say what the Cost of the Building will be, as it is not yet fully determined with what Materials to build, whether with Brick, or Stone.

We have discovered a considerable Body of good Stone at the Distance of about three quarters of a Mile from the Spot proposed for the Building; and some who have examined it judge there will be Stone enough to compleat it; how that will prove we can better judge when we have got enough for the Cellar and Rustick, or Ground Story; and all acquainted with Buildings of this Nature may judge for themselves of the Expence of it, I suppose none will esteem it to be a very little Thing; and likely the judicious will think, when they consider the Nature, Use, and Design of the Building, that it is not injudicious to prefer Stone to any Thing else, if good Stone may be conveniently had. It is proposed to finish it in the most plain, decent, and cheapest Manner, after the dorick Order, and all may be assured that it shall be performed with all the Prudence, Care, Fidelity, and good Oeconomy which I am Master of. The Public may expect a faithful Account of Expences as often as shall be reasonable, and of the whole when it is finished.

By what I have thus imperfectly represented it is easy to see what is now my Object, viz. to begin and finish this large Building, compleat what I have began in putting a suitable Part of these Lands under proper Cultivation, and the sooner this be done the sooner will the School have the Comfort and Benefit proposed by them.

Another Barn will likely soon be Necessary, as also a House, and Accomodations for a Dairy, &c. and though the Expences to accomplish these Things must necessarily be great, yet the Fund thereby laid will be lasting, and I hope sufficient to support a large Number of Indians, and pious Youth who shall devote themselves to the Service of the Redeemer with their whole Hearts, in a pleasing Succession to the latest Generations. And also by what I have said I trust Gentlemen of Consideration and Penetration will see that now is the Time if ever for the Friends of this Institution to lend a helping Hand, and especially as I believe none will think it prudent to abate our endeavours for the Pagans, our first and great Object, on Account of these extraordinary Expences which are subordinate to that End. Would not such Abatement of our immediate Endeavours with them at least endanger the Reputation of the Cause, give the Enemy an Advantage to put greater Embarrassments in our Way, and render the Success of future Endeavors more improbable? But I think this Objection of the Greatness of our present Expences can have no Force in it, since they are only for that which is on all Hands allowed to be Expedient and Necessary, and especially if we consider that by the execution of the Plan proposed, those Expences will likely soon be amply refunded. As for Instance, Twenty Shillings will clear, stock and fence an Acre of Land, and that Acre, when thus put under Improvement, will be worth Twenty Shillings per Annum. I dont mean that all these Lands can be put under Improvement so Cheap, or that all will be so profitable when they are brought under Cultivation, but that this is the Case with a considerable Part of these Lands, and I don't say this at Random, or by Guess, for it is found to be so in Instances not a few in these Parts, and I hope will be confirmed by my own Experience, so that the School will soon loose the principal of the Money laid out by neglecting to make this Improvement of it.

When I think of the great Weight of present Expence for the Support of sixteen or seventeen Indian Boys, which has been my Number all the last Year, and as many English Youth on Charity; eight in the Wilderness who depend upon their Support wholly from this Quarter; which has been the Case a considerable Part of this Year—such a Number of Labourers—and under Necessity to build a House for myself (as the House I have lived in was originally planned for a Store-House for the School, and has been for some Time used for that Purpose, and must be henceforward devoted to it) and Expence for three, and sometimes four Tutors, which has been the least Number that would suffice for the well instructing my Students, I have sometimes

Founding the College 21

found faintness of Heart. . . .—But the Consideration which above all others, has been, and is my sovereign Support, is that it is the Cause of God; and God most certainly has, and does own it as his own, and in him, and him only, do I hope to perfect his own Plan for his own Glory. And whatever his Plan may be (and we yet see but the Beginning of it) he will accomplish it, let the Devices, Counsels and Machinations of Men, or Devils against it be what they will. And I wish I may always be disposed with the Temper and becoming the Character of a Servant to have my Eyes ever to him— Under these Apprehensions, I can't be anxious about the Event. God has done great Things for it hitherto, & I may not go back, but wait upon & hope in him to maintain, support and defend it, & perform what is wanting for it in his own Way and Time. Certainly his Hand has been conspicuous, in the Beginning, Rise, and Progress of it, through so many dark Scenes. When in it's Infancy and was the Object of Contempt, it was the Hand of God that opened, and disposed the Hearts of so many on both Sides the Water to such pious & charitable Liberal ties for the Support of it. —It was the Finger of God that pointed out such a wise, godly, honourable, and friendly Patronage for it in Europe—And what but a Divine Influence should move my worthy Patrons with so much Chearfulness to accept that important Trust in London, and with such Steadiness, disinterested Zeal, prosecure the Design hitherto—It was the Hand of God that advanced it's great Friend and Patron, the Right Honourable William Earl of Dartmouth, to the American Administration, at such a Time, and while he was in such Connection with this Seminary—It was the Hand of God that opened the Heart of our gracious Sovereign to shew his princely Munificence towards it in his Royal Bounty of two Hundred Pounds Sterling, and more especially in ratifying a Charter endowing it with all the Powers, Immunities, and Privileges of any University in his Kingdom, by which the Interests of it are most effectually secured, and those who are graduated in it have not an empty Title, but by Law have Claim to all those Rights and Privileges belonging to Graduates in any University within the Realm of Great-Britain.—Was it not the Hand of a gracious God that advanced so important and beneficial a Friend as his Excellency Governor Wentworth to the Chair in this Province, and disposed him as a nursing Father to patronize this tender Cause in its Infancy in this Wilderness? . . . Certainly the gracious Hand of God has been very evident to all acquainted, in that Regularity and good Order which has uninterruptedly subsisted here. . . .

FROM THE NARRATIVE OF 1775

THE PROGRESS of Husbandry on this Farm, the last Year, has not been equal, in every Respect, to my Hopes, by Reason that the Season proved so wet, as not to favour some Branches of it. However, the Progress of it, and Benefit by it, has been very considerable.—I have raised and reaped upon the School Land, the last Year, about 300 Bushels of choice Wheat—but the Crop of Indian Corn fell much Short of my Expectations, being but about 250 Bushels—I have fitted and sowed, the last Season, about 25 Acres of Wheat on new Land, and about 15 Acres of Rye; but have done it under the Disadvantage of not being able sufficiently to burn the Trash upon the Surface, which occasioned much more Labour and Expence in preparing the Ground, and the prospect of a Crop is much less.

I have cut 60 Tons of good Hay the last Season, and have a Prospect of a very considerable Addition to that Quantity the next, if Providence shall favour it.

I have begun to prepare, and have a Prospect, that I shall fit about 60 Acres of new Land to sow with Wheat the next Season. I have improved about 12 or 14 Oxen, and about 20 Cows, the Property of the School, and have a Prospect of Plenty for their Support for Summer and Winter, and I find already the great Benefit of having wherewith to do it this Winter, without the Fatigue and Expence of going 40 Miles for my Hay, as I have been forced to do 'till this Year.

I have been obliged to employ a large Number of Labourers to bring the Affair of the Farm to such a Ripeness, besides those, employed in building my own House, and other Buildings, necessary to accommodate my Students, and must employ a large Number the ensuing Year to compleat that which I have begun, and make such Fences as will be necessary to secure Improvements.

I have been, and now am making Provision of Boards, Bricks, Stone, &c. for the new College [building], proposed to be erected here, and expect, by the coming Spring, to have expended all that has been generously contributed by this Province, and others for that Purpose; and hope God will graciously open other Resources, by which I may be enabled to accomplish that most necessary Design, without which the Growth and Progress of this Institution must be stinted....

There has been an Addition of 29 Students to this College, at, and since, the last Commencement, (instead of Eight, who received the Honours of it, and left it last August) besides the Addition made to the School before mentioned.—And such an Increase of this Seminary, and the encouraging Prospects of its Utility, has, and likely will increase the Necessity of a new Building to accommodate the Students and as there is yet no sufficient Provision otherwise made for this Necessity, I cant but indulge a pleasing Thought, that there are Gentlemen, whom God hath honoured with Ability, and who are not forbid such an Act of Charity by particular Connections, who, if they should give themselves the Trouble to enquire fully into the Necessity of this Case, would esteem themselves happy, in the opportunity to return the Honours and Bounties of Divine Providence, they have received to their great Benefactor, by a liberal Disbursement for this Purpose. And I wish, I hope, and Pray, that this Paragraph may be kindly directed to the Eye of such a benevolent Soul, and the hint induce him to consider quite seriously, whether it is not a Matter well worthy his Attention, and Enquiry; and I am persuaded, if he be once so far gained, he will not find either his Sense of Obligation, or his Disposition to such an act of Charity, to be at all diminished by a most thorough Examination, and the fullest Understanding of the Case.—For this Favour I wait upon God; and bow the Knee in humble Supplication, to the Father of Mercies, who has so signally owned his Institution hereto, and has enabled and disposed Instruments, as there has been occasion to minister Supplies, from Time to Time for its rising Necessities, and who has the Disposal of the Hearts, and Substance of all, as much as ever, in his Hands, and at his Sovereign controul.

A Letter From John Ledyard

❧❧❧ John Ledyard, explorer, adventurer, entered Dartmouth in 1772 intending to become a missionary to the Indians, but he found college discipline not to his liking and in the spring of 1773, after unpleasant exchanges with the President, he departed abruptly, traveling down the Connecticut by canoe. From his home in Hartford, Conn., he wrote the President a long letter that was often incoherent, frequently insulting, in complaint of Wheelock's criticism of his conduct in Hanover. "Now Doctor Wheelock," he wrote, "I take what you have said with regard to my pride very ill natured, very unkind in you... your eyes discerning no further than the Coat and Breeches." Ledyard concluded his letter with the farewell to the college that is printed below and that one would like to think he meant. The original is in the Dartmouth Archives.

—Doct^r I can no more. a few words & farewell.—So far as I know myself I came to your College under influences of the good kind—whether you S^r believe it or not,—the Auquaintance I have gaind there is dearer than I can possibly express!—farewel dear Dartm^o—delightfull repose for Innocence & true felicity—sweet society, love, & peace,—that you may flourish like the Bay tree, be like an Apple Tree in the midst of the Woods—of whose fruit I was so happy as to taste, but now no more—that you may flourish in immortal green—that you may be the Sinai to this Continent & give her examples of that kind of Education that the World knows not of—that you may surmout, yea far transcend the fondest hopes & sanguine desires of the nearest concern'd—that you may be Bless d indeed with that which is better than Corn & Wine—New Covnant increas—is certainly, tho' the weak yet constant & ardent supplication of your beloved tho' un-

fortunate *Son.*,—Doct^r my heart is chaste as new fallen Snow. farewell!—yea thro' Time & Eternity farewell' & may the God of Abraham Isaac & Jacob Bless you & yours.
—I am Hon^d & Rev^d S^r
tho' sorely besett, y^r obliged
& dutifull young Servant
JOHN LEDYARD

Commencement, 1774
JEREMY BELKNAP

>>> A Harvard graduate who had been so impressed by one of Eleazar Wheelock's *Narratives* that he considered becoming a missionary to the Indians, Jeremy Belknap at the time of his visit to Dartmouth was minister of the Congregational Church in Dover, N.H. He is best known for his three-volume *History of New Hampshire*, but his claim for remembrance also rests on his being one of the founders of the Massachusetts Historical Society (1791), the first society of its kind in the United States. "The Journey" was edited by Edward C. Lathem (Hanover, 1950). The original manuscript is in the Massachusetts Historical Society.

THURSDAY, AUG. 18, 1774. At six o'clock this morning I set out on a journey to Dartmouth College. There having been considerable rain the night before, which suceeded a long and severe drought of four weeks, the weather cleared up about eight o'clock.... Went through Allen's Town and Buckstreet, so called, into Suncook or Pembroke; a very pleasant well settled town on Merrimack River. Lodged at Lieut. Conner's. The street here is strait, about three and a half miles and mostly level.

Friday, Aug. 19. The company I expected to meet here not being arrived, I was in no hurry to proceed.... A great fog rose off the river in the night and continued till nine or ten o'clock, which is common here at this season and is a sign of a fair day. About ten o'clock, set out in company with one Mr. Walker, a trader, crossed Merrimack River into Penicook or Concord; a beautiful town about forty years old, large intervals and fine land....

About five o'clock arrived Brigadier Gilman, Mr. Jaffrey, and Mr. Sherburne.* I joined company with them and rode to Boscawen.

* Peter Gilman, Speaker of the House of Representatives, and George Jaffrey, member of the Royal Council of the Province of New Hampshire, were charter trustees of the College. John Sherburne, a member of the New Hampshire Assembly, on recommendation of Gov. Wentworth was elected to the board at its meeting during this Commencement.

Lodged at Capt. Gerrish's but slept not, the bed being preoccupied by innumerable vermin.... Coming into Orford we saw an high mountain just before us, against which a large black cloud broke and poured down a torrent of rain upon us for half an hour together. There was also some thunder.... Many slate rocks on the descent to Connecticut River.

Connecticut River at Orford is twenty-five rods wide and about seven feet deep at this season.

Tuesday, Aug. 23. Cloudy and drizzly. I went over the river to New York side [what is now Vermont] to view a mountain there concerning the height of which we could not agree as we stood on the other side. I found myself much decieved in the appearance, it proving to be in reality double the height which I supposed, as we judged by a nearer inspection and a comparison of the height of trees both under and upon it. Here was a spring of the coldest water I ever tasted and a beautiful, regular, and extensive bank as if laid out by art, about six or seven rod from the side of the river and parallel to it.

Connecticut River sometimes shifts and alters lands, as I observed in Pemisewasset, so that there have been litigations about property occasioned thereby.

About nine or ten set out again.... Stopt at one Green's at Lime; viewed his pearl ash works. Were met by a number of gentlemen from the College. Rode through the rain and got to Dartmouth College in Hanover about quarter after two o'clock. Dined with the President, who appeared somewhat disappointed at the governor's not coming.*
After dinner walked down to Connecticut River opposite to the College where is a ferry. Observed on a tree where the bark was cut off the figure of an Indian painted, which was done by one of the Indian scholars. At evening prayers, by the President's desire, I preached a sermon in the college hall from Heb. 11. 8, 9, 10 "By faith Abraham, etc."

---

* On July 14, Gov. Wentworth had written to Wheelock from Portsmouth: "Such is the distracted State of the Colonies, that I cannot engage to be at Commencement; However, if possible, I will be there."

Supped and lodged at the President's. In the evening the front of the college was illuminated.

The plain where the College stands is large and pleasant and the land good. The college is about seventy or eighty feet long and thirty broad, containing twenty chambers. The hall is a distinct building which also serves for a meeting house, and the kitchen is in one end of it. The President's house stands on a rising ground east of the college, and to the north of this is the place proposed to build the new college near a quarry of grey stone which is intended for the materials of building. There is another quarry much larger about three-quarters of a mile distant. The tutors are Messrs. Woodward, Ripley, Wheelock and Smith; the two former are married to the President's daughters. Several tradesmen and taverners are settled round the College in good buildings, which gives the place the appearance of a village.

Wednesday, Aug. 24. Walked to the mills about a mile distant. Here are a saw and grist mill and a house in which six scholars reside who take the mills to the halves and live a kind of philosophic, laborious life. They maintain themselves by their labor. Their house, which is entirely of their own construction, is a curiosity. It consists of one room and one chamber; the stairs outside. The chamber is arched with boards for the better sound of the voice in singing. The chairs and tables are contrived in an odd manner, and they have a wooden clock. At the door is an upright pipe with a spout like a pump, which is continually running with brook water conveyed down a covered descent; so that they have only to hold a vessel under it and it is immediately filled. They have a neat poultry house built of sawed strips of wood in the form of a cobb house with four apartments.

I went round and visited all the Indian scholars, most of whom could speak good English. One little boy was so shy that he would not be seen. Here is a likely, ingenious French man, Joseph Marri Verrueil, who came hither of his own accord, and being taught to read the Bible and judge for himself, has now become a thorough Protestant.

The President appears to be much affected with the reports that are circulated concerning the badness of the provisions, on which account some have left the College. Last evening he entered into a large and warm vindication of himself, declaring that the reports are ALL FALSE, and that he did not doubt but "God would bring forth his righteousness as the light, and his judgment as the noon day." He has had the mortification to lose two cows, and the rest were greatly hurt by a contagious distemper, so that they *could not have a full supply of milk*. And once the pickle leaked out of the beef barrell, so that the *meat was not sweet*. He had also been ill-used with respect to the purchase of some wheat, so that they had *smutty bread* for a while, etc. The scholars, on the other hand, say they scarce ever have any thing but pork and greens, without vinegar, and pork and potatoes; that fresh meat comes but very seldom; and that the victuals is very badly dressed. The trustees have drawn up something of a vindication after a full enquiry into this matter.

I observed in the President's prayers such expressions as these, speaking of this institution: "Thou thyself hast founded it, Thou hast preserved and supported it when its beginnings were small, and in the opinion of many contemptable, and Thy gentleness hath made it great." There seems to be also too much said in the public exercises concerning *its enemies*, and the College is constantly spoken of as in a state of victory over them, which serves to keep alive a spirit that I think ought to be discouraged.

About eleven o'clock the Commencement began in a large tent erected on the east side of the College and covered with boards, scaffolds and seats being prepared.

The President began with a prayer in the usual *strain*. Then an English oration was spoken by one of the Bachelors, complimenting the trustees, etc. A sylogistic disputation in Latin on this question: *Amicitia vera non est absque amore divina*. Then a cliosophic oration. Then an anthem, "The voice of my beloved sounds, etc." Then a forensic dispute, *Whether Christ Died for all Men*, which was well supported on both sides. Then an anthem, "Lift up your heads, O ye gates, etc." The company were invited to dine at the President's and the hall. The Connecticut lads and lasses, I observed, walked about hand in hand in procession, as 'tis said they go to a wedding.

Commencement, 1774

P.M. The exercises began with a Latin oration on the state of society by Mr. Ripley. Then followed an anthem. Then an English *Oration on the Imitative Arts* by Mr. J. Wheelock. The degrees were then conferred, and in addition to the usual ceremony of the book, diplomas were delivered to each candidate with this form of words "Admitto vos ad primum (vel secundum) gradum in artibus pro more academiarum in Angliä vobisque trado hunc librum una cum potestate publice prelegendi ubicunque ad hoc munus avocati fueritis (to the Masters' was added *fuistis vel fueritis*) cujus rei hoc diploma membrana scripta est testimonium." Mr. Woodward stood by the President and held the book and parchments, delivering and exchanging them as need required.

Reverend Mr. Benjamin Pomeroy of Hebron [Connecticut] was admitted to the degree of Doctor in Divinity.

After this, McGregore and Swetland, two Bachelors, spoke a dialogue of Lord Lyttleton's between Apicius and Darteneuf upon *good* eating and drinking. The Mercury performed his part but clumsily, but the two epicures did well; and the President laughed as heartily as the rest of the audience, though, considering the circumstances, it might admit of some doubt whether the dialogue were really a burlesque or a compliment to the College.

An anthem and prayer concluded the public exercises. Much decency and regularity were observable through the day in the numerous attending concourse of people.

There is a very fine brass horizontal dial fixed on a post in the President's yard. It was given by Capt. Holland; it cost ten guineas. The latitude of the place: 43° 38' N.

I saw the hut where the President first lived. It is a log house about twenty feet square, but will soon rot, it being built mostly of beech sticks. This is called "the first sprout of the College." The scholars built huts round it to live in. 'Tis really surprizing to observe the improvements that have been made in four years.

The college library is kept at Mr. Woodward's. It is not large, but there are some very good books in it. The seal is also kept there. They have two good globes of eighteen inches and a good solar microscope.

Thursday, Aug. 25. The trustees were upon business all day. Col. Phillips gave £600 LM for the Christianizing [of] the Indians.*

I attended with several others the examination of Joseph Johnson, an Indian educated in this school, who with the rest of the New England Indians, are about moving up into the country of the Six Nations, where they have a tract of land fifteen miles square given them. He appeared to be an ingenious, sensible, serious young man, and we gave him an approbamus . . . . After which, at three o'clock P.M., he preached in the college hall, and a collection of twenty-seven dollars and a half was made for him. The auditors were agreeably entertained. . . .

---

* John Phillips, founder of Phillips Andover and Exeter Academies, was a generous benefactor of the College and a trustee from 1773 to 1793.

A Student in the Wilderness
JOSEPH VAILL

>>> The hardships of Joseph Vaill's student years—he was a member of the Class of 1778—must have toughened him, for he lived until the age of 88. After college he spent 58 years as pastor of the Congregational church in Hadlyme, Conn. His account of his student years is incorporated in Isaac Parsons's *Memoir of the Life and Character of Rev. Joseph Vaill* (New York, 1839).

SOMETIME in the month of June 1772, a plan was proposed by Mr. J. O., who had removed the preceding year, into the neighborhood of Dartmouth College, for several young men to procure a College education, and to defray their expenses, by tending a saw-mill and grist-mill, the property of the College, which he had taken to run on shares. A brother of Mr. O. had before this, become a member of Dartmouth College. I had been thinking of a public education for some time, and had been desirous of obtaining one; but no way seemed to be open to me for it. Two of my acquaintance concluded to make trial of Mr. O's plan, and I felt inclined to join them in this new and arduous enterprize. But numerous and seemingly insurmountable difficulties lay in the way: As my father was considerably advanced in life, (turned of fifty) and had no other son except one who was then an infant about six months old, and had involved himself in debt to a considerable amount, for the purchase of a suitable settlement for me that I might live near to him. He had seven daughters, most of whom were dependent on him; and on learning my plan to leave home for the purpose of acquiring an education, my parents started such strong objections, that I felt it to be my duty, at first, to give it up. Still the subject was on my mind continually through the summer, and I was not satisfied to abandon it. At length, I signified by letter, to Mr. J. O., my desire to go and pursue his proposed plan, and received an answer from him in the forepart of September, which fixed my determination to go forward. My father offered me one half of his property, if I would relinquish the idea of leaving him, and remain on the farm; but I replied that I had rather give up my claims to any part of his estate than not go. My friends, in general, regarded it as a visionary and wild undertaking which would soon be given up in despair; and dissuaded me all in their power.

My father told me that, as I was of age, he had no legal right to control me, and should leave me to do as I thought best. He did not refuse to assist me so far as he was able; yet he was not in circumstances to afford me much pecuniary aid. Having made the best preparation I could under my circumstances, I set out, with three others, for Dartmouth College, Sept. 28th, 1772. I took my axe with me, and such articles of clothing and a few such books as were most necessary.

Four of us started in company, taking one small horse with us, on which the youngest and most feeble of our company rode most of the way. Three of us travelled on foot, and for part of two days, each footman swung his pack, soldier-like. But, at length we contrived to place our packs on our horse. The distance we were to travel was computed to be one hundred and eighty miles. I had only about fifteen shillings in money in my pocket to bear my expenses on the journey; and as this proved insufficient, I received some more from one of our company. We travelled, on an average, about thirty miles a day. I had never before been twenty miles from home, nor gone on foot a whole day at a time. I became excessively weary, and at times almost ready to lie down in the street. On the third day, as we went from Hartford, on the east side of Connecticut River, we reached the Chickopee River in Massachusetts; and finding the bridge gone, three of us forded this river. One rode the horse over, and ascertained that it was not dangerous, on account of its depth. We pulled off our stockings and shoes, and waded across, a distance of about ten rods. The water was cold, the stream rapid, and the bottom covered with sharp and slippery stones. We reached Claremont in New Hampshire, on Saturday night, and put up at a small tavern, over the Sabbath, on the beach of Sugar River. The Landlord was an Episcopalian. A meeting was held at his house on the Sabbath. On Monday, Oct. 5th, we reached the College Mills.

The Mills were one mile south from the College. They stood on a large brook, and near to them, was an interval of fifteen or twenty acres of land, which interval was nearly surrounded on one side by a high hill of a semicircular form, which extended from North East, to South West. This hill was thickly covered with forest trees. The road from the Mills to the College, after about sixty rods of level land, passed directly up this hill which was about one fourth of a mile from the bottom to the top, and thence through a hemlock swamp, nearly half of a mile in width, before it reached the plain on which the College stood.

We found Mr. J. O., living alone in a small framed unfinished house, which had been built for the residence of the man who should tend the College Mills. A more solitary and romantic situation can seldom be found. The howling of wild beasts, and the plaintive notes of the owl, greatly added to the gloominess of the night season. Mr. O. was supplied with some provisions and utensils, sufficient for one who lived in his solitary condition. His lodging was a box made of boards, called a bunk, with a ticken filled with pine shavings, and a sufficient covering of Indian blankets. For the first week we strangers took each one a blanket and slept upon the floor;—but in a short time we furnished ourselves with bunks and straw beds, and with utensils sufficient to take our meals in a more decent manner.

The first four or five weeks we spent in tending the mills, and in clearing away the trees near our house, which furnished a supply of fuel for the winter. One of our company soon gave up the idea of studying, and returned to Connecticut before winter. Three of us now entered on the study of the Latin Grammar, and continued to pursue our studies through the winter. Our tutor was a brother of Mr. J.O., who was a member of the Sophomore Class in College. We gave him his board for his service in teaching us;—and we had no other instructor till we entered College. During the first winter, we studied in our cold house, and used pine knots to burn for lights, instead of candles, for a part of the time. I lodged in the chamber, with one of my class-mates. We ascended a ladder placed in our small entry. My pillow was a duffed great coat, and our covering narrow Indian blankets. We did our own cooking and washing until the latter part of March, when a young married couple came from Connecticut, and lived in our house, and superintended our domestic concerns. Having repaired a small cottage near by, built in part of logs, we removed into that to study and lodge, where we remained during the next summer, suffering many inconveniences, and undergoing many privations.

On the return of spring in 1773, as soon as the ice dissolved, we resumed our sawing. We sawed about sixty thousand feet of pine boards, and *stuck* them up. We also tended the grist mill in our turns. We had one dollar per thousand for sawing and stacking the boards, and half the toll for grinding. We also burned over several acres of ground, and cleared them for tillage,—we sowed a part with clover seed for mowing and pasture, and planted yearly about one acre of corn, besides our garden. Our corn-field was never plowed. We employed our hoes in planting the corn, and we dug our field when the corn was up, with our hoes. The first spring after we commenced our settlement there, the *measles* broke out in our family, and proved fatal in the case of one of our number, who was thrown into a quick consumption, which terminated his life in about six weeks. This was an afflictive Providence to us all.

In the first summer, we built a new convenient house. One of our number and myself constructed the chimney; and for want of cattle, we backed the stones from several rods distance. The mantle-tree stone, two of us carried on our shoulders nearly a mile; and the jamb-stones, we backed some distance. By the time we had finished our house, which was in September, my health was very much reduced; and I experienced a severe attack of the dysentery, attended with a burning fever; and for several days, my life was greatly threatened. But through a merciful Providence, I was at length restored to health. Thus, I continued to labor and study for two years, before I, with one of the company, entered College. My hardships were excessive, and especially in the spring, when, after studying through the winter, we turned out in the latter part of March, two of us at a time, and tended the saw-mill for about six weeks together. In the second spring we sawed about seventy thousand feet of boards; and in the third about ninety thousand. We made it our rule to saw every evening, except Saturday and Sabbath evenings, till ten o'clock, and in the mean time, some one, in his turn, tended the grist-mill.

About two years after we began our enterprise, two young men from Massachusetts joined us, one of whom brought on an excellent cow, which furnished us with milk and butter for most of the year, and greatly contributed to our living more comfortably.

After I entered college, I went twice a day to recite with my class in College, which made me four miles travel each day. We recited to our Tutor immediately after morning prayers, and again at eleven o'clock; and some part of the time we had three recitations in a day. In the winter, we rose frequently at five o'clock, and in the shortest days at six o'clock, and having united in morning prayer in our family, I set off for College, having to face the North West wind, which was cold and piercing in that climate; and not unfrequently, I had to break my path through a new fall of snow, a foot in depth or more. Considering the severity of the winters in that cold region, it was marvellous that I did not freeze my limbs, or perish with the cold, especially as I was but thinly clothed for that climate. After my admission to College, I tended the saw-mill about six weeks in the spring, which was chiefly vacation; and in summer, in addition to going to College twice or three times a day, I made it my rule to labor about three hours in the field or garden, or some other kind of manual labor. I had scarcely a moment's leisure from one day, week and month to another. My hardships were excessive, and especially in the Spring, in tending the saw-mill. I was frequently exposed to being drenched with water when mending the trough or buckets of the water-wheel; and in one instance, I experienced a narrow escape from being torn in pieces by the saw.

I continued at the mills and pursued my studies and labors until the month of June 1777, when I was in my Junior year, which completed the term of about four years and a half. . . .

My design when I set out to procure an education, was that I might be prepared for the work of the ministry. This object I kept continually in view, after I entered on the prosecution of my plan. My mind was habitually impressed with the importance of living a religious life, I daily kept up secret prayer, and paid a greater attention to reading and hearing the word. I gained more clear and satisfactory views of the doctrines of the Gospel, and of the nature of regeneration, and Christian exercises from the discourses of our President, Dr. Eleazer Wheelock....

In the winter after I entered College, there was a revival of religion among the students. The awakening was more general in the Freshman class, though there was a solemnity among nearly all the members of College. A number of my class-mates, and several others, were brought to indulge hope of their conversion.... Notwithstanding the little evidence I had gained of my conversion, I ventured to join the College Church sometime in 1775, while a Sophomore; and I hope, by the amazing grace of God, that notwithstanding my great remains of the body of sin and death, my criminal short-comings and abuse of distinguished privileges my experience has borne some faint resemblance to the light of the morning, which shineth more and more unto the perfect day....

The College was frequently in a state of alarm and especially so after Burgoyne, with the Northern army had taken the forts of Ticonderoga and Crown-point. Such was the confusion among the students, as well as apprehension on the part of the faculty, that College exercises were often interrupted, and in several instances, they were suspended, and the students permitted to return home; or they were sent for by their parents, or called for to join the militia, or to enlist in the army. For as many as two years before I graduated, frequent interruptions and embarrassments attended our College course.

In the spring of 1778, I returned back to the College; but not finding provision made sufficient to board all the students in the commons, a number of us of different classes, agreed to purchase our own provisions, and to hire our board dressed at a private house not far from the College, and we continued thus to live until commencement, which was the fourth Wednesday in August. I then took my degree with my class; and to pay up my College bills which remained unpaid, I was obliged to hire some money, which brought me in debt about twenty dollars, at the close of my College life.

On the Demolition of Dartmouth College
PHILIP FRENEAU

🍂 Near the southeast corner of the Hanover Green, Eleazar Wheelock built in 1770 the structure that he describes in his 1771 *Narrative* and in which he lived with his family for three years. Then in 1773 the building was enlarged to become the College Hall, housing both the commons and the chapel. Unrepaired, neglected, it fell into a sorry state, and on December 3, 1789, the students, in what was described as a "nocturnal visitation," tore it down. To the New York *Daily Advertiser* on March 22, 1790, Philip Freneau, "poet of the American Revolution" and a romantic adventurer outside the world of verse, contributed his poet's version of the event on Hanover Plain.

O N NEW-YEARS eve, the year was eighty-nine,
All clad in *black*, a Dartmouth college crew
With crow-bar, sledge, and pick ax did combine
To level with the dust their antique hall,
In hopes the President would build a new:
Yes, yes, said they, the ancient pile shall fall
And laugh no longer at yon cobler's stall.

The clock struck seven—in social compact join'd,
They pledg'd their sacred honors to proceed:
The number seventy-five this feat design'd,
But first some oaths they swore by candle light
On Euclid's Elements—no bible did they heed
One must be true, they said, the other might—
Besides, no bible could be found that night.

On the Demolition of Dartmouth College

Now darkness o'er the plain her pinions spread
Then rung the bell an unaccustom'd peal:
Out rush'd the brave, the cowards went to bed
And left the attempt to those that felt full bold
To pull down halls, where years had seen them kneel,
Where *Wheelock* oft at rakes was wont to scold
Or sung them many a psalm in days of old.

Advancing then towards the tottering hall
That now at least one hundred years had stood
They gave due notice that it soon should fall—
Lest there some godly wight might gaping stand;
(For well they knew the world wants all its good
To awe the sturdy sinners of the land,
And shame old Satan, with his sooty band.)

The reverend man that Dartmouth college awes
Hearing the bell at this unhallow'd hour,
Vext at the infringement of the college laws
With lengthy stride out-sally'd from his den,
And made a speech (as being a man in power)
Alas! it was not heard by one in ten—
No time to heed his speeches, or his pen.

"Ah, rogues, said he, ah whither do ye run,
"Bent on the ruin of that harmless pile
"That, all the war, has brav'd both sword and gun?—
"Reflect dear boys, some reverend rats are there
"That now will have to scamper many a mile
"For whom past time old Latin books did spare,
"And Attic greek, and manuscripts most rare.

"Relent, relent! to accomplish such designs
"Our Dartmouth college fare is much too weak—
"For such attempts folks drink your high-proof wines,

"Not wretched *switchel* and vile *hogo* drams
"Hardly sufficient to digest your Greek—
"Come, let the fabric stand, my dear black lambs—
"Besides, I think we have no battering-rams.

Thus he—but all his sighs and tears were lost
To work they went with pick-ax, spade and hammer,
One smote a wall, and one dislodg'd a post,
Tugg'd at a beam, or aim'd at pigeon holes,
Where Indian boys were wont to study grammar:
Indeed, they took great pains, and dug like moles,
And work'd—as if they work'd to save their souls.

Now to its deep foundations shook the dome
Farewell to all its learning, fame, and honor!
So fell the capitol of Heathen Rome
By Goths and Vandals level'd with the dust—
And so shall die the works of *John O'Connor*,
Which he himself will even outlive, we trust
But now our story's coming to the worst:

Down fell the Pile!—aghast these rebels stood
And wonder'd at the mischiefs they had done
To such a pile, compos'd of stone and wood,
To such a pile, so antique and renown'd,
Which many a prayer had heard and many a pun—
So, three huzzas they gave, and fir'd a round,
Then homeward trudg'd—half drunk—but safe and sound.

ON THE CAMPUS

Outrage and Riot

AMOS KENDALL

⇶ This chapter of college in President John Wheelock's Dartmouth is taken from the *Autobiography of Amos Kendall* (Boston, 1872). A member of the Class of 1811, Kendall became a lawyer, an editor, a businessman. He was a confidant and adviser to President Andrew Jackson—a member of his "Kitchen Cabinet"—wrote many of Jackson's Presidential messages and served for five years as his Postmaster General.

A FEW WILD fellows had amused themselves one night by collecting the cattle on the common and shutting them up in the college cellar. It was not an uncommon occurrence, and the faculty had not generally taken any notice of it. On this occasion they ordered the young men occupying the rooms above the entrance into the cellar to remove the obstructions and let the cattle out. They were among the most orderly students in college, some of them members of churches, and all young men who never participated in nightly frolics. They obeyed the order; but their natural indignation at being required in open day to undo the nightly mischief of others was soon inflamed, as well by their own reflections as by the comments of their friends and the derision of their less orderly fellow-students. The result was a general determination to put the cattle into the cellar again, to come out as they might.

Kendall was not one of the young men on whom the indignity had been put; but they were his associates, and he fully sympathized with their resentment. On the evening of the 19th of June [1810] he had gone to bed early, having an attack of sick-headache. Between nine and ten o'clock his chum came in, and told him they had resolved to turn out that night. He got up, dressed himself, and with his chum sallied out to take part in the fray. It was not ten o'clock, and the moon was shining brightly. Now, that even the church-members were engaged, the lovers of frolic turned out in force, and soon more than a hundred young men, most of them somewhat disguised, were perambulating in squads the common and roads adjacent, and driving cattle and horses towards the college. Some of the animals had been driven into the cellar, when President Wheelock, unobserved, approached the entrance. Seizing one of the young men by the arm, he spoke, and being recognized, was tripped up and fell upon the ground. He was not further molested, but deemed it prudent to make a hasty retreat. About a score of live stock had been driven into the cellar, and a party were engaged in carrying and rolling stones, taken from a fence just at hand, with which the entrance had been so far filled as to be impassable, when another party appeared with a horse and a number of cattle. The question was, Shall the obstructions be removed and this additional lot driven in? It was known that the faculty had assembled at the President's house, and their appearance on the ground was momentarily expected. Nevertheless, it was determined that these new recruits should go in at all hazards. Probably more than sixty young men were on the spot; and about half of them were assigned to prevent the interference of the faculty, while the residue removed the obstructions, drove in the cattle, and filled up the entrance. Amos Kendall was one of the party assigned to the duty of defending the working-party.

The cellar-way was under the rear of the main college building, and in full view of the rear of the President's house; but a board-fence intervened, in which was a gate, and through that gate the faculty were expected to approach should they venture to interfere. The defensive party of students stationed themselves, armed with stones and brickbats, a few rods from this fence, with the understanding that in case the faculty made their appearance, advancing from the rear of the President's house, they should hurl their missiles against the board-fence, which demonstration it was believed would deter them from advancing.

The party at the cellar-way had removed the obstructions so that the entrance was passable, and were in the act of driving in the reinforcements of stock, when the two tutors made their appearance from the rear of the President's house, advancing toward the gate. Stones and brickbats rattled against the fence, but the brave men kept on, passed through the gate, and were rapidly approaching the array of students. At this crisis, more than half of the defensive party took to their heels, but the residue, knowing that the entire object of the movement would be defeated should they prove recreant, aimed their missiles directly at the tutors, who immediately ran behind the chapel, which was just at hand. No violence was offered them after they turned their backs, though Kendall and a few others followed them as a *corps* of observation. After a short consultation the tutors retired, evidently in despair of stopping the disturbance.

Kendall had been quite sick all the evening, and now, perhaps not altogether satisfied with the extremes to which the affair had been carried, retired to his room and went to bed. The next morning there was a mound of stones covered with earth over the cellar-way, and, near by a large stack of newly mown hay, brought from an adjacent meadow. Under the windows, at the end of the passage in the building above, were piles of small stones. These were significant indications not only that the students did not intend to let the cattle out themselves, but might resist their unconditional surrender by others.

The morning exercises and recitations passed off in customary quietude. About eleven o'clock there was a visible movement among the citizens of the village, and a rumor circulated that they were preparing to release their imprisoned live stock by force. Nearly all the students in college collected in the main building, and, barricading the doors, were ready for defence. The faculty appeared in a body, and walking around the building, accosted the students standing in the windows, requesting some, and commanding others, to open the doors. The general answer from those addressed was, that it would not be safe for them to attempt it. At length all the faculty retired, and soon afterwards Professor Hubbard, a most amiable man much beloved by the students, approached one of the end doors with an axe in his hand, and, unresisted, knocked out the panels. He then crawled in through the breach he had made, removed the fastening, and opened the door. The rest of the faculty then joined him, and, treating the students with the utmost courtesy, they took possession of the passages and sent word to the citizens that they might come and dig their cattle out. No aid was asked of the students in this operation.

The faculty were greatly excited by these events, and showed signs of a disposition to inflict condign punishment upon the leaders therein. But their tone soon changed. Calling up a young man of irregular habits who had been recognized on the ground by one of the faculty, they required him to state the names of others who were present. In the hope of saving himself, he named several of the most orderly young men in college, some of whom were brethren in the church with the President and professors. As soon as it was known that the inquisition was on foot, a meeting of students was held and a committee appointed, of whom Mr. Kendall was one, to prepare and send to the faculty a memorial setting forth the extenuating circumstances. This duty was performed. But the most effective step was, doubtless, the concerted determination of the orderly young men engaged in the affair to admit their participation and frankly state their reasons. The following is substantially the result of the examination of a church-member, one of those who had been required to undo the mischief of others, viz.:—

President. Your name has been furnished us as one of those who took part in the recent riot. Is the charge true?

Student. It is.

Pres. What could have induced you to take part in such a scandalous affair?

Stu. Your own injustice. I had always obeyed the regulations of the college, took no part in any of the mischievous frolics of other students, was punctual at recitation and studious to preserve the character of an upright and religious man. Notwithstanding all this, you put upon me and others like me the indignity of undoing the mischief of others, and subjected me to their taunts and sneers. Our friends sympathized with us in our natural indignation, and proposed, as the most appropriate mode of making known our resentment, to aid us in putting the cattle back again, and it was done.

Pres. What apology have you to make for your participation in this affair?

Stu. None whatever.

Having been answered in this style by three or four of their most worthy students, the faculty made no further inquiry. They dismissed the young man first called up, and another who was seen to carry into the college building a plank with which one of the doors had been barricaded, imposing upon the others summoned a fine to pay for damages done to some of the cattle and to a stone fence, a rod or two of which had been used for filling up the cellar-way. A general contribution of about twenty-five cents by each student paid the fine, and thus the affair ended. It was a lesson to the faculty by which they doubtless profited in their subsequent conduct towards their more orderly pupils. . . .

A Cycle of Webster Letters

>> The painful father-and-son correspondence that appears below was exchanged by Edward Webster and the great Daniel, a United States Senator at the time. Edward Webster was graduated in 1841, studied law, and at the outbreak of the war with Mexico recruited the first company of Massachusetts volunteers. A major, he died in Mexico of typhoid fever in January 1848. The letters, as edited by E. C. Latham, were published in the *Alumni Magazine*, November 1962.

Dart Coll., 1838

MY DEAR FATHER,

During the winter & spring terms of my Freshman year to gether with other students I got drawn very largely into debt and before I was aware how far I had gone I found myself in debt to a large amount Knowing that it must of necessity grately hurt your feelings and also asshamed of my own folly & weakness, I have let them remain till this time in all they amout to $225. since the time in which these debts were incured I have been trying to pay them with the pocket money which you have been kind enough to give me[,] only spending as much as I was obliged to in order to appear decently and as I know you would wish a son of yours to appear here.

It is with great reluctance now My Dear Father that I broach this subject to you. As I am well aware that I disregarded the good advice you had given me and suffered myself to be led away by silly boys & willy store keepers and also knowing the state of your business and money matters I am still more reluctant

You knew the dangers among which I was thrown and warned me but I neglected your warnings but now I come like the Prodigal son of old and ask your help & forgiveness with promises of better conduct and a more rigid compliance to your wishes in future[;] and My dear Father if you would tran[s]mit me money enough to discharge them

I should be very thankful to you and I can assure you that I am very sorry for what I have done, and you may res[t] assured that the like will never occurr again as this has taugh[t] me a lesson which I never shall forget—

And Dear Father
I remain your affectionant
and henceforth duitiful son
EDWARD—

Marshfield Sep. 8. 1838

MY DEAR SON,

Your letter, respecting your own private affairs, has caused me very great grief. I am shocked, not only at the folly, & guilt, of contracting such a debt, but at the misrepresentations, which you must have repeatedly made; as you have always told me that you owed nothing, which the means I furnished were not competent to discharge. Your letter has remained several days, unanswered, because I had not made up my mind what answer to give. My first feeling was to withdraw you from College, & to let you take care of yourself hereafter. But your letter shows an apparent spirit of repentance, & if I were sure that I could trust *that*, I might be inclined to overlook the enormity of your misconduct. But how can I be sure that you have *now* told me the whole truth? How can I trust your present statements?—Besides, how was this debt created? Was it by gaming, or other immoral habits,—or by mere thoughtlessness, & folly?

I have concluded to go up to Boston, tomorrow or next day; & then, either to go directly to Hanover, or to write you again. In the meantime, I want to know more about the manner of contracting this debt; & I expect the whole truth. I would not expose you to public reproach, nor cast you off, for slight cause; but with all my affection, I will not excuse misconduct, and, especially, I will not put up with any degree or particle of misrepresentation, or concealment of the truth. On the receipt of this, you will immediately write to me, directed to

Boston; & when I receive your letter, I shall determine what course to pursue.

Your affectionate, but
distressed father
Danl Webster

Hanover Sept. 13. 1838

My Dear Father,

I recieved your letter yesterday I was aware that it could not but grieve you very much and that was the reason why I never told you before and also made the misrepresentations which you speak of, and Sir I can quiet your fears about my repentance not being real and affected for I certainly do feel very sorry, and penitent, and you may rest assured that the like will never occur again

You wish to know how the debts were contracted, & I will tell you the *truth* now. You say that you dont know but it was by gaming? It was not for I never gambled for a *cent* in my life nor do I think I ever shall for I never could have been lead away as far as that if any one had tried me, for I detest the practise and always did. a good deal is for such things as nuts & raisins, crockerey, cigars, candy pantaloons chess men backgammon boards knifes and some *wine* a very little of which I can say with a clear conscience I drank my self, riding on horse back and other ways for pleasure, and I am sorry to say very few of the articles were of any use.

the *only* immoral thing which I have purchased is wine, the students with whome most of these debts were contracted have graduated so that there would not be the same temptations if I would yeild to them which by the help of a firm resolve I hope I never shall.

I should be very sorry to be taken away from college, but If you think best I should be willing to go, with the education you have been kind enough to give me and my bodily strength I feel I should be able to take care of myself. If I do not improve upon trial I do not wish nor ask for any further indulgence. and as to the money part of it if by any means by keeping school or in other way I could make that up to you in a measure or in full I should be most happy to do so, And I remain my dear Father your

most affectional and *deeply*
penitent son
EDWARD WEBSTER

Boston Sept. 21. 1838

MY DEAR SON

I rec^d your letter, two days ago, and have made up my mind to put entire trust in your statements—to clear off your embarrassments—& to give you a fair opportunity to retrieve whatever may have been amiss: & to pursue your studies—

I now trust, My Dear Son, to hear nothing of you, hereafter, except what may be gratifying. You must see, now, that you for your living, & your character & happiness hereafter, you must rely on yourself. If I can get you through with your education, it will be as much as I shall be able to do. I owe a good deal of money, & am at present receiving but a small income from my profession.

If you intend yourself for the *Bar*, you must begin, early, to contract a habit of diligent & ambitious study. You must be emulous of excellence. An ordinary lawyer is not an enviable character. I believe, verily, that you have sense and ability enough to make you quite respectable—& I pray you, My Dear Son, keep your attention steadily directed to your progress in your studies.

Your mother will be glad of your letter, which I receive this morning. It has come back from Marshfield, we both happening to be here. She returns tomorrow, & I go to N.Y. this P.M. We look for Fletcher [a brother] shortly. You will have notice of his arrival—& while here, we shall expect you to come & see him. Some of us will write, to fix the time.

I enclose 3 checks for, $100—& 100—& 50—being 250 in all. You may use these, as you have occasion—tho' I should prefer that you should not use the whole of them before the 1st or 5th of October—

[DAN^L WEBSTER]

The Coming of the Civil War
EDWARD TUCK

⇶ When Edward Tuck 1862, died in 1938 at 95, he was Dartmouth's greatest benefactor, and because he had lived in France for much of his life he seemed a figure of legend to most Dartmouth men. The Amos Tuck School of Business Administration, given in memory of his father (Class of 1835) and the recipient of all but one of the letters printed below, is the most visible of his benefactions in Hanover. The letters, edited by E. C. Lathem, were published in the *Alumni Magazine*, October 1961.

Hanover, April 14th 1861.

MY DEAR FATHER:

This has been a very exciting day here, although Sunday and that too in a place where, of all others, one would least expect excitement on the Sabbath. This noon the Telegraph confirmed last night's rumor that Fort Sumter had been unconditionally surrendered with other news which you of course know. The more interested of the Professors were on the alert for the dispatch, as well as the students and it seems that the minister was likewise, for this afternoon he very aptly introduced the subject and preached as good and practical a sermon, closing with a most earnest appeal, as I ever heard.

Everybody talks of war, 9 out of 10 profess willingness to "go down and fight" and I've no doubt a majority of these talkers would really go if things came to the worst. Two or three really think of taking up their standing and joining some volunteer corps. Frank Hobbs positively declares he will but that's not much sign that he will do it. What do you think the prospect is?

We have had some rain here to-day, but more, probably, in the mountains, for the river is very high, almost into the road on the Vermont side and above the Breakwater on the Pier. It is rising at the rate of 4 inches an hour, or did this afternoon, but, as the ice is all out, the bridge is in no danger. The swift current looks very handsomely....

As the Tribune gets here a day later than the Boston Dailies, I should prefer the latter and if you will stop it, I will change. The Tribune contains much interesting matter which is not to be found in the other, but I do'nt find time more than 3 days in the week to peruse it as I should like to. . . .

With love to all, I am

> your affectionate son
> NED.

Hanover, April 28th 1861.

MY DEAR FATHER:

We have finished one week more of the term and there is left only 1 ½ weeks before I come home. They are driving us very hard, having 3 recitations and a lecture per diem, making 4 hours in the recitation room. I shall be glad when we get a fortnight's rest.

A warrant has been procured from the State to form a company and already between 30 & 40 have enlisted, among them are Ingraham & Bailey, the first & second of our class. It is to be composed solely of students and for that reason I suppose would not be called out unless affairs came into a very bad state. The only objection to this plan is that the 3 upper classes joining together, some of those who graduate this year might want to go into the service before those now in College.

All those who have now signed the paper are determined fellows and the most of them over 21 yrs. of age. I should admire to put my name on the paper but, after your letter of a week ago or more, I have concluded I must get your permission. If it was a company of citizens, as well as students, it would be a different matter, but as it is I wish you would give me permission.

Guns are to be procured from the State probably next term, at any rate as soon as the demand for them upon Government can be filled. The Sophomores & Freshmen have formed companies and are to have uniforms, but not signing any warrant to serve the State, would probably disperse if there was danger of fighting. The Soph. Company numbers about 50 & the Fresh. 60 or more.

Nearly all the Southern students are gone and 3 have enlisted at the South. Very many graduates of '60 & '59 and of those who have entered and not finished their course are known to be in arms. . . .

A meeting was held yesterday at which Profs. Aiken & Patterson spoke. Mr. Balch offers $1000 to assist in the equipment of forces.

This reminds me that I shall need some money to settle my bills. . . .

With much love, I am
your affectionate son
NED.

Hanover, June 16th 1861.

MY DEAR SISTER:

I suppose Father is not with you today. I rec'd a letter yesterday from him telling me of his proposed visit to Washington, to help his friends, he said. He didn't mention what his address would be, so that I shant write him till I hear more.

The war spirit has entirely evaporated at Dartmouth, leaving in its stead a spirit of destruction & deviltry.

You remember perhaps the long brick convent-like building in the rear of Dart. Hall. Several attempts had been made to set it on fire by firing it from below but as every partition was of brick and the least possible amount of wood-work had been used in its structure, the attempt was unavailing, until last Thursday night, when it was set inside the roof just under the eaves.

About $11\frac{1}{2}$ o'clock the alarm of fire was raised and on jumping from my bed everything was illuminated with the blaze. A very still night was chosen, else there would have been danger. After it burst through the roof, it burned an hour & a half, with half the college collected round it battering down the brick walls and laughing at the numerous jokes perpetrated at its expense. The faculty were in the background but were quiet. The bell-ringer knew what was burning and for that reason no bell was rung & no alarm raised away from the buildings.

Some inconvenience was experienced yesterday but a large wooden shanty was erected during the day and a new site for a permanent edifice has been selected.

It was the most ludicrous sight I ever saw, the students coming down from their rooms many of them with nothing on but their slippers & hat and a quilt or shawl wrapped round their bodies bringing their pipes, which they lighted from the fire amidst great enthusiasm. An immense amount of brick was used in the building and it was amusing to see the half-clothed beings prying over the walls. It looks now, or did look before it was enveloped in the wooden shanty, like the ruin of a jail closely filled with cells. It was undoubtedly a good thing that it was "removed."

Last night a skeleton was stolen from the Medical College and suspended from the ceiling in the Chapel, directly over the Student's seats. Unluckily for the perpetrators of the deed, it was discovered before Prayers & removed, but it had to be cut to pieces, some of which remained in the Chapel, together with a large hole through which a rope had been let down, fastened to the beast and pulled up again. I have procured, fortunately, a collarbone to preserve as a trophy. It will be very hard for those who are found out, if any there are, as the skeleton, an immense one, was worth $50. to say the least and has hung for a long time in the Lecture Room at the Med. Coll. building and will be missed for that reason.

I have taken up, I see, a good deal of space telling you of these things but it is all that has happened that I think you would be interested in.

The young ladies here of yr. acquaintance wish to be remembered &c. &c. Since receiving so much wholesome advice under the paternal roof I do not, of course, allow myself to be inveighled by the fair sex in any manner. The hearts of Hanover young ladies must be, I think, entirely insensible, neither being affected nor producing any effect, as none of them have ever left the state of single blessedness, but pass through the successive stages of blossom, maturity & decay as easily as Shakers.

Our church doesnt commence till 3 ½ o'clock but tis time to be getting ready. So with love to all I am

yr. affectionate bro.

NED.

Hanover, July 14th 1861.

MY DEAR FATHER:

We are now entirely thro' study for Junior Year. The Examination is the only bugbear we have to look forward too & that will be over this week. The week after is of course Commencement week.

You will come up on Tuesday, I suppose. . . . I shall not myself be here as I have been chosen a delegate to our annual Ψ.U. Convention, which is to be holden at Yale. I would like to stop here but presume I shall enjoy that trip, having always desired to visit Yale, & this being a trip at half price. . . .

With love to all, I am
yr. affectionate son
NED.

Hanover, Sept. 29th 1861.

MY DEAR FATHER:

I have not heard from you since Tuesday but suppose you have been busy about matters & things & have not been able to write me. . . .

What do you think of matters in Missouri & Gen. Fremont's campaign? I wish that I was enlisted in some capacity. I wrote this last sentence without thinking, for I dont intend to express such sentiments unless there is some chance of my fulfilling the wish, which I fear there is not at present.

The President's son Nat. is here to-day. He is Colonel of the Vt. 6th which goes before long. He was Lieut. Col. of the Reg. which started a few days ago but just as he was leaving he heard of his promotion. Another son of the Prex. is surgeon of the same regiment. . . .

We took up last week, rather unexpectedly on account of the illness of Prof. Long, "Edwards on the Will," which I believe you studied when you were here. It is quite difficult but I guess I shall find no more trouble with it than with the others. I have got along very well this term in our studies, especially in Prof. Long's department.

I have lately been taking a review of the life of Washington. I have been reading the first & second volumes & part of the third for a long time past, principally in vacations. I have taken notes on the whole work, with the exception of about 50 pages in vol. 4th which I have not completed, in my review. You can judge better of the fulness of the notes from the quantity of them; I have written over thus far nearly 12 pages of large size writing paper, such as you gave me in vacation. I shall hereafter take notes on all my historical reading & wish I had done so with Prescott's works. . . .

yr. affectionate son
NED.

Hanover, Oct. 13th 1861.

MY DEAR FATHER:

I was quite surprised to hear from you that George Gill had left college & also that Gage had "collapsed under the present excitement." They are both in regular standing & are present and recite at recitation as usual. There must have been some misunderstanding between you & Mr. Gill or else George was premature in his statements. Three of them, White, Gage & Gill, tho't of taking commissions to get up a company but are not yet suited with their offer & are more than likely to stay thro' the term. Perhaps you had better not mention this to Mr. Gill if you are sure that you understood him correctly, as it might be unpleasant for George.

But our boys are still going. Two Juniors have appointments (commissions) as Lieutenants of Cavalry, in Vt., very good places. I have heard of two Sophs also as being in Cavalry Co.s somewhere. I believe I wrote you that a Junior had gone as Adjutant of Vt. 6th.

Our boys (Seniors) have formed a drill club, under the instruction of Brig. Gen. Jackman, the head of Norwich University, drilling an hour every afternoon. I have joined it, as I thought a little military knowledge could do one no hurt.

To show how our boys take hold of it, it is enough to say that out of 40 only, who are back this fall, 26 were at Norwich yesterday at the first lesson & 4 more will go to-morrow. The lessons will continue 3 or 4 weeks, at $1.00 per week. What do you think of it?

Professor Long has been very sick for 2 or 3 days & is not expected to live. His death will be a great loss to the college, being a much sounder man on many subjects than any other man in the Faculty. If another Fairbanks or Varney is made to take his place, this institution may as well give up the ghost.

How was the matter of the Library settled by the Trustees last summer? The college faculty have not yet seen fit to open it.

Last week evening prayers were abolished, much to the gratification of all concerned. The morning exercises are a little lengthened by the introduction of singing but not enough to counteract the good of no evening exercises.

The Catalogues are out but I have not sent you one as I tho't that the President would. If you have'nt one, let me know.

We didn't read our compositions on *Wit* till last week. Your ideas were quite serviceable to me, although by considerable study I worked up the matter into a very different form from that you sent it in, making it a more serious thing....

yr. affectionate son,
NED.

...I hope you wont think Gage's ideas of going to "*War*," foolish. His reason will be, if he goes, that he cant get a school for the winter & must get money some way or other, & fighting would be the easiest, as he could get his diploma even if he were shot. Some of our best men will go between now & Spring. I dont think we shall graduate 40.

Hanover Nov. 4th 1861.

MY DEAR FATHER:

I have only two more Sundays to spend in Hanover this fall. Our Examination takes place a fortnight from to-day & probably I shall get home a fortnight from to-morrow. I had tho't some of going by Lowell, as our Class photographs are to be taken by a man there, Warren, and those of us who can do so prefer to go there on our way rather than wait till he comes here in the Spring. I shall be governed entirely by the trains: If I can't go without staying over one night, I shall not go....

A Sophomore, Kimball—died here last Friday of typhoid fever.

Saturday morning, as is customary on such occasions, the students formed in procession & escorted the body to the Depot. It was a little singular that two of his classmates went home the same day to attend the funerals of brothers who were killed at Ball's Bluff. Don't you think that somebody was to be blamed for that defeat?

I am afraid that the terrible gale we had Saturday night may have reached down the coast to the Naval Expedition. But to-day we shall probably hear something from it. Everything most depends upon it, I suppose, for it must be that Mc[C]lellan won't wait any longer to make his advance movement if that succeeds. Will Gen. Scott's resignation affect the cause in any way, do you think?—

The class voted last Tuesday not to drill any longer, after having taken lessons two weeks. We had time to get an insight into nearly all the company movements & some of them we could go through very well indeed. It will be of great advantage to us if we are ever put where we want to drill recruits. . . .

yr. affectionate son
NED.

Hanover, Nov. 10th 1861.

MY DEAR FATHER:

In a week & 2 days, I shall be in Exeter. This term has gone faster than any I have ever spent here, not only to myself alone but to most everybody, for all speak of its seeming shortness. . . .

The war news is getting to be quite exciting. By a new arrangement we get two mails a day here now, one being brought by the midnight train & opened early in the morning. By this we get the Boston evening papers the next morning after they are printed.

I have just finished reading Motley's Dutch Republic. Our class is now purchasing donations for the Libraries. We subscribe $5.00 apiece & pay in the Spring, having the books sent us now, which we distribute among ourselves during the winter. I am in hopes to get some valuable works from the Library & the donation both, but we draw by lot & according to Tuck luck, I am the very last man in the Class, to draw from the Library & expect the same luck in the donation.

My expenses this Fall will be large, but they include a new outfit from top to toe. My board bill will be $39.00 My overcoat $21.00, under-coat $14.00, pants & vest, $10.00, washing-bill $3.25, Daily-paper (about) $1.95, expenses home $5.00. I have on hand $5.00 which will undoubtedly go for something I don't now think of. The whole amounts to 89$, which will cover everything.

I shall write you most likely by Saturday to let you know when I shall get home. . . .

I may go down in a coach (as most of our Class will do) to W. Lebanon to meet the train that goes down at 2 in the morning, on Tuesday, in which case I shall get home at 11 ½, or I may wait till the 2nd train, not getting home till 5 or 7 P.M., via Lawrence.

With love to all, I am
your most affectionate son
NED.

In President Bartlett's Time

EDWIN B. FROST

≫ What student life was like at Dartmouth in the 1880s is described in *An Astronomer's Life* (Boston, 1933), the autobiography of Edwin B. Frost. Following graduation in 1885, he taught at Dartmouth (physics, chemistry, astronomy) and later at the University of Chicago. He was director of the University of Chicago's famous Yerkes Observatory for twenty-seven years.

IN JUNE, 1882, we [Edwin and his brother Gilman] with a few others, took the entrance examinations for Dartmouth College. Most of the men entered from academies or high schools by certificate and without examination. These boys had the advantage of being drilled so that they would do creditable work in their freshman year. We worked on these examinations for three days, morning and afternoon. This was about a month before my sixteenth birthday. We were certainly lacking in the study of English grammar and English literature, although we were well drilled in Latin and Greek grammar. We were admitted, and I remember that Father told us to forget our books until the college term opened in September. . . .

When college opened in the autumn, it had less novelty for us than for most of our classmates. We had hung around the outskirts of the crowd at all college sports enough to be familiar with them, and we had seen so many freshmen come in and adapt themselves to the new life that we were inclined to regard ourselves as somewhat sophisticated. This was not the case in the classroom, because we had not been used to reciting before other students and we were both rather shy. The schedule was: Algebra, Latin (Livy), and Greek (Herodotus, Æschylus, and the lyric poets). While I realize very fully the limited acquaintance with the classics which the average boy picks up during the six years of Latin and four years of Greek under the old academic

63

system, I nevertheless have no moment to regret for the time that I thus spent.... I never was a good scholar in Latin and I could never see reason in the sequence of Latin composition. I know, too, that most of the students abhorred it....

I always liked Greek better than Latin. One of our instructors was Professor John Henry Wright, an excellent scholar who had lately come back to teach at Hanover after completing his studies in Germany. He thought that there was virtue in the German lecture method and tried it on us in Greek composition. Thus we had to take notes, and were obliged to write down *verbatim* his introductory paragraph, which I committed to memory. When called upon to make some remarks at our reunion forty years later, I thought it would be amusing to repeat that paragraph: 'The object of this course is, by a series of exercises, interspersed with notes on various matters, first, to secure familiarity with the Greek mode of expression, and second, to make more vivid, exact, and comprehensive, the knowledge to be gained by reading.' Several of my classmates called out, 'Letter perfect.' Naturally, that was the only thing about the course that I did remember. It is sometimes easier to commit a thing to memory than to forget it.

In the spring term all freshmen were required to take a practical course in surveying. This was one of the most interesting of all courses, both to those naturally industrious and to those naturally lazy. We went out in groups of about four each in charge of one of the more trustworthy students. We used the plane-table for a survey of the campus and laid a base-line measuring the distance to Mount Ascutney, which is a fraction under twenty miles from the observatory. We wound up with making a survey of some irregular piece of land with a rail fence and plenty of bushes, requiring offsets.... For well over a hundred years in the history of the college this was a required exercise....

I think that family prayers were suspended in our house when two or three of us had to make a hurried scramble to get to chapel at three minutes to eight. The bell rang for four minutes, then tolled for three minutes and ended with a double stroke, after which no entrance was permitted, and those who arrived too late could only gnash their teeth.

Students often came to chapel without full completion of their toilet, but a large overcoat covered a multitude of omissions. It was always arranged that classes immediately followed chapel, and there was a hasty exodus from the building to the various classrooms. Most of these were heated by an iron stove and there was a small room adjacent, called the 'guard-room,' wherein lived the student charged with keeping up the temperature in the classroom. This system of heating seems rather crude today, but it was on the whole very efficient and we seldom had cold rooms. The student who acted as stoker also served as a monitor, checking off attendance at certain classes.

The morning exercises in the old chapel in the central part of Old Dartmouth Hall were always likely to have some unexpected finale. The president and faculty sat on a raised platform at the front with only one entrance on either side. There was never quite complete certainty whether the organ would work or might have been tampered with in the night so as to emit sounds not appropriate in a religious exercise. Back of the stage a window-curtain might fall during the service, bearing incriminating remarks about certain students or the faculty. Or a sheet might be found in the hymn-books having some 'grinds' on an unsuspecting college officer or upon a member of the student body who might be in temporary disfavor.

Then there was always the question of emergence. The juniors sat on the south side and behind them the freshmen, with the seniors in front on the north and the sophomores behind them. President Bartlett usually gave a pretty fair hint as to when the final prayer was approaching the end. It took the form of the phrase, 'Hasten the time when all the earth shall,' and so forth. This was parodied once in the college annual, 'Hasten the day when prexy will pray some other way than "Hasten the day." ' The form of ending became a matter of speculation to those inclined to wager. Someone therefore set the president wise and he frequently used an alternative phrase, 'May the time soon come,' so that sporting chances were still taken. But when these final phrases came from the lips of the august president, the juniors who sat in front of me had their hats ready and no time was lost. Not a second after the Amen began, they started for the door. And it was with some delight that the freshmen followed them so closely that the front array was generally pushed from the stone steps and carried off, as it were, on a wave of descending piety to the walk below. Once in a while there was a sprained back or leg as a result of this prompt dismissal, but on the whole there was a business-like air in hastening to the classrooms and an apparent ardor for learning which would hardly have been expected. This procedure had been followed for over a century. I always remember Josiah Quincy, of the class of '84, who sat not far in front of me and could be seen for the last few minutes of the prayer getting his little derby in position so that he would have a grand start.

After sophomore year was finished, we were allowed some electives, and my natural tendency toward the study of the physical sciences led me to choose all the laboratory work possible in the ground floor of Reed Hall. The college really had some remarkable equipment, especially in the line of optics. This had been purchased chiefly by Professor Charles Young and his father before him. I took great pains with my notebook on the physical experiments, which I illustrated much more elaborately than was necessary, little realizing that in a couple of years I should be installed as an assistant in the same laboratory.

One of my special pleasures in college was the opportunity of being in the classroom of Professor Arthur S. Hardy who taught us analytic geometry, calculus, and analytic mechanics. He was a remarkable teacher and a many-sided gentleman—poet, novelist, and author of a volume of quaternions. He gave up teaching about 1895 and became editor of the *Cosmopolitan Magazine* in New York. Shortly thereafter he was appointed Minister to Persia and so journeyed to Teheran. Later he was transferred to the position of Minister at Athens, and thence after some years to Berne, and finally retired from the diplomatic service after having been Ambassador to the court of Madrid for some time.

Senior year at Dartmouth in 1886 provided rather a large range of electives. I had been greatly interested in a course in descriptive astronomy given by Professor Charles F. Emerson (familiarly known as

'Chuck'), and had up to then used the telescope, with which I had been more or less familiar for many years. This term was probably the only one in which I had a higher rating than my brother, and to pass ahead of him required being about at the head of the class. I was considerably in doubt as to whether my work would be in the line of physics or astronomy.... It happened that at this time (in August, 1885) a new star, or Nova, was suddenly discovered by an English astronomer. It was in the heart of the Great Nebula of Andromeda and was a star of about the seventh magnitude. It thus became the only individual star distinguishable in this nebula, which at that time we supposed to be a purely gaseous body.... Among astronomers, as well as the public generally, it was thought that we might be observing the sudden transformation of the nebula into a star along the lines of the theory of Laplace. I was familiar with the appearance of the nebula and was immensely excited over the new phenomenon. Perhaps it was this that led me somewhat definitely to enter the field of astronomy rather than that of physics. I had just passed my nineteenth birthday at this time and had a right to youthful enthusiasm.

It had been the requirement at Dartmouth that every senior should deliver before the college an original oration during the course of the year. This exercise occurred at one-thirty on Wednesday afternoons under the conduct of the professor of English literature, who censored in advance the speeches to be presented. After the two or three so-called orations were over on a given Wednesday, the rest of the afternoon was free. This made the audience somewhat restive, as all the boys had some program of activity to set in motion as soon as the last speaker had finished, and it was a highly critical audience, not hesitating at all to applaud at the wrong place as circumstances might seem to require.

When my turn came, I had the temerity to choose as my topic this remarkable new star in the Andromeda Nebula. Perhaps it was out of consideration of my youth, for I was the youngest in the class, that the audience was tolerant and let me by without any undue disturbance.
...

In June, 1886, we graduated in the regular course, after a year of hard, interesting work. I specialized in physics and received 'final honors' therein, while my brother received his in mathematics. We had to write theses as a part of the extra requirements. My brother gave the salutatory address and I ranked somewhere around sixth in the class. I made rather a juvenile speech on the influence of astronomy on literature. Graduating day was quite an ordeal for the audience, for not less than fifteen of us spoke, and we followed the ancient practice of appearing in dress suits, though the time was forenoon. . . .

Country Schoolmaster
FRED LEWIS PATTEE

⇒⇒ The library at Pennsylvania State University was named for Fred Lewis Pattee 1888, who taught English and American literature there from 1894 to 1928. During a long life (he died in 1950) he was a prolific writer of critical essays, novels, literary history, memoirs. The recollections printed here are taken from his autobiography *Penn State Yankee* (State College, Penn., 1953).

THE MARVELLOUS BEAUTY of Hanover Plain with its mountain setting thrilled me more and more every year of my stay there. On the South, etched like a cameo against the sky, was the sharp peak of Ascutney, once in a sonnet written in senior year hailed by me as the Soracte of the college setting:

> "Behold Soracte white with winter snow"—
> Ah, sunny poet of the Sabine Farm,
> I never read thy memory-haunting psalm
> But what Ascutney, lying blue and low
> Upon the South, and clad in mellow glow
> Comes back to me.

The campus with its ancient elms and its bordering maples a blaze of scarlet and yellow in autumn, made an ideal setting for the old Dartmouth Row, strictly academic like the architecture of the buildings. Behind it all arose sharply the observatory ridge crowned with the commanding old pine, during our day vigorous and seemingly, like the very college, a landmark forever. But lightning was to destroy it. Now in its place stands the round tower, first suggested by President Bartlett. Our class built the second section. Below it was the picturesque glen known as the Bema woods, with many trees dedicated to college classes in a ceremony following the "sing out" when the Juniors furnished the lemonade for a "wet down."

No college had more facilities for walks and outings. One might explore the Vale of Tempe, follow Stump Lane through a matchless stand of white pine to the Connecticut River, "frog it" around the five-mile square, or one might climb Balch Hill and view the town from the upper air. And endless were the possibilities of the great river, the Connecticut, often in the spring filled with logs that sometimes jammed against the Ledyard Bridge even threatening the old structure. Near enough to the college for a week-end trip were the Franconias, with Mooselauke, and farther away Mount Washington and the Presidential range. Few of us, however, dreamed of actually visiting them.

Intense loyalty to Dartmouth came early to all of us. When the president addressed the student body as "Men of Dartmouth," it always brought to me a strange thrill. The spirit of the fighting old college that had been planted in the forest of the frontier by a man who had had a vision was instilled into our very souls. . . .

In every way the college adapted itself to the young Vikings it had in charge. . . . Board was $3 a week and room rent $10 a term. I left college with what seemed to me a tremendous debt—$550. All my other expenses I had paid from money earned at college or during vacations. Using the experience I had gained in [a] printing office, I made for the college the blank books used in the college examinations, and I peddled through the dormitory rooms blocks of paper and various kinds of stationery. One summer I waited table at Revere Beach, another summer at Nantasket Beach out of Boston. In my junior summer I worked as a hayfield hand at $1.50 a day and, haying over, I got a job running a boring machine with a gang that was building a pulp-mill in Bristol. During two winter vacations I taught school, once in Candia, N.H., and once in Maine. It had long been a college tradition to allow students to teach 10-week terms in rural schools during the mid-year vacations. One of the jokes of my era had it that Cape Cod had been educated by Dartmouth winter pedagogues, and as a result many of the fair Cape Cod sirens wore Dartmouth fraternity pins, later to be exchanged for wedding rings. Be this as it may, dozens of Dartmouth students turned schoolmasters, were found all over New

England during the winter months. I have no doubt that "the master of the district school," who, according to Whittier in *Snow Bound*,

> Sang songs, and told us what befalls
> In classic Dartmouth's college halls,

was one of these embryo pedagogues let loose for a winter term to lighten the darkness of a rural school.

To make this teaching plan possible, the Christmas vacation had been lengthened to four weeks, and by incurring an absence of six weeks, the student would have time to complete a 10-weeks school term, the absence to be made up on his return in early March. Such absences, however, raised havoc with one's grades. My own standing, because of my two winter absences, was affected to the degree that I did not make Phi Beta Kappa (honorary membership was awarded me by the chapter in later years) and in a graduating class of 65 I was able to be only number 17. During my senior year, which was unbroken, I was number six.

The school in Maine which occupied my junior winter was secured for me by a teacher's agency run by two seniors who had bought the business from the preceding senior class and who in turn, for a consideration, would pass it on at the end of the year. Of the inner workings of this agency I was soon to learn. I had registered with them early in the fall, signing an agreement to pay to the agency a percentage of my salary in any school they provided for me. Accordingly early in December I was told that a school had been found for me at Bowdoinham, Maine, and that I was to open it the day after Christmas. In high spirits, therefore, I started for Maine little dreaming what was ahead of me. Bowdoinham I found was a town on the Sagadahoc, a branch of the Kennebec. It was a tide-water town with a unique fertilizer mill run by a tide wheel so adjusted that it could be used for power both on the incoming and the outgoing tides. A shipyard was there too, but unused during the winter.

I soon found that I was not expected in Bowdoinham. It seems that the student at the head of the agency, an experienced teacher with a wealth of recommendations, had engaged the school for himself, and just before my arrival had telegraphed the committee that he had broken his leg and had sent me as a substitute. All at once I found myself in an embarrassing position. The committee was divided. After a meeting discussing the situation, Dr. Cheeny, a physician of the old school much loved by the community, called me in and looked me keenly in the eye. "What is the truth? Tell me squarely," he said. I told him all I knew and after a searching interview he said he would let me open the school. There seemed to be nothing else to do. The school was to open on Monday and I was the only teacher in sight.

Then came another attack on my nerves. The school was a "teacher-killer," so I was told by every one I met. The boys one winter had thrown the master from a window and he had landed head down in a snowdrift. Walking up to view the school house Saturday afternoon, I was stopped four or five times, welcomed to Bowdoinham, and then showered with advice: "They are a tough lot and the only way is to begin licking 'em the very first day. Thrash 'em or they'll thrash you." I did not sleep well the Sunday night before the opening.

As I viewed the 70 boys and girls, all of them of high school age, I realized that I had tackled a job that needed experience, and I was a mere college junior who had taught only one term in a small school. In one corner sat eight or ten strapping young men who worked during the summer in the shipyards, raw-boned Yankee lads boiling over with life and mischief. My first problem was discipline, and unconsciously I did the one thing needed to rule the turbulent youngsters. I took no pains to conceal the fact that I was a member of the Dartmouth track team with a record for the two-mile run, and that I played football in the fall. I weighed then 185 pounds and had no more fat on me than a fox hound. I talked athletics with the boys, told them how to organize teams, and how football squads are dieted and handled. They were impressed, but action was needed to convince them. A half dozen of the students were better men than I was physically and they knew it. The test was not delayed. One morning I found the key-hole plugged and the door unopenable save by a carpenter, with the school lined up to see what I would do. From the academic standpoint I did the wrong thing. I was melodramatic in those days, full of adventure stories, and I felt that difficulties must be met not with argument but with action. Accordingly I made a flying-tackle rush at the door, the strength of which I knew, and smashed it down. Then in true Oliver Optic fashion I stripped off my coat and shouted, "If you are men, come on one at a time. If you are yellow rats, come in a bunch." I laugh when I think of it now, but it worked. For a moment no one stirred, then the leader, a giant of a shipyard worker, came to me and said, "We's only jokin'. We didn't mean nothing. Don't go to work and get mad." Thereupon I laughed and said, "Oh, I didn't mean nothing either. I was only just joking too. Hurry up; the bell's going to ring." I had no more trouble. A glorious fellow I found the leader after that. His name was Jake Rideout—I still remember it. The 10 weeks over, he came to me and half bashfully said: "Kinder wish you wan't goin'. We sort er like ye." The local paper gave me a three-inch write-up, praising my work, but the paragraph was evidently put into type by the printer's devil. The editor had written, "The Prof. was well liked by his pupils," but as it appeared in type it read—"well licked." . . .

No Room at the Inn
WILLIAM W. GRANT

>>> After graduation from Dartmouth in 1903, William W. Grant went on to the Harvard Law School and to a lifelong practice of law in Denver. He was a trustee of the College for twenty years. His recollections are from his autobiography *Such Is Life*, privately printed at Denver in 1952.

THE QUESTION then arose where was I to attend college? I had a strong hankering for Stanford, with a minor pull for Colorado University. My father, however, resolved the matter in his usual peremptory way, as though writing a prescription.

"You," he said, "tend to be lazy. New England is the educational background of America. I came from the South and went into the Confederate Army at fifteen instead of going to the University of Virginia where Pa was going to send me. The New Englanders are hustlers. I shall send you to Dartmouth College. You will be in the educational background of the country and you will learn to hustle. The college is small and incidentally you can get a good education if you want it, and nobody can ever take it away from you." . . .

I said, "Yes, sir." . . . The die was cast, and I was entered at Dartmouth. . . .

Two suits were purchased for me at The May Shoe and Clothing Company, the only time up to then I had had such a lavish wardrobe. A dashing young clerk assured my stepmother that they were very collegiate. They were my first complete suits with long trousers. Previously, odd trousers with my old coats had been the order of the day. The great day finally came, the tenth of September, 1899, and I was off on the long four-night and three-day trip to Hanover, New Hampshire. I remember the exact day because Mrs. Henry Merriam and the General lived next door to us, and she gave me a book to read on the train—"When Knighthood was in Flower" by Charles Major—with her card and the date on it. . . .

I rode on a pass over the Rock Island to Chicago. My father had been one of the road surgeons since the early eighties. I left Denver at eleven p.m. and arrived in Chicago full of cinders and dirt the second morning after. It was the first time in ten years I had been out of Colorado since coming to live there, except once to Davenport for Christmas. I then went over the Lake Shore to Springfield, Massachusetts, and thence by Boston & Maine to White River Junction, Vermont. I was there hustled into a stage coach and rode in a blinding rain for four miles over wretched, muddy roads, arriving at Hanover about midnight. My, I felt bad!

A chubby, young fellow, obviously one of the students, was acting as night clerk. No rooms were to be had. I looked around the lobby. There were windows on one side, a door and front wall on the next side, on the third, the desk parallel to the first side, and on the fourth, a number of miscellaneous doors leading to all the retreats customary in such cases. There were a few worn leather chairs and sofas scattered around. The Wheelock Hotel—named in honor of the founder of the college, Eleazar Wheelock—was undoubtedly in its day one of the worst, if not the worst, hotel in the United States. The thought of sitting in that lobby all night made me regret not having gone to Stanford or Colorado or anywhere else. But it was useless to repine. I couldn't have gotten away because I didn't have carfare, if for no other reason. Why had I chosen to leave Denver at all? All thoughts of having gone to Dartmouth for good, sound reasons, even to learn to hustle, were as nothing to my consuming homesickness just for Denver.

The clerk sensed my distress. He glanced at the register and said cheerfully, "It's a hell of a long way to come and then roll in here on a night like this, ain't it? You can have my room. I get board and lodging for working here at night."

He took me up four long flights to an octagonal room in the top of an octagonal tower. It was, if possible, even more bleak than the lobby. It was a large room with a dirty, tumbled bed somewhere around the middle of the room, without even the dreary pictures or fuzzy prints that are still characteristic of hotel rooms everywhere. I thanked the clerk, whom I subsequently knew as Fat Archibald. At least he had given me the best he had. When he left the room, I shuddered. After looking over the bed casually, I pulled the coverlid up tight, took off my coat and shoes, and covered myself with the heavy overcoat I had brought along. I went to sleep probably more dismal than at any time in my life theretofore.

I woke up about six-thirty to a damp day and looked out the window on a sodden campus of eight or nine acres. On the west, a row of dignified old New England houses, in the midst of which was Sanborn Hall, Professor Sanborn's old house remodelled as a dormitory; on the north, a gaunt, old Congregational Church, with some slight evidences of beauty inside of a puritanical severity, flanked by a row of houses, one quite beautiful and known as the "Choate House" because Rufus Choate lived there when in college; on the east, four very handsome college buildings, the center one Old Dartmouth Hall, the first of the college buildings; and on the south, Bissell Hall and the hotel, both of unspeakable ugliness. Scattered around in the background were college buildings of all kinds of incongruous design and construction. Wilson Hall, the library, had been erected on a foundation of Hostetter's Bitters. . . .

The college at that time had about six hundred and fifty students in attendance. The location made up for the lack of beauty in the buildings. On a plateau about a hundred feet above the Connecticut River, surrounded by dense pine forests, with Mt. Ascutney and the White Mountains rising a few miles in the background, the prospect was fascinating. A village with few inhabitants except those who worked for the college. It seemed a long way from anywhere . . . , with no feminine society within any distance except by rail. Trains were available at White River Junction and an occasional one at Norwich, Vermont, across the river, at all kinds of ghostly hours, such as eleven p.m., two a.m., six a.m., etc. White River Junction had a horrible frame station where slabs of cold pie, cold beans and other assorted delicacies were served morning, noon and night. A regular course of eating at the Junc was calculated to insure life-long dyspepsia.

That morning I matriculated, and all regrets vanished when I met Dr. William Jewett Tucker, President of the College and one of the very few really great men I have ever met. He had a dignified, personal charm that was irresistible. He had every freshman come to his office when his matriculation was complete, had him sit down, put him immediately at his ease, and talked to him in a most informal and attractive way. He had close-cropped, white hair, a short, white mustache, cleancut features, and the most piercing blue eyes I have ever seen—eyes that were sympathetic and kind, but capable of darting forth shafts that went right through you. He came closest to the cloud compelling Zeus of all the men I have ever seen.

He it was who put Dartmouth on the road to becoming the great institution she is today. After meeting Dr. Tucker no boy ever regretted coming to Dartmouth. I certainly did not. Inside of two or three weeks he knew every freshman by name on sight. How heartwarming it was to go down the street, touch your hat to him and have him say in that kindly, firm voice, "Good morning, Grant." The President knew you, even though lewd fellows such as sophomores and upper classmen might ignore you! The students of his time literally idolized him....

My freshman year I had mathematics—a review of algebra, geometry, plane and solid, and trigonometry; English—when to use "shall" or "will"; Adams Sherman Hill's Rhetoric; German; Greek Archeology, Latin—Valleius Paterculus and others; all interspersed with lectures on hygiene and matters of that sort. We were divided into sections in English on the basis of one hundred questions on "shall" or "will." I answered them all "will," on the assumption that they were divided half and half. I was right and landed in the lowest group.

On my twentieth reunion, I ran into Professor Worthen, our math teacher. I said, "Professor Worthen, you don't remember me. I am Grant, 1903." He replied, "Oh, yes, I do. I remember you perfectly. If it hadn't been for me you would have flunked freshman math."...

Sophomore year I took Greek—Sophocles, Aeschylus, Plato's Apology, Euripides, and Aristophanes' Birds; Latin—various comic writers such as Plautus and Terence; physics; English; and German. It seems rather an overdose of languages, ancient and modern. At the same time, had I had some of my later experience, I would have taken more economics and government.

Junior year things slacked off a bit. I took Early English—Chaucer's poetry, Palgrave's Golden Treasury, under the remarkable Professor Charles Francis Richardson, affectionately known as "Clothespins" because of his great height and long legs; anthropology—Keane's Races of Mankind, under Professor Wells; a memory course of classic English selections under Professor Laycock; several special courses in Greek and Latin literature; astronomy, under Professor Frost of the Yerkes Observatory. As a Dartmouth graduate, he used to come to Hanover every year for a semester.

Senior year I had field geology under Professor Hitchcock; a course in sociology; more English under Professor Richardson; more German; modern European history, under Professor Justin Smith; more Greek; a course in elementary jurisprudence; and various other courses I can't recall.... I got the highest mark I received in college from Professor Colby for an essay on "The Spanish Code in the Philippines," and for an English essay on a subject and for a professor, neither of which I now remember. I also had a course in economics in which I learned nothing.

Professor Richardson was easily the best teacher I had in college. Everybody passed his courses. One day he paused and said in his dry, rather cynical, clipped, nasal tones, "Young gentlemen, I know this is considered a cinch course. It is so because I choose to make it so. Long years of experience have taught me that by teaching in this way a few men acquire a genuine taste for English literature. The rest of you don't count, and nobody cares about flunking you." The effect was crushing. He went on, "I often wonder why it is that dogs, without any special effort to educate them, show such infinitely greater intelligence. Take my dog, Geist, for example." (Geist was a small, brown Dachshund.) "In my daily, rather long walks he has faithfully followed me for a number of years, with certain diversions of his own. I decided to follow him for an afternoon. I am ashamed to disclose to you the intimate nature of some of the information—concerning some of you, incidentally—which I have come into possession of, to say nothing of my fellow members of the faculty and their household arrangements.

"My walk was very much longer and more fatiguing than usual, and confined for the most part to alleys and kitchen entrances. I know, for instance, that the wife of a fellow professor is going to have a reception and what she is going to have in the way of refreshments. I know which faculty wives are thrifty and which are extravagant by what they put in their garbage pails. I may say Geist has no use for the former. If I were a tramp, the information I have accumulated would be invaluable from the standpoint of subsistence handouts. If I were teaching something required for you to get a living, I am confident Geist would be a much better teacher than I merely by force of example. But as I am trying to teach you something that will add to the joy and satisfaction of living, I must continue to carry on. As you know nothing of today's assignment, I will now dismiss you with the somewhat dim hope that you will know a little more tomorrow." . . .

Professor Justin Smith's course in modern European history was inspiring. The Professor himself was completely out of the ordinary. There was none of the local carelessness either as to clothes or manners. . . . He was a large man, about six feet two, and he must have weighed well over two hundred pounds. He had a full, bushy, immaculately kept black beard. He was always dressed in the height of elegance—a morning coat, figured waistcoat, striped trousers, patent leather shoes, immaculate linen, winged collar, stiff white shirt, bright colored four-in-hand tie with a quietly expensive pin in it—generally a pearl—a stiff hat and a silk-lined, Oxford gray overcoat. He was a tremendous swell. As he sat at his desk before a room full of boys, he looked like a super Cossack beautifully habited in modern garb.

Different teachers have different methods. Professor Smith would look at an unprepared subject—one felt like a subject awaiting the stroke of the knout—with such withering scorn and spoke with such biting irony that he got more work out of a class than any professor in college. We really worked. Our terror at approaching semester exams was so obvious that it impressed even him. He finally said to us, "I am handing you today a series of ninety-eight questions. The examination will be taken from among those questions."

I have never seen in a class of boys such feverish activity at the library, such continuous discussion in groups, such lively attention to sources, so many subsidiary lectures from the well-informed among the students. The class as a whole did very well in the exam. It occurred to me afterwards that the ninety-eight questions pretty well covered the entire topic subject to examination.

Professor Smith began his course bluntly and abruptly. "Mr. Jones," he said, "how would you define 'history'?" A discussion immediately started which lasted the whole semester. I recollect Carlyle's definition, "History is how man, out of the chaos of actuality, realizes his ideals, social, political, and religious." I should call Professor Smith a driver and a highly successful teacher. He knew no persons. To him we were simply items and all alike, even football players—but we learned.

All in all, the teaching was first class and the personal attention was everything a student needed. I have considerable doubt as to whether close, personal attention is always desirable after high school. Certainly in law school and to a large extent in college men do better on their own than by being continually propped up. When there is a definite deterioration, it should, of course, be pointed out and steps taken to check it. In my sophomore year I had a summons one morning to go to the President's office. I went in with a minimum of formality. Dr. Tucker glanced up, took a paper from his desk and said, "Grant, I notice you are weak in physics. Otherwise, you are doing quite well. This indicates to me you can do better in physics. You will have to make more of an effort. You have come from farther west than any boy in college and you can't let your preparatory school down. The standing of schools on the accredited list depends on how well their graduates do. That's all." Dr. Tucker never asked you, he told you.

If anyone should ask me what I got out of college, I should say that at Dartmouth I learned to live with other people—rich and poor, mostly poor, clever and not so clever—with a regard for their own and my own limitations; to be absolutely independent with perhaps too much disregard for appearances; to appreciate learning and scholarship for their own sakes; to acquire some degree of mental discipline; and, finally, to consider that without Christianity real spiritual and moral progress was impossible. I still think so, and my whole experience of life confirms it. I have no doubt that listening to Dr. Tucker preach nearly every Sunday for four college years and at chapel every morning had a very definite influence on every student within the sound of his voice. He was never other than vigorous, emphatic, persuasive and stimulating. . . . I shall always be grateful for having had the opportunity to listen to Dr. Tucker. . . .

As the Century Turned
DOUGLAS VANDERHOOF

≫ The extracts below are from student letters written by Douglas Vander-Hoof 1901, published, in versions edited by E. C. Lathem, in the *Alumni Magazine* in June 1963. He became a prominent physician in Richmond, Va., taught at the Medical College of Virginia, and was for a time president of the Dartmouth Club of Virginia.

FRESHMAN YEAR

September 13, 1897—We arrived at Norwich at 8-15 this A.M. & then for 25 cts I had myself & all my baggage conveyed right here by coach....

I registered (at college) today & found out that my bill for the first term is $22^{00} but Pres. Tucker told me that if I stood 85% for the first term, that this bill would pay for the whole 3 terms. In fact there would be 1^{00} coming to me as $106 (the tuition with library fees) less $85—my scholarship—is $21^{00}....

I told Pres. Tucker that I wanted something to do to earn my way. He said that nothing could be done the first term as I knew nobody & nobody knew me. But he said to keep my eyes open.

September 17—Well, I am now fully started in Dartmouth College—had two recitations and a lecture today—Saturday & Wednesday afternoons there are no classes. We arise about seven A.M., go to breakfast & then at 7-^{57} to chapel. Attendance at chapel is compulsory so the whole college meets together, the different classes being seated by themselves. Pres. Tucker presides & the service consists of the reading of a few lines from Scripture, a hymn & a prayer.

The opening exercise of the College was held in the old chapel in old Dartmouth Hall.... At this meeting the Pres. spoke of affairs of interest to the College & to college men.... I only wish I could tell you all he said. He is a splendid *manly* man, & makes an ideal president for a boy's college. There's not a man here who does not respect & look up to Pres. Tucker.

October 27—Things have been in a dreadful state here. Boys have had hardly any sleep, food or rest for the past two days. But at last the chinning season is over. And I am supremely happy in the thought that I shant have to live thro' two such days again. I have joined the Theta Delts. . . .

October 31—Yesterday afternoon I went walking with a fellow named Sawyer, a Theta Delt. We went over the golf grounds & past the links. There are a few "Medics" here who are trying to introduce golf but the students don't take hold of it very eagerly. . . .

Your idea about chinning is correct only you don't half realize what it is. One fellow gets hold of you and talks three quarters of an hour and before you have gone a block another gets hold of you and so it goes on. Then you are invited to come around to the different frats in the evening where you meet all the fellows and where you are feasted and "jawed" and sit in a circle with about five or six fellows around you telling you what they will think of you if you don't join their frat etc.

November 7—Yesterday afternoon there was the annual Sophomore-Freshman football game, and altho the sophs had some crack players we held them down pretty well, being beaten only 10 to 6. Trude played a splendid game for the freshmen. There was considerable feeling displayed between the classes which ended in a "rush."

Just before the game we held a spirited class meeting but decided not to rush unless the sophs began it. But I dressed all prepared with my oldest clothes. After the game the sophs took a stout stick, used as a cane, and ran to the campus with it. Then as many of their men as possible got hold of the stick and the rest tried to keep us off. It was a very fierce rush, much fiercer than any last year, I am told. We went right into them and fought and pushed for a full half hour.

I went into it with all my might and as a result have a very stiff neck, am lame all over, especially my sides, and have a black & blue spot on my temple. I managed to work my way in in the first part of the rush

& got a hand on the cane. Then two sophs got hold of me one on each side and took me by the collar & pulled steady until I was completely choked. There happened to be no freshman at hand to keep them off and as a consequence I was "choked off." My old vest was ripped down the back & my old shirt, one of those you made me long ago had the band badly torn. My feet were so stepped on that the eyelets of the bicycle shoes that I wore had to be pried up with a knife before I could unlace them.

Well, the rush was declared a tie, each side having 17 hands on the cane, but I am quite sure the Freshmen won, altho the seniors who acted as judges said 17 apiece in order not to prevent the regular cane rush which comes off in the spring. For if we had won this rush the fellows might not wish to risk another.

January 19, 1898—I have now found out my approximate marks in my various studies and will tell you them—Math- in exam VG. and in daily work "E."—Latin-exam G., d.w. VG.—French-exam "E." and d.w. "E." You cant realize my joy at obtaining such marks three "E's" think of it. . . . You understand that "E." means 92% or over, V.G. 85%–92% and G. 75–85— . . .

I have started boarding at the Kyea (pronounced Key) Club and this afternoon went around & saw Mr & Mrs Kyea. They are very nice old people as I was told they were. I had a very long talk with them and seem to impress them as being all right so that they promised me a position to wait on table at the first vacancy which should occur.

January 30—34° below Zero yesterday morning! How's that. . . . Everything is on runners. Have not seen one wagon wheel since I struck town [following the Christmas vacation] and I guess we wont see the ground again until we get down on the campus and shovel off the snow for the first baseball game in the spring.

Last night the "kid faculty" gave an amateur theatrical performance at the "Gym." The play, "A Midwinter's Night Dream" was written, music and all by "Ed & Mary" i.e. Prof. and Mrs. Frost. Almost all the young professors and their wives took part in it and as it was an invitation affair was very select, of course. Very few of the students were invited, only a few Seniors.

February 9—This afternoon there was a mass meeting in the old chapel in Dartmouth Hall to talk over the honor system. It has been brought up several times and the Faculty have just finished acting on it and have submitted our constitution as amended by them. I am very much in favor of adopting the system where[by] each pupil will be put on his honor, and by which I firmly believe the standard of the college will be raised. . . .

After the regular meeting was over a base ball rally was held & it was decided to levy a tax of 2.50 on each student, for the support of the team. . . .

Then after this meeting there was a rush for the doors and as soon as the first ones got out they immediately began bombarding the rest with snow balls. As I with the rest of the Freshmen was up in the gallery I couldn't get out as everybody was lined up outside with snow balls ready to throw half a hundred balls at the first head to appear. Many jumped out of the back windows and a general fight ensued. Consequence, seventy four panes of glass broken—think of it. . . . Watching my opportunity, I jumped out of a rear window and altho' twenty snow-balls were thrown at me I got away unscathed. Harold did not fare so well being hit on the bridge of the nose with a regular cannon ball.

February 17—All Tuesday night and yesterday a blizzard has raged and no one here in college remembers one so severe. . . .

Last night there was great excitement here. Prof. Dow's new 16,000 house burned to the ground. It was just completed and his young wife was in Boston purchasing the furniture.

We were in fraternity meeting and heard cries of *fire*! One of the boys was sent down and came back with the report. The hall was cleared in less than a minute We had to run thro' untrodden snow way above our knees and I must have fallen down ten times.

Nothing could be done to save it, altho they brought out a little hand hose cart and played a single stream on it. It was a terrible night, the wind was blowing a gale and the only thing that saved the neighboring houses was the fact that the wind was not blowing towards them. When a fire starts in this town there is nothing to stop it.

April 13—Spring weather is here now and you begin to see the fellows lying around on the campus, smoking their pipes and watching the 'Varsity base ball squad practice. We are going to have a good nine this year and have great expectations of winning the championship of the tri-angular league, consisting of Williams, Amherst & Dartmouth.

April 24—I was greatly surprised this afternoon at Vesper Service, how seriously "Prexy" views the war upon which we have now entered. His talk was very impressive and you could have heard a pin drop at any time during the half hour in which he spoke. I have thought right along that the war would not last more than a couple of weeks at the most and that it would entail just simply our navy in its normal state. But during the last few days many of the boys have received summons from their regiments, etc and it was on this issue that "Prexy" spoke.

He said that we who are undergraduates are at present in the greatest crisis of our lives, and that it is for us to carefully consider wherein our duty lies. He said that before any of us enlisted we should consider two things. I Any sensative attachment which might keep us at home II Wheth[e]r we were enlisting in an opportunity or a necessity.

He dwelt on the fact that quite a number might leave with their regiments next week and when he ended I felt "all broke up" and several fellows went away with tears in their eyes. His talk was mainly to prepare us for what might be in store for us, and also to prevent many from enlisting "in an opportunity and not a necessity" i.e. to prevent many from enlisting just for the adventures. The necessity may come but only the opportunity is here now and there are many besides college men to fill the ranks at present.

May 5—Last Monday morning nineteen fellows went off from college to join their regiment at Concord N.H. . . . We all marched down to the station in regular military style and cheered them off. It was a very solemn affair and I noticed that all the boys were pretty quiet on the way back from the station.

SOPHOMORE YEAR

September 21, 1898—My studies so far have been decidedly easy. I have German, English (with a 5 page essay every week), Biology History and Physics. But before long I suppose it will be necessary to buckle down in good shape. There are quite a number of new professors on the faculty.

My biology course is going to be intensely interesting. We start in with microscopic work on the minute structure of the lowest forms of animal life. English is going to be a good deal of a bore but I shall do what I can with it. History is hard and exacting but interesting

Physics tho' difficult is going to be a favorite with me and German will be quite easy. I have secured two monitorships which will just about pay my washing bills.

October 12—Down at the Keay club matters are just as they were before. None of the waiters have their tables full. I have been putting a great deal of my spare time in looking for boarders but to no avail. The only way I can explain matters is this. The board at the Keay club is 3.50 per week. A good many of the clubs only charge 2.75 to 3.^{00} while on the other hand there are a good many $4.^{00} & $5.^{00} clubs. Now the wealthy fellows all go to the high priced clubs and the poor ones frequent the cheap clubs and that leaves hardly any one for Keays. As it is now I am earning just ½ my board, but I shall be untiring in my efforts to fill up my table.

Yesterday I had my conference with "Eric the Red" [Herbert D. Foster]. He is my history prof. and about once every month he calls up the class one by one at appointed times and asks them questions on their outside readings and also examines their notebooks. I had quite a "spiel" with him and he told me that my work had been very good and that my map of Europe in 476 A.D. was the best that had been ever handed in to him.

October 19—We had a mass meeting last Thursday called by the Seniors to forestall any action of the faculty in abolishing hazing. It is said that our class did more hazing than any other class in the history of the college. Pres. Tucker was very much displeased and decided to put a stop to it, and when he once determines to do anything he never stops until he accomplishes his end. Every member of our class was called up before the dean at different times and questioned. In this way & thro' outside sources it was narrowed down to about 15 sophomores among them several baseball men and other prominent fellows of the class. I told the dean that I had been out several nights but had made the freshmen do nothing very disagreeable.

At the mass meeting speeches were made showing how useless it would be to take any action contrary to Prexy's way of thinking and rather than have hazing abolished by the faculty—we submitted to the inevitable and passed resolutions for its abolishment from Dartmouth College forever. Hazing in a way is a good thing for some fellows who come up here in all the glory of their High school graduation & think they can run everything. But indiscriminate hazing is a very bad state of affairs. . . .

We had another mass meeting of the college today, called by Prexy. He congratulated us on our action and said that further action against the sophomores would be suspended.

November 6—I guess that there is no danger of our freezing this winter. We are now getting our steam from the central heating station which is over a block away and we have to keep the windows open all the time.

November 16—This evening just after supper the college bell began tolling. It was to announce the death of ex-president Bartlett. He was president before Prexy Tucker and was in the 81st year of his life when he died. He was a fine old man and is acknowledged to be among the three greatest scholars of the present time. I have heard him speak several times and he was an exceedingly brilliant man. They say that the reason he was not an entire success as a college president was that he lacked tact—a quality that Prexy Tucker possesses to a wonderful degree. Pres. Bartlett used to go at every body with an open blade & of course made many enemies. There will probably be a large funeral & the whole college will escort the procession.

February 5, 1899—I am very much interested in my work in Biology and am once more very enthusiastic over the prospect of being an M.D. I really think that it is the profession best suited to me, and I shall elect all my studies with that end in view.

February 22—I have some good news to tell you. Dr. Jennings, our Biology instructor has appointed me as his assistant in the laboratory.

As the Century Turned 89

I guess he realizes that I am working very earnestly in my biology, with a definite end in view. I did not ask him for the position as I did not know that he required an assistant, but he asked me if I should like to do it and I told him that as I was earning my way as far as possible, it would be most acceptable. He gives me twenty cents an hour but just now it wont amount to very much as there is not over 2 ½ or 3 hours work to do in a week. Still 50 or 60 cents a week amounts up at the end of a term and then it may lead to better things if I prove very useful to him, which I hope to do.

March 5—I am taking life very easy, eating my meals in my room etc as the result of the German measles which are all over college and as this weeks Dartmouth says is the "popular disease."

April 23—We are having hot summer days now and the boys are all out in negligée shirts etc This is the only time of the year for Hanover. The seniors are now wearing their caps and gowns and their senior canes have arrived. They are large heavy *sticks* with a carved Indian's head for a handle. The fellows all carve their names on the canes so that each cane is literally covered with nicknames etc and makes a most pleasant souvenir of ones last days at College.

May 15—Our carnival was the greatest success imaginable for everything turned out successfully We won our debate from Williams—beat her twice in baseball—had some good parades—in one of which the editors of the "Dartmouth" rode in a tallyho-& four & had our pictures taken. Then 1901 won the cane rush!!! It was very fierce & was 'way ahead of any thing of last year. . . .

To crown carnival week—Prexy Tucker returned to Hanover today after being abroad since the first of the year. He was accorded a great ovation in Boston by the alumni there & his reception was no less boisterous here. The whole college met him at the top of the hill with the band etc—He is in the best of health and enjoyed a very pleasant vacation.

JUNIOR YEAR

September 19, 1899—Sunday night I had a chill & yesterday was in bed all day with a bad head. Dr. Frost called last night & said he would send

Dr. Kingsford, of the Hospital, down to draw a little of my blood to determine, by microscopic examination, if I had malaria or typhoid fever. It is now 3^{00} P.M. & the verdict has just come. He found typhoid in my blood. . . . Dr. Frost thinks I am going to have it very lightly, but in order to have the best care he will take me to the Hospital this afternoon

September 24—The check arrives very opportunely as it costs a good deal to be sick here in Hanover. The Hospital is 12^{00} a week I believe. . . . If there is no change for the worse I hope to get out of here in another week altho that will be a very short time for a fever case.

September 25—Dartmouth has just received a gift of $300 000.00 from an alumnus in Prexy Tuckers class. Income to be used entirely in increasing the curriculum.

November 12—In the same mail with this letter I send you a couple of photos. Our "Aegis" comes out just before Christmas. You know, every junior class gets out an "Aegis" which is just a book of fun etc containing accounts of the fraternities, athletics, literary & dramatic side of college life etc, with pictures of all the members of the class.

December 13—Have decided to remain in Hanover during the Christmas vacation, altho' they all say that after one such experience one would rather go anywhere than repeat the performance. . . .

In your last letter you ask for information about my studies. Well, my best course is under "Billy" Patten in Biology. We have just finished a stiff book on the theories of the cell . . . & now are supplementing this work with general theories of heredity, of the transmission of acquired characters—Darwinism & Weismannism etc. . . .

My other biology course is under Dr Moore which is a course in Cryptogamic Botany. . . .

In Chemistry we are just beginning a systematic study of the elements—inorganic chemistry. This leads next year to courses in organic chemistry & toxicology (criminal poisoning) etc which will be of great benefit if I study medicine

Economics is hard. . . .

Now comes my only "snap" course, English 7, required Junior study. "Clothespins" Richardson give us two lectures and one quiz a week. It is a splendid *general culture* course[:] Lectures on Chaucer, Shakespeare, Milton Dryden etc & selected sympathetic readings.

Besides all this [as laboratory assistant] I have four two hour classes of the sophomores in biology under "Squirt" Jerould.

January 22, 1900—Prexy announced this morning of a new school of Finance & Administration which was to be established here next year for those who want post graduate work not in any professional but business lines.

February 4—Several nights ago Harold and I went over to the dancing school at Norwich. He is very anxious to learn to waltz well, & I said I would go over with him, just for the fun of it as they always have a dance after the lesson. There was a funny old teacher who played the violin as he taught. The great trouble was the striking lack of girls, but such as were there were good dancers, & I didnt seem to have any trouble getting partners & had a fine time; but the whole affair cost a dollar so I guess I wont go over there again very soon.

February 9—Last Tuesday I took my first lesson in skeeing and was out all Wednesday afternoon. Wednesday however there was a very hard crust formed on the snow, which made the skeeing lots of fun unless you happened to tumble—Well, in going down a long steep hill, my skees got crossed & threw me on my face—Well, you ought to have seen me go. My face was pushed into the crust & my feet went right over my head, turning a complete somersault. To relieve your mind I will say that the bruises are only skin deep, but a tatooed man's face is not a circumstance to mine—my nose & right cheek & both upper & lower lips—But skeeing is lots of fun. . . . As I wrote you Whit & "Billy" Mason & I each had a pair of skees made & they only cost 1.^{05} which I think was very reasonable. . . .

The Davison block burned down during the night and about 30 men roomed up stairs, some of whom lost everything, including pianos etc. Half of the college was out to the fire & helped all the boys carry their stuff out & also the contents of the drug store & dry goods store below. Sib & I slept thro' it all, not even hearing the bell or all the shouting . . . .

February 11—. . . my fraternity has honored me by electing me the head of the chapter, the first Junior to be elected. I have to prepare a long written inaugural address for next Wednesday evening.

March 1—The first day of spring was ushered in by a big snow storm which has kept the snow plow busy all day around the Hanover streets . . . . But we never consider it spring in Hanover until after the Easter vacation . . . .

March 26—You cant realize how overjoyed I am to think I was elected [to Casque and Gauntlet] as it really represents the pick of the whole class and will mean a great deal for me. Of course I haven't been initiated yet as that doesn't take place till June but the fellows want us to be around to the house as much as possible.

April 26—Yesterday I succeeded in putting a few more beauty marks on my face Played ball in the afternoon & in trying to catch a pop fly with the sun in my eyes the ball slipped thro my hands & struck my cheek bone with considerable force—But that is quite a common accident in ball playing. My razor got obstreperous however & took a small slice out of my chin. So that together with my scars from skeeing I look like a German student, the hero of many duels.

June 17—Am not going to stay for Commencement, as I am in such a hurry to get home to see you all that just now a week will seem a month. Then too I am in a hurry to get started on my summer's work . . . .

Such a week this has been! First exam last Tuesday—plugged Monday night till quarter of three, but rushed it all right—got some sleep Tuesday night—plugged Wednesday night & Thursday night did not go to bed at all—for C & G. initiation came that night & when I got back about 5-30 A.M. I had to sit right down & plug for my Friday exam at 9^{00}. Another exam yesterday kept me up Friday night until eleven, when I was so played out that I went to bed with an alarm clock & got up at four the next morning—& got to bed last night at one, & tonight it will be lucky if I reach bed by two as tomorrow the sophs have their exam in biology II & expect to have my hands full [tutoring] tonight Have got to plug tight all day tomorrow with logic coming Tuesday A.M. & chemistry Wednesday A.M.—but then it will all be over.

But it is worth it all, for I have rushed all my exams cold so far which, however, was due fully as much to the good work I have been doing in daily work as to my cramming.

A Return to Hanover
BEN AMES WILLIAMS

❧ Ben Ames Williams 1910 was a story-teller and a good one, writing novels one after another that were entertaining best-sellers and that were sometimes adapted for the movies. "A Return to Hanover" was printed in the *Alumni Magazine*, February 1926.

THERE ARE a good many old saws to the effect that familiarity breeds contempt, but it is probable that they err on the side of exaggeration. It is not so much contempt which results from familiarity as something which can better be characterized as indifference. Probably this is a fundamental psychological fact; and it is all the more tribute to college life in general, and to Dartmouth in particular, that in this particular case the rule does not apply. Those who know Hanover best are usually those who enjoy it most, and this is even true of the four years of undergraduate life. But it is nevertheless the case that Dartmouth, and presumably other colleges, have one great drawback. You cannot fully enjoy them while you are a part of them. They are too close to you. You have no perspective, and the result is that you become blind to a good many charming aspects which they wear. . . .

To return to Hanover as I did after an absence of ten years is to perceive the existence of beauties unsuspected till that time, to discover a friendliness in the atmosphere and a charm in the perpetual associations of a very definite and valuable therapeutic quality, which may be hard to define but which must nevertheless be felt by any visitor. . . . I shall always remember very vividly a certain trip to Hanover during the latter part of February with Mrs. Williams, and with our two boys serving in a general way the part of an interpretative chorus, opening our eyes when they needed opening, making clear to us the true inwardness of our own reactions, and incidentally setting us now and then very definitely in our place as oldsters who can only look back and whose pleasure must therefore be always tinged with sadness as compared with that exuberant anticipation which is the fair portion of those years when one looks forward to college and need not look beyond at all.

Even the trip by train from Boston had about it something which differentiated it from other railroad journeys. Before half the distance was done, the landscape to be seen from the car window began to assume familiar and suggestive contours. The day was bright and cold and perfectly clear, yet the sun was sufficiently warm so that when we stopped at a station we could see water dripping from the snow-laden eaves, and pools of water blackening the boards of the platforms. Even the cinders and smoke were less offensive when they came to us chilled by their passage through the cold air; and the smooth surface of the white clad river, broken here and there by black blotches where swifter water had prevented ice from forming, had something about it which invited an adventurous foot.

As the towns became smaller, the names of the stations began to be familiar, and even before we came to Lebanon the boys themselves had caught the infection of our own eagerness, and we had all piled into coats and overshoes twenty minutes before we reached the Junc.

The ride by train from the Junction to Hanover, after a change of cars there, might almost have been calculated for the very purpose of taking the joy out of life; but it was possible to avoid this, and we took one of the automobiles with snow shovels strapped to the tire-carrier at the back, and thus covered the remainder of the way, plunging through the uneven roads, crawling to one side when it became necessary to let other cars pass, feeling communicated to our bodies through the tires and the frame of the car that curious, firm and exhilarating resilience characteristic of packed snow which makes it possible to walk on such a surface almost tirelessly. After we had passed the woods about Wilder, we began to see the parallel marks of skis on the white breasts of the low and friendly hills, and these marks became more frequent, till in the valley below the village they were an interlacing network of inviting trails. The boys had skis at home, but their only opportunity to use them had been in backyards where a slide of twenty feet was an event. The testimony on the hillsides confirmed our promise that they should go skiing here, and the tumult of their plans, and the glamor of their boasts as to what they would do began for the first time to fill Mrs. Williams and myself with some misgivings as to our ability to keep pace with them. . . .

I first came to Hanover on the midnight train in the fall of 1906, and I remember walking up the hill from the station carrying my suitcase, knowing nobody in town, and not even sure where I would sleep that night. Lon Gove, I believe, was in charge of the desk at the Inn when I applied there, hopefully enough, for accommodations. He told me every room was full, and I slept that night, or what remained of that night, on a seat in the writing room, a seat which abutted against the wall at one end, and at the other had an unnecessarily high arm; and which was, over all, only about four and one-half feet long, while I was myself thirty percent longer.

Even before we went up-stairs to our rooms, on this later occasion, I took the boys in to see that seat which will always be one of my most vivid memories of Hanover. Bud said "Gee," and Chuck said "Gosh," and they both looked at me with a measuring eye, as though estimating just how much of a feat it had been for me to pass even the tag-end of a night within such bounds. . . .

After dinner we sent the boys to bed, and then crossed the street to the movies, and although there were no moving pictures in Hanover in 1906, the fellows who jeered at the more blatant absurdities of the film displayed this night spoke with the same voices as those of fifteen years before. Thus there was no sense of strangeness in discovering movies in Hanover. They had already assumed that atmosphere of venerable respectability which made it easy to believe that they had always been here. I suppose this is a characteristic of every new thing in Hanover life, that it ceases to be a new thing by being added on to other things which are old and very familiar. To be conscious of this fact was to feel very definitely the eternal character of the College. I was reading the other night something about the Dartmouth College case in which, if my memory is accurate, John Marshall uttered that definition of a corporation as both immortal and individual. When he did so, he had Dartmouth College in mind, and there has always seemed to be a peculiar truth in this characterization, and a peculiar satisfaction in feeling that you are, for all the transient character of your own life, a unit in that immortal and individual corporate existence, a part of that eternal flowing stream. . . .

When we were presently abed I lay a long time awake, while from the Campus through this still and friendly cold of the night there came the occasional sound of the whistle of some solitary man returning to his room, the snow squeaking under his slogging feet, or the murmur of the voices of two or three fellows in conversation, decreasing as they drew away towards the Chapel, lost at last in the embracing night while the sounds of their feet were still audible. And I heard once or twice someone shout a hail or a farewell to his fellow, and I caught the far blare of a saxophone from some fraternity house up toward the hospital. And now and then the door of College Hall slammed echoingly, and I could hear the steps of the man who had come out as he crossed the wide veranda and descended the steps, and the squeaking note of the packed snow as he hurried on his way.

In the morning, the first clang of the Chapel bell awoke me. As a Freshman I lived in Wheeler Hall, and that first note was my rising gong, and it was easily possible in the seven minutes intervening between the first stroke and the final double peal of the tolling bell, for me to get into my clothes and get to Chapel. But to do that it had been necessary to awaken with no preparatory rubbing of the eyes or indolent yawns. So this morning I awoke and sat up in bed. I was on the point of leaping to the floor when memory came back to me, realization of the fact I could lie still and let the damned bells ring. So I lay down again, and relaxed luxuriously; and the second bell added its clamor to the first, and their interweaving sounds had about them a fierce and insistent and intoxicating summons. And when the third struck in, it seemed impossible that any man could sleep through such a din. It seemed impossible that any man could want to sleep through it. There was something joyful about it, something exuberant and youthful, full of an avid appetite for life, full of invitation. The spell which the bells laid upon me became almost intolerable, and I was on the point of changing my mind and getting up after all. I did go so far as to get out of bed and go to the window and stand there, watching the long black lines of men crossing the Campus paths towards the Chapel and there converging so that these many streams flowed into one and this one disappeared at last into the distant portico. But while I still stood at the window, the shouting clamor of the three bells ended, and the tolling began; and immediately I felt a sense of anti-climax, as though my emotions had been worked to a fever pitch only to discover in the end that there was nothing to be excited about after all...

I went back to bed, and with that final decisive double stroke of the great clapper, my eyes closed; and almost before the reverberations of the bell had ceased vibrating through the still morning air, I was asleep again.

If it had not been for the boys, we might well enough have slept till noon, but that was in their opinion a wholly fruitless way to spend the morning, and we presently found ourselves dragged out of bed, and so came down-stairs to breakfast. And afterwards on the Inn veranda selected skis, and with them across our shoulders went down below the village where the hills are not too long nor too severe, and where it was possible to give the boys some paternal instruction.

I entered upon this business confidently enough. It is quite true that when I was in college, to go skiing meant simply to walk out to a convenient hill, stick your toes through the loops, slide down the hill, keep your feet if you could, pick up your skis, climb to the top again, and repeat till satisfied. This much at least I supposed I could safely show the boys, and I expected to see them tumble as extravagantly in the soft snow as I had myself been used to do. They were a disappointment to me. They refused to fall; or when they did fall it was in a manner perfectly innocuous. They had at first been humble enough and willing to learn, but before we had been there more than a few minutes, they had reached the point of patronizing Mrs. Williams' efforts; and when she successfully accomplished the first hill they both said in tones calculated to be reassuring:

"Pretty good, Mother. Pretty good."

I felt a certain chilly foreboding, felt a curious certainty that before the day was done they would even so be patronizing me. But I managed to avert this consummation all morning; and we went back to the Inn for dinner, all of us warm and tingling, and the older of us feeling quite definitely that we had had enough for a little while.

After dinner we suggested this to the boys, but they had no notion of submitting to such a curtailment of their activities, so while Mrs. Williams stayed behind, I set out with them once more. But I had learned to be wary, so I chose a route which I was sure was well within my powers, and at the first opportunity suggested that we abandon the hills and strike a trail which ran from the Junction road through a winding valley to strike the Lebanon road below the gym. I calculated on this being hard work for them, thought it might somewhat dampen their enthusiasm; and in this I was correct. Their skis did not fit them properly; they were forever losing one or the other; and even if I went slowly, what was slow for me was fast for them. They became weary and dejected, and from this I was so unwary as to acquire a false confidence. I began to exult in my apparent victory, and to emphasize it by urging them to new efforts.

Disaster overtook me at a point within a hundred yards of the road that was our destination. Here, on the right-hand side of the valley we were following, boys had heaped a pile of snow at the top of a steep little pitch, and thus constructed a low jump with a landing on the almost perpendicular slope below. I suggested in my arrogance that the boys try this jump. The snow was deep. There was no likelihood that they would suffer anything worse than a tumble. Bud was frankly unwilling to undertake the adventure, and while I tried to hearten him, Chuck, who is apt to be the more silent of the two, listened with a thoughtful attention. I told them how easy it was, and I assured them that even though they fell, they would suffer no harm, and I elaborated upon this theme, confidently enough, until Chuck struck me basely in the rear by suggesting:

"Why don't you do it, Daddy, and show us how?"

I had gone too far to withdraw. There was no escape for me in any quarter, and that little jump which had seemed so innocent when I was urging them to attempt it, grew before my very eyes till it was as impressive as that appalling structure beyond the golf links. As between the two I think I might have even chosen the other. There the end would at least be decisive and immediate. Here I was not likely to be killed, was much more likely to be maimed and to drag out a miserable existence for years. I tried explaining that my skis did not fit me, that the jump was too short for me to bother with, that they would never learn by seeing others do what they should do themselves. But they combined against me and overpowered me with my own arguments; pointed out that my skis fitted better than theirs did, and that what was easy for them would be less than an incident for me.

Matters reached a point where it was better to die bravely than to confess my own fears, so I climbed to the run above the jump, and without giving myself time to draw back, set my skis in line and let go. I remember—will I ever forget—that moment immediately before I struck the take-off, that moment when I saw the two boys twenty or thirty feet below me, watching with wide eyes, a cool curiosity in their countenances as though they were already estimating how many pieces there would be left for them to carry home. And my skis struck the take-off and spurned it beneath them, and I was in the air.

It was at this moment that I decided not to make the jump after all, let the boys think what they would. It was better to be despised than to be dead. But the only effect of my decision was to make both of my skis slip sidewise and in opposite directions, and I saw them rise in the air in front of me and cross at an appalling angle. Then I was fathoms deep in soft snow, bruised in a dozen places, and with snow packed firmly inside my collar, up my sleeves, and under my belt. By the time I fought my way to the surface, I had realized that I was not defunct, so I stuck my head out of the drift and struck the snow off my face and laughed a loud and boisterous laugh.

"There you are," I cried.

It was Chuck who delivered the verdict: "Pretty good, Daddy," he said, in a tone full of patronage. And I humbly gathered up my shattered skis, and led the way to the road, and we trudged back to the Inn while the two boys discussed with some merriment the appearance which I had presented at various stages of the enterprise....

The next day—it was chinning season—we were able to enlist the services of two Freshmen as chaperons, nurses, and guardians for the boys; and we saw them off with a relieved sigh at the thought that someone else would have to take them skiing now.... We ourselves went sedately for a walk, chose to go afoot along the ski trail through the Vale of Tempe. And on the outward journey we had easy going, and went blithely, and the loveliness of the winding path laid a spell upon us so that we talked little, were content to submit to the embraces of the healing silence all about. But when we came to return, the temperature had risen; the sun had warmed the snow, and we began to break through the trail and to flounder knee deep in snow at almost every step. Thus progress was difficult, and weariness increased to a point that was for me distressing and must have been for Mrs. Williams torment.

It is a testimony to the influence of Hanover that neither of us particularly resented the experience. There is something about the place which strengthens the soul.... Until a man has been out of college ten or fifteen years and has ... come back to the familiar scenes, he has not begun to discover all that Dartmouth has to give him. It is a very definite evidence of this fact that no one ever leaves Hanover after such a stay without planning, perhaps in vain, but planning nevertheless, when he will come again....

The Diary of a Freshman
DEXTER MARTIN

❊ Dexter Martin 1936 became a teacher of English after his graduation from Dartmouth. He has taught in many institutions, among them South Dakota State University. His diary appeared in the *Alumni Magazine* in November 1932.

FIRST WEEK

Monday: Dartmouth, in its first splendid vagueness, came into sight this morning as the White River bus rounded the last curve. Then, passing through the jumble of students and stores, we stepped out by the campus—Hanover soil at last! The simple green and white grandeur of the old Hall and its brother buildings was on our right: before us stood the wonderful new library, its tower rising above the elms; and on our left was the Administration Building whence we would push off on our College Careers.

I had read that freshmen are always bewildered, and one might very well be during the hasty hour or so of registration, matriculation, scrabbling some second-hand furniture together, hitching trunks upstairs, feeling tempted to use the fire rope to escape the innumerable solicitors, listening to the ponderous advice of sophomores, and their quaint tales of smothered freshmen, wondering, etc.

I had also read that freshmen are always lonesome. But that fascinating five-minute mixture of strangeness and familiarity between us newly met roommates and a few involuntary services to upperclassmen also moving in showed me that all freshmen are intent upon making friends and that most upperclassmen are not averse to you. (The furniture is standing up manfully and the walls have just been enlivened with pictures of Lincoln and Greta Garbo.)

Commons opened for supper. There, the obviousness of eating

The Diary of a Freshman 103

subdues whatever inferiority we may feel. And so it's also in the darkness of the movies. The show was a real talkie with the picture quite subordinate to the audience. Having shook the peanut shells out of my hair, had a shredded wheat and now to bed.

Wednesday: Unlike yesterday's Daily Puzzle, the Aptitude Test, placement exams, are suspiciously easy.

Tonight we walked to the Vale of Tempe, a place as lovely as its name. The dewy grass, the sweet cool shock of air among the pines, the pines themselves, each star-tipped, and, returning, a mighty outpour of moonlight upon the buildings—such composed our first excursion into the poetry of Dartmouth.

Thursday: Webster Hall was impressively thronged this morning for the opening exercises. Not even the tinted autumn leaves outside could match the colors within. Professors in black robes trimmed with scarlet and yellow and blue sat before us—the white-clad Palaeopitus ushers moved among the green-coated seniors—and, as we arose for President Hopkins' entrance, the bright sunlight enriching clothes and faces made the whole room flash with very youth. More than 2,000 voices lifted the hymns. More than four thousand hands applauded the opening address, which, I learned afterwards, was the first ever to have been thus accorded, a measure of its impression upon us.

In the rush this rainy afternoon the sophomores, with four-to-one odds against them, surprised the freshmen by speedily capturing two of the five footballs. But their numbers could not avail for we won the rest.

Seized by Delta Alpha tonight with fifty other freshmen, I was made to march around the town hollering, "Nerts!", and was paddled to bed very late.

Saturday: The monotony of the Dartmouth touchdowns in the classic collision with Norwich was relieved by the parade of the Norwich cadets and the undressed-up freshmen. Our dormitory having laboriously hauled a Ballyhoo-backhouse around the track, we were a bit disgusted when not ours but the cleanest float won the prize.

Sunday: Two days of steady argument with my roommate culminated today in a decision to change my room. I wanted to live with anybody but him—perhaps a big jolly jig with a smile like a split tomato (he would just match the curtains)—someone not intelligent enough to be annoying. Followed a talk with the Dean and interviews with three unmated freshmen whom I thought best to leave so. Returned home this evening, there was silence for a while. Then my roommate turned to me and said, "What do you say we forget about these last two days?" Cider and tobacco and high talk before the fireplace now.

SECOND WEEK

Monday: Classes today.—Having felt rather neutral the past week, we were pleasantly surprised to be introduced into the curriculum thus by one of the professors: "Well, boys, this is a hard course. But take it easy. Informality will be stressed—smoking is allowed in conferences. Friendship as well as knowledge is fostered here." (Incidentally, this is the first year that freshmen have been allowed to smoke on the streets.) Every professor, in addition to his knowledge, seems to have something individual so that the extensive conference system is especially welcome to us.

Tuesday: The dormitories have such a peculiarly club-like atmosphere that it is very easy to make acquaintances. Across the hall lives one who has been a wine-taster in France and can talk of Yquem, Pomard, and Falais; there is a penny-pitching game always going on upstairs; a sailor rooms below; a connoisseur of phonograph records plays foreign recordings nearby; a student next door knows Chinese and can prattle in an alarming manner; and there is a collector of first editions, a cinemaniac, a poet and an artist around.

Thursday: Life can never settle into a routine here. Every day something turns up: evening lectures, the D. C. A. and the D. O. C. freshman feeds, details about a girl in White River, art exhibits in Carpenter and the Tower Room of the Library, in some classes whole books to be read in a week, dormitory football games, fraternity initiations for sophomores such as measuring Main Street with a fish or the distance to Lyme in ski-lengths, etc.

Saturday: With a couple of friends, also members of the Outing

Club, I hiked around the hills today, catching glimpses below us of the white and red college among the turning leaves and, once, hearing a faint echo of "Eleazar Wheelock" chanted by the football crowd at the Vermont game. The air was like the inside of a snow-apple, very cold at night when we later slept on Mt. Mooselauke. No meat tastes better than that cooked over an open fire and flavored with dirty hands.

The Camel

EDWARD M. HOLMES

⇒ The Camel was Edward Holmes's first and last Model T. After graduation in 1933, he sampled various occupations, job-hopped as he put it, finally settled in teaching and made the University of Maine his base. He has written short stories, essays, criticism. "The Camel" was printed in the *Alumni Magazine*, November 1962.

HAD SHE BEEN one of those clownish affairs so often sported by high-school and college boys of the late twenties, had she been a first-stripped-down-then-grotesquely-ornamented Model T, with electric doorbells, a siren, three horns, "The Road to Roam" or similar legend printed on one door and dice and gin bottles stenciled on the others, had she been one of those artifacts (like flapping galoshes, hip flasks, and raccoon coats) by which the young of John Held Jr.'s day tried hard to convince themselves and everyone else they were Flaming Youth—then one would hardly take the trouble to write about her. Too many of the same.

But *The Camel*, which fought its battles with undergraduates, the police, and the New England weather in the early thirties was, I believe, more nearly unique than most Model T's of any time. My roommate [Darwin S. Bates 1933] brought her home one fall day in 1931 from somewhere in the wilds of Vermont and promptly extracted $7.50 from my desk drawer as my exact half-share in the purchase price. After we had registered her and written home, Darwin's father announced that, like it or not, we were going to carry liability insurance. A year's premium cost us three times our initial investment, a fact which bore witness to a deplorable lack of faith, on the part of the insurance company, in *The Camel* and the camel drivers.

But perhaps it is just as well that the agents never saw her in action, for *The Camel* had no neutral. I mean, none whatever. It was possible, of course, to stall her (though it went against our grain to descend to that trick), or to switch off the ignition and come to a fairly abrupt halt, or to juggle the gears, first a little reverse, then a little ahead, then reverse, then ahead, and so on, keeping *The Camel* in a most uncertain and nervous state of equilibrium, but this hesitation-waltz was exceedingly wearing for *The Camel*, the local constabulary, pedestrians, and even Darwin and me.

Trying to start her and come through the process with no fractures was even worse. Self-starting was simply out of the question, especially in cold weather, and we could not park her on hills *all* the time (as it was, Darwin had to rescue her once from the clutches of the Hanover police who had hauled her off to the dump, presumably as a piece of refuse obstructing Route 10 traffic). Cranking was the only method left. It wasn't bad when someone was at the controls, but when either of us was alone the problem was almost impossible. Only a person bent on suicide would have cranked *The Camel* with no one in the driver's seat to put his foot on the reverse pedal.

Darwin, who was strongly endowed with Yankee ingenuity, albeit he hailed from Ohio, chewed this problem over in his English major's brain and concluded (nay, demonstrated) that the thing to do was to jack up one rear wheel, grab the thing by the spokes, twirl it, and away she would go. But supposing a fellow were alone, how was he going to pick up the jack? And anyway, we didn't have a jack; Darwin had borrowed a physics professor's (our landlord's) for the demonstration. What we finally did, of course, was invade the dramatic club's carpenter shop and build one of two-by-fours. It was six feet long, shaped like a somewhat flattened big dipper, with a slight bend at the fulcrum, jointed, braced, and bolted. Moreover it worked.

Starting *The Camel* now involved the following steps: (1) Place jack under rear axle and bear down until *The Camel* tilted back (and slightly up) on the jack's now upright stanchion; (2) retard spark and gas; (3) spin the rear wheel—forward, that is. When *The Camel*, driverless, had started, and she very often did, one dove for the now toppled jack, wedged it firmly between the spare tire and the body of the moving *Camel*, vaulted over the back into the tonneau (no top, of course), took a low hurdle to the front seat, and corrected *The Camel's* direction before two wheels were over the curb. *One* wheel over the curb was par for the course.

To practice this technique, Darwin and I, with possible emergencies in mind, chose a street that separated his fraternity house from the Mary Hitchcock Memorial Hospital. But we had no accidents, and within an hour or two felt ourselves competent at solo starting.

The campus by this time was used to *The Camel*. Everyone had stared at it (as had others anywhere from the White Mountains to Copley Square where *The Camel* had been ignominiously towed in circles behind a taxi until she consented to start). Everyone had stared at the hoodless engine, at the air-cooled radiator (waterless always when the mercury stood at ten or more below zero) and then had gone more or less quietly about his business. But with the new jack, *The Camel* drew some unwonted, and unwanted, attention.

Alone I started her in our Ringling-Brothers-Barnum-and-Bailey style one March day on the straightaway in front of Dartmouth Hall and gained the wheel just in time to avoid head-on collision with that long, sleek, black roadster customarily driven, and certainly owned, by President Ernest Martin Hopkins. Who was driving it, I was never quite sure. Within a few hours, however, Darwin, whose name was officially attached to our license number on the college records, was summoned to the dean's office. He accepted punishment—removal of permission to drive for the rest of the year—with stoic calm, and of course never mentioned me. His ethics in such matters were beyond reproach.

I chauffeured Darwin a considerable number of miles in both intramural and inter-state traffic in the next two months. It was a beautiful spring.

Then with minor regret we sold her, still for $15.00, to a syndicate of California juniors looking for cheap transportation home for the summer, and let them take the license plates into the bargain. The last we saw of *The Camel*, she was loaded to the gunwales with boys and baggage, roaring away in the direction of Vermont's Rutland Mountain, where, so far as Darwin and I were concerned, she disappeared forever into the great Golden West. The world may have seen her like somewhere, some time, but if so, I have yet to hear about it.

You Can't Go Back Again—
But in a Way You Can

WILLIAM ROTCH

William Rotch 1937 is publisher and editor of *The Milford Cabinet and Wilton Journal* in Milford, N.H. His account of his return to Hanover appeared in the *Alumni Magazine*, in February 1960.

I'M GLAD that the Freshman Green Book confirms that I have a son at Dartmouth. It is hard for me to believe, too.

You can think a lot about Dartmouth, but you can't go back. You can pretend, but you are not fooling anyone.

I remember visiting a few years ago at B.U.—but it could have been on any campus—standing by a classroom building. My crew cut was short, my collar turned up at the proper collegiate angle; I was, I fondly believed, the picture of the typical undergraduate, waiting for someone to ask: "How did you do in the exam..." Instead a diffident student approached. "Pardon me, Sir, but could you..." No, I couldn't. You can't go back.

But in a way you can.

You can if your son enters Dartmouth.

You have planned on it for a long time, everything seems under control. Then one day you find yourself driving into Hanover, and there's the spire of Baker, and all of a sudden funny little emotions begin to take over, and you feel sort of choked up, and you look for a parking space, trying to appear very much in command of the situation.

The lawns are the same incredible green that you remember, and the same students appear to be strolling across the campus. You walk by Robinson Hall and look in at the DOC office. The automatic pilot takes over—that automatic pilot conditioned by four years in Hanover. It guides you across the street to the Library, and even into the men's room at the foot of the basement stairs, just where it used to be.

The same parents, the same clusters of undergraduates and their dates, are discussing the Orozco murals.

You start to bound up the stairs at Woodward. The first flight is easy. The second and third are a little steep. Everything is so natural. A couple of students come down the hall, and without thinking you say "Hi," and then wince slightly at the polite "Good morning, Sir."

You live through some long-forgotten experiences as you read those serious letters home asking advice on the merits of going out for *The Dartmouth* and for Cabin and Trail. There are the same adjustments to roommates and professors; only the slang is slightly different.

There are new problems—ROTC, and the lingering uncertainty of the draft. But you live it all again, the concerts, the bonfires on campus, and you smile reminiscently as Crouthamel walks by and your freshman son points and whispers: "There's Big Jake."

You are asked: "What should I do about skis?" (This really is a problem, if you have priced them in recent years.) You listen to talk about exams, the hour exams, the finals, and you nod in sympathy at the picture—duly transmitted for the benefit of parents—that life at Dartmouth has become a cold, monastic existence dedicated to study.

There are the football weekends, and the dormitories fill with the chatter of girls. This really is different, and the girls now are so young. But then some Sunday night after a weekend you bring your boy back to the campus and you recapture the mood. The lights shine in Baker, you glance into dormitory rooms where students sit hunched over desks, and you shiver a little in the wind which blows down from Moosilauke.

You wish—and you know you can't—pass on to your son all that you think you've learned in the last twenty years or more. And you know you wouldn't if you could.

But you're living it again, and you know you can't go back, but in a way you can—and it's a funny, mixed up, sad, and thrilling feeling.

VISITORS

An Anti-Slavery Apostle
PARKER PILLSBURY

⁂ More than fifty years after his unhappy experience at Dartmouth, Parker Pillsbury published his autobiographical account, *Acts of the Anti-Slavery Apostles* (Concord, N.H., 1883), in which he told of a visit to Hanover in 1841 in the company of Stephen S. Foster 1838. This former Congregational minister and anti-slavery worker held no grudge. In the copy that he presented to the College, he wrote: "To the Library of Dartmouth College from the Author with sincere wishes for its great usefulness, prosperity and prominence."

IN PROSECUTING our mission [of spreading the anti-slavery cause], Mr. Foster and myself found ourselves at Hanover, and the gates of Dartmouth college, from whence Foster had graduated only three years before, and with more than ordinary college honors. I had never before seen the interior of that, nor of any other college, in my life; and to academies and high-schools I was scarcely less a stranger.

The annual meeting of the Grafton county [anti-slavery] society had been already held, but in the south part of the county, a full day's drive from Hanover, and a similar convening seemed desirable in the northern section, and Hanover was the selected place. It was a full week, however, before any house could be found in which to assemble, and the committee were at length, after that delay, compelled to call our meeting at the dancing hall of the principal hotel. Neither church nor college would open to us a door, nor condescend to give us any reason why we were so summarily denied.

At the time appointed, however, the convention assembled in encouraging numbers, was duly organized, opened with prayer, and we proceeded to business. Henry C. Wright, of Philadelphia, formerly a Congregational minister, Mr. Foster, and myself were present as principal speakers, though all persons present were cordially invited, as was our invariable custom, to participate in the discussions. The first resolution presented was to the effect that in any moral conflict, strength and success depended, not so much upon numbers, as on inflexible adherence to principle. An interesting debate ensued, which occupied the remainder of the morning session, when the resolution passed unanimously, and we adjourned till afternoon.

At two o'clock we again assembled, when after prayer the following resolution was offered:

Resolved, That every person in the nation, north or south, who is not an open abolitionist, is by his influence, sustaining and perpetuating slavery, and should be regarded by every friend of humanity as a virtual slave-holder.

This resolution was the order for afternoon.... And as church, college and village made a large part of the audience after closing all their doors against us, the original resolution was rejected, by small majority. In the evening, our resolution read as below:

Resolved, That American slavery is a complication of the foulest crimes; robbery, adultery, man-stealing, and murder; and should therefore be immediately and unconditionally abolished.

The college students crowded themselves together and were very disorderly, both before and after the exercises began, clapping, hissing, and hooting, in most indecent and vulgar manner. Mr. Foster opened the discussion in an address of wondrous eloquence and power of argument, showing how slavery was all the resolution charged and a great deal more, and that logically, morally, every way, the slave holder must be robber, adulterer, man-stealer and murderer. Then he illustrated what these crimes meant in slavery; how a man-stealer must be as much greater than a horse or sheep-stealer, as a man is better and greater than sheep or horse. Then he asked: "How much greater is a man than a sheep?" "Who in Dartmouth college can solve that problem? Who?" And yet, he declared, "those monsters are hourly stealing the very Christ who died for them, in the person of his little ones. For inasmuch as they do it to the poorest, blackest of his children, they do it unto God! And to Christ his Son. All this, not to speak of the other capital crimes mentioned in the resolution. And who perpetrates these

An Anti-Slavery Apostle 117

outrages? They are ministers, bishops, elders, doctors of divinity, deacons, and church members, presidents and professors of colleges and theological seminaries." And he declared, "those at the north who fellowshiped such as christians and christian ministers, are bad as they. They voluntarily make themselves man-stealers and robbers, adulterers and murderers, in position, all of them; and many of them in heart. We do not see them do the deeds, and so we hold them innocent. But what would you say if President Lord, of your own college, should be seen carrying home at night, a stolen sheep? or buying one he knew had just been stolen?"

From that time, the order and quiet of the convention were no more. But the disturbance did not begin then, it was only mightily increased. It commenced before the opening prayer, and did not wholly cease during the evening. There were those, not all boys, who, during some of Mr. Foster's most thrilling appeals, and blood curdling descriptions, would keep up their scraping, whistling, and snickering, as though they were in some cheap circus or minstrel show....

For a time we were completely silenced by the uproar. The editor of the *Hanover Amulet*, who happened to enter at that moment, said in his next paper: "Judge of our surprise when we entered the hall where we supposed every heart beat in unison with sympathy for the oppressed, to find general tumult and confusion," which *tumult* continued through the evening with greater or less atrocity to the very last....

But no explanation which Mr. Foster could make availed anything. For a long time, he had no hearing at all. When he obtained the ear for a few moments, he abjured utterly, any disrespect to President Lord or to the college. He only wished to impress on the minds and hearts of his hearers, the awful wickedness of slavery, and not less of the north, especially the northern church and clergy, in fellowshiping as christians, these monsters of iniquity—that for Dr. Lord he had only profound respect; and with good reason, he said, for he had ever been as a father to him, both while he was at college and since he graduated; and that sooner should his tongue cleave to the roof of his mouth than be guilty of uttering one word to his injury; but all to no purpose. He was constantly hissed and insulted till he closed his remarks, and afterwards, if he attempted to speak, until we closed the meeting.

Henry C. Wright was not much better received, though in most pathetic word and tone, he depicted the condition of the enslaved, completely, hopelessly, and to their last breath, in the power of those who had been proved beyond all possibility of doubt, robbers, and adulterers, man-stealers and murderers; cruel, remorseless, relentless as death. Mr. Wright was heard, with more or less interruption, nearly half an hour.

The next speaker was . . . from some place in Massachusetts. In rather a sneering, contemptuous manner he asked, not the mob, but us who had called the meeting, if he might speak. . . . He, of course, . . . strenuously opposed our resolution, and presented a stupidly modified and diluted substitute. The solemn and pathetic address of Mr. Wright had produced a deep and desirable impression on many minds, and the object of the substituted resolution and its mover was to efface it. His low, vulgar wit, the farthest possible remove from the searching description and appeal of Mr. Wright, was loudly cheered and applauded by the uproarious crew for whose benefit it was uttered. . . . We asked our opponent whether to shoot down, or tear in pieces with trained blood-hounds, a poor slave who, under cover of night, was quietly, peacefully fleeing to Canada for freedom, was not murder? "No," he said, "not *legal* murder," and this answer elicited applause loud and long, making the floor to tremble under our feet. From this time, if not indeed long before, all sense of honor, propriety, decency, was disregarded. The women present had before retired in disgust, and it seemed probable that we who had called the convention would no longer be suffered. But Foster determined to make one more effort at a hearing. Seizing on a moment of comparative silence, in a loud voice he proceeded to say that he had a few days before visited Hanover, to secure a place for this convention, but was unable to procure any place whatever that was controlled by the college; that he then applied for this tavern hall, and, after some delay and deliberation, he secured it, at the not unreasonable price of three dollars a day; that it had been our intention to continue the convention two days and evenings, but such had been the confusion and uproar of this evening, and such the manifest intention, if possible, to hinder the orderly and quiet prosecution of our business, the meetings will be closed to-night; *and the responsibility of disturbing and breaking up an open, free-discussion, anti-slavery convention, may rest on those to whom it justly belongs.*

These remarks, in good, strong, earnest tone and spirit, made a deep impression. Many had not before comprehended the position in which they had placed themselves and their college. One young man, afterwards a professor in a theological seminary, rose and attempted what proved a most lame and impotent defence of the rioters. He said it was the custom of the students to express their approval or disapproval of whatever passed before them in this way; that an attack had been made on Dr. Lord, an honored and respected officer of the institution, and it was not strange that those who honored and venerated him should thus manifest their disapprobation. And besides, the students themselves had been reproached, and took this method to express their displeasure at that also. One or two others also spoke to about the same import; one adding to other charges, that our "speeches were wild and windy," and another, that they "were long and tedious."

Glad at seeing any change for the better in the temper or methods of our opponents, I ventured, for the first time during the evening, to occupy a few minutes, and began by assuring the meeting that it was not strange, since the president and college professors had driven the poor slave to the tavern hall as the only place where, with their approval, his friends could assemble to plead his cause, the students, imitating their spirit, should come here also to drive us from this, the slave's last refuge. I reminded them that this, like all our meetings, was open to free and friendly discussion; unlike most assemblies, as free to our opponents as our friends. We learned afterwards that the committee of the Congregational meeting-house, which was also refused us, was composed in part of the college faculty, the very chairman of the board being one. I said further, what surely was always true at that time, that we found the most violent opposition to the anti-slavery cause among the so-called "educated ministry," and that from this time we could not be surprised at it, for here at college, they see the doors of meeting-houses, vestries, lecture rooms, shut against us, and commence their hostilities by driving us even from tavern halls. Here to-night, I said, we see what the candidates for the ministry can do through hatred to our movements, and in imitation of the spirit of those under whose tuition you have placed yourselves; and everywhere we are seeing and feeling what you may do when you come to be ministers. I said that my own life had been anything rather than a student's life; that, though I had traveled and lectured extensively throughout New York and New England, singularly enough, I had never, till to-day, seen even the outside of a college (we thought of that, exclaimed one in the crowd); and I hoped as to moral character, that what we saw here, was not a fair specimen of our higher institutions of learning; though I felt compelled to say, that, judging from the spirit and position of the clergy and most of our educated men on the great questions of moral reform, I feared most of our large seminaries of learning had not been much misrepresented by the students of Dartmouth college, here to-night. It did not surprise me that by this time the tumult was renewed by some of the younger portion of the disturbers, nor did I greatly regret it, for I felt that my rebuke was as necessary as it was richly deserved; and that kind of hostile demonstration only clinched tighter the argument. Many endeavored to hush the confusion and some cried loudly, "Hear him, hear him." But I had closed my remarks, and kept my feet till it was possible to be again heard, and then moved that the convention be now finally adjourned; which was immediately put, and carried unanimously. And with that closed my first and last connection with any college. And now the question is answered; *at what college I obtained my education?* The answer; my *collegiate* education, at Dartmouth; and all in one day. There needed no more.

Choate's Eulogy of Webster

HENRY J. RAYMOND

>> Henry J. Raymond, a founder of *The New York Times*, had early made part of his reputation as a newspaperman by his excellent reporting of Daniel Webster's speeches and his friendship with the statesman. He journeyed to Hanover for the Commencement of 1853 to report for the *Times* the eulogy of Webster by Rufus Choate 1819. The report was printed in the paper on July 30, 1853. Herewith are excerpts from Raymond's account and brief excerpts also from his report of the two-hours-and-a-quarter-long eulogy, including Choate's attribution of the now familiar "It is, Sir, as I have said, a small college. And yet there are those who love it."

THE EXERCISES of the Annual Commencement of Dartmouth College occupy the attention of this vicinity of the country during the present week. They are invested this year with an extraordinary degree of interest, in consequence of the appointment of a Eulogy upon Mr. Webster pronounced by Rufus Choate, whose name is now almost universally recognized, since Mr. Webster's death, as that of the most eloquent American living. The expectation of this event has for some months engaged very general attention throughout New-England. The appointment was made very soon after the death of the illustrious statesman, and was at first fixed for the 4th of July, but was changed, I believe, upon Mr. Choate's suggestion, that it would more appropriately occur in immediate connection with the Anniversary of the College where Mr. Webster received his early academic culture. . . .

I came from Boston on Tuesday, and by way of Concord, and through the beautiful section of New-Hampshire, where so much of Mr. Webster's early life was passed, and which is still full of the memorials of his character and his recreations. The Railroad passes within a few rods of his farm in Franklin, which is much more beautifully situated than I had expected to find, and which justifies, by its shaded

121

verdure, the attachment which he evinced for it throughout his life. The house is of good size,—painted white with green blinds, and stands in one corner of a large level plain, skirted on one side by a splendid row of elms, and shut in by hills upon the other. Mr. Fletcher Webster and his family came upon the cars here, like very many others, on their way to Hanover. We passed several of the little lakes where Mr. Webster was wont to gratify his passionate fondness for fishing,—ran along under the shadow of Keersage Mountain which forms a conspicuous landmark in this section of the State, and came out upon the Connecticut at one of its most beautiful points,—just where it is joined by the White River, coming down from the heart of the Green Mountains. The spot is called the White River Junction,— and upon a high, level plateau, facing the East, and commanding a superb view up and down the valley of the Connecticut, the several roads that here unite, have their point of meeting. I anticipated that Hanover would be full—for it is a small village, with only two hotels, and those of not over a *ten horse power*, and therefore likely to be overwhelmed as under an avalanche, by a crowd which in New-York would disappear utterly within half an hour after its descent. Finding a large, airy looking and every way inviting hotel upon the plain, only four miles from Hanover, I stopped there for the night, as did several of my fellow-passengers from Massachusetts, with whom I was fortunate enough to form a very pleasant acquaintance. To one who had just left the intense activity, the ceaseless stir and commotion of New-York life, the exceeding quiet and perfect stillness of this lonely and picturesque hotel, was a luxury of itself well worth the journey.

The next morning I went to Hanover and found the whole place alive with expectation; wagons of all kinds were pouring in from every quarter of the country; booths had been erected upon the College green, at which refreshments of all sorts were lavishly disbursed; the two little hotels were bursting with the unwonted pressure from within; the students were rushing insanely about under an agitating consciousness of their close connection with this extraordinary scene: the place resembled a bee-hive, when it had become too populous for its limits, and its inhabitants were just upon the eve of swarming. . . .

Choate's Eulogy of Webster 123

Mr. Choate's eulogy was delivered in the afternoon. The hour appointed was 3 ½ o'clock. Ladies were admitted to the gallery at 2 ½. But long before 2 o'clock the Church was fairly besieged by an immense multitude eager for admission, and fearful that they would be unable to effect it. Very vigorous and efficient police arrangements had been made for the occasion, and were successfully carried out. The procession, formed at the College Chapel, entered at a little before 4. Among those present were ten graduates of the Class of 1813, who left College fifty years ago. The house was jammed to its utmost capacity, and presented a most animated and interesting view. The galleries were devoted wholly to the ladies, and among those present were very many of exceeding beauty; while the lower parts of the building were filled with gentlemen.

The pulpit had been clothed in black;—a desk upon the platform in front of it was also draped; and over the pulpit hung a portrait of Webster, the frame clothed in crape, and with the inscription beneath, "I STILL LIVE." Emblems of mourning were hung in other parts of the Church. After an opening prayer by Rev. Mr. Fisher, of Cincinnati, the band played a dirge, and then Mr. Choate rose to speak. His appearance, . . . is singularly striking. Of rather more than medium height,—thin, and apparently of feeble frame, —with large eyes, close, curling black hair, a face flexible in all its features, and expression, and marked by evidences of severe and incessant study, and betraying in every movement, and in every glance, the nervousness and intense, energetic earnestness of his temperament, his opening words and manner are quite sufficient to excite expectation of something quite different from the common-places of eloquent public speaking. And this expectation is never deceived. The whole structure of his mind is eminently original. His voice is rich, sweet and strong; his manner, unstudied, sometimes ungraceful from its abruptness and nervous vigor, is always impressive; his sentences, winding into every nook and corner of the subject, and desperately bent, as it seems, upon hunting out and bringing into light the remotest shades and relations of meaning connected with it—long, involved, parenthetical, and often broken apparently, are yet always correct and wonderfully exhaustive; and his language is classical in its words and phrases, and inevitably exact. He is, undoubtedly, the most thoroughly and profoundly educated man in public life; and his orations, no matter what may be the subject or the occasion of them, are masterpieces of a peculiar and consummate art. He resembles Burke more nearly, in many of the great characteristics of his genius, than any other writer; and if he is inferior to him in that unmatched wealth of intellect which marks Burke as the miracle of his age, he is not unequal to him in that profound and pervasive culture which makes itself in every word he selects, and in every sentence he utters.

One fault he has which no one closely connected with the Press, or conscious of the agency it must exert upon the tone and scope of public thought, can be expected to forgive;—and that is the supreme indifference he shows to the presentation of his speeches to the public eye. He never speaks when he can possibly avoid it, without the most careful preparation; but the moment he has done, he seems to lose all thought or care for what he may have said. None of his speeches are accessible in books or in pamphlets, although they would stand, if collected, among the best and most instructive productions of English literature;—nor until the recent energy of the Press, somewhat reckless and *outré* in its modes, it must be confessed, but effective in its results, showed him that without some personal care for the matter himself, he must go to the world in the mangled and distorted shape, which was all the desperate, panting, but inevitable Reporters, could possibly give him, could the public get anything from him even in the form of newspaper reports of his speeches. Fortunate in writing a hand which no human being not gifted with Champollion's skill, and with more than his patience of study, can possibly decipher,—and speaking with so great rapidity, and using such infinite and apparently inextricable convolutions of style, that a reporter might as well attempt to follow chain-lightning as to report his words; he seemed absolutely on that height seldom attained, where the press could not reach him. But he has been at last forced to yield; the prospect of having his exquisite sentences and sentiments so mangled and butchered for the public eye, that he himself could not recognize, though he could not repudiate them, was too much even for his resolution; and the Press is now indebted to him for manifold courtesies not less serviceable to himself than to the public at large.

I am consequently able to send you a full report of his Eulogy on Mr. Webster, prepared with a good deal of care, and revised by himself for the Press. It will be read, I do not doubt, with universal interest and admiration.

After the applause by which he was greeted had ceased, and quiet had been restored, Mr. Choate spoke as follows in eulogy of Mr. Webster.

It would be a strange neglect of a beautiful and approved custom of the schools of learning, and of one of the most pious and appropriate of the offices of literature, if the College in which the intellectual life of Daniel Webster began, and to which his name imparts charm and illustration, should give no formal expression to her grief in the common sorrow,—if she should not draw near, of the saddest in the procession of the bereaved, to the tomb at the sea, nor find in all her classic shades one affectionate and grateful leaf to set in the garland with which they have bound the brow of her child, the mightiest departed. Others mourn and praise him by his more distant and more general titles to fame and remembrance,—his supremacy of intellect, his statesmanship of so many years, his eloquence of reason and of the heart, his love of country, incorruptible, conscientious, and ruling every hour and act:—that greatness combined of genius, of character, and manner;—of place, of achievement, which was just now among us, and is not,—and yet lives still and evermore. You come, his cherishing mother, to own a closer tie, to indulge an emotion more personal and more fond,—grief and exultation contending for mastery, as in the bosom of the desolated parent, whose tears could not hinder him from exclaiming, "I would not exchange my dead son for any living one of Christendom." . . .

We are among the scenes where the youth of Webster awoke first and fully to the life of the mind. We stand, as it were, at the sources physical, social, moral, intellectual, of that exceeding greatness. Some now here saw that youth; almost it was yours. *Nilum parvum videre!* Some,—one of his instructors,—some possibly of his classmates or nearest college friends,—some of the books he read,—some of the apartments in which he studied, are here. We can almost call up from their habitation in the past, or in fancy, the whole spiritual circle which environed that time of his life;—the opinions he had embraced, the theories of mind, of religion, of morals, of philosophy, to which he had surrendered himself,—the canons of taste and criticism which he had accepted,—the great authors whom he loved best, the great trophies which began to disturb his sleep, the facts of history which he had learned, believed, and began to interpret, the shapes of hope and fear in which imagination began to bring before him the good and evil of the future. Still, the same outward world is around you and above you. The sweet and solemn flow of the river gleaming through intervale here and there, margins and samples of the same old woods, but thinned and retiring; the same range of green hills yonder, tolerant of culture to the top, but shaded then by primeval forests, on whose crest the last rays of sunset lingered; the summit of Ascutney; the great northern light that never sets; the constellations that walk around and watch the pole; the same nature, undecayed, unchanging, is here. Almost the idolatries of the old Paganism grow intelligible. "*Magnorum fluminum capita veneramur,*" exclaims Seneca. "*Subitur et ex abrupto vasti amnis eruptio aras habet!*" We stand at the fountain of a stream. We stand, rather, where a stream, sudden and from hidden springs, bursts to light—from which we can look along and down, as it were, on our own Connecticut, and trace its resplendent pathway to the sea; and we venerate, and almost would build altars here! Almost it seems as if here we might learn the secrets of his supremacy. We know that God gave him an excellent spirit, and an understanding above that of other men. That ultimate fact we accept and repose on; yet more we would know, if we could, and hither we should come to know it. . . .

It would not be unpleasing, . . . to enumerate the names, at least of some of the great causes by which his fame was built, and try to convey some impression of the novelty of the questions involved, and the importance of the principles adjudged. But there is only one of which I have time to say anything, and that is the case which established the inviolability of the charter of Dartmouth College by the Legislature of the State of New-Hampshire. Acts of the Legislature, passed in the year 1816, had invaded its charter. A suit was brought to test their validity. It was tried in the Supreme Court of the State; a judgment was given against the College, and this was appealed to the Supreme Federal Court by writ of error. Upon solemn argument the charter was decided to be a contract whose obligation a State may not impair. The acts were decided to be invalid as an attempt to impair it, and you hold your charter under that decision to day. How much Mr. Webster contributed to that result, how much the effort advanced his own distinction at the bar, you all know. Well, as if of yesterday, I remember how it was written home from Washington that Mr. Webster closed a legal argument of great power by a peroration which charmed and melted his audience. Often since I have heard vague accounts, not much more satisfactory, of the speech and the scene. I was aware that the report of his argument, as it is published, did not contain the actual peroration, and I supposed it lost forever. By the great kindness of a learned and excellent person, Dr. Chauncy A. Goodrich, a Professor in Yale College, with whom I have not the honor of a personal acquaintance, although his virtues, accomplishments, and most useful life, were well known to me, I can read to you the words whose power, when those lips spoke them, so many owned, although they could not repeat them. As those lips spoke them we shall hear them nevermore, but no utterance can extinguish their simple, sweet and perfect beauty. Let me first bring the general scene before you, and then you will hear the rest in Mr. Goodrich's description. It was in 1818, in the 37th year of Mr. Webster's age. It was addressed to a tribunal presided over by Marshall, assisted by Washington, Livingston, Johnson, Story, Todd and Duvall—a tribunal unsurpassed on earth in all that gives illustration to a bench of law, and sustained and venerated by a noble bar. He had called to his aid the ripe and beautiful culture of Hopkinson, and of his opponents was William Wirt, then and ever of the leaders of the bar, who, with faculties and accomplishments fitting him to adorn and guide public life, abounding in deep professional learning and in the most various and elegant acquisitions, a ripe and splendid orator, made so by genius and the most assiduous culture, consecrated all to the service of the law. It was before that tribunal and in presence of an audience select and critical, among whom, it must be borne in mind, were some graduates of the college, who were attending to assist against her, that he opened the cause. I gladly proceed in the words of Mr. Goodrich:

"Before going to Washington, which I did chiefly for the sake of hearing Mr. Webster, I was told that, in arguing the case at Exeter, N. H., he had left the whole Court-room in tears at the conclusion of his speech. This, I confess, struck me unpleasantly—any attempt at pathos on a purely legal question like this, seemed hardly in good taste. On my way to Washington, I made the acquaintance of Mr. Webster. We were together for several days in Philadelphia, at the house of a common friend; and as the College question was one of deep interest to literary men, we conversed often and largely on the subject. As he dwelt upon the leading points of the case, in terms so calm, simple and precise, I said to myself, more than once, in reference to the story I had heard, 'Whatever may have seemed appropriate in defending the College at *home*, and on her own ground, there will be no appeal to the feelings of Judge Marshall and his associates at Washington.'" The Supreme Court of the United States held its session, that Winter, in a mean apartment, of moderate size—the Capitol not having been built after its destruction in 1814. The audience, when the case came on, was therefore small, consisting chiefly of legal men, the *elite* of the profession throughout the country. Mr. Webster entered upon his argument in the calm tone of easy and dignified conversation. His matter was so completely at his command that he scarcely looked at his brief, but went on for more than four hours with a statement so luminous and a chain of reasoning so easy to be understood, and yet approaching so nearly to absolute demonstration, that he seemed to carry with him every man of his audience, without the slightest effort or weariness on either side. It was hardly *eloquence*, in the strict sense of the term; it was pure reason. Now and then, for a sentence or two, his eye flashed and his voice swelled into a bolder note, as he uttered some emphatic thought; but he instantly fell back into the tone of earnest conversation, which ran throughout the great body of his speech. A single circumstance will show you the clearness and absorbing power of his argument.

I observed that Judge Story, at the opening of the case, had prepared himself, pen in hand, as if to take copious minutes. Hour after hour I saw him fixed in the same attitude, but, so far as I could perceive, with not a note on his paper. The argument closed, and *I could not discover that he had taken a single note.* Others around me remarked the same thing, and it was among the *on dits* of Washington, that a friend spoke to him of the fact with surprise, when the Judge remarked: "Everything was so clear, and so easy to remember, that not a note seemed necessary, and, in fact, I thought little or nothing about my notes."

The argument ended; Mr. Webster stood for some moments silent before the Court, while every eye was fixed intently upon him. At length, addressing the Chief Justice Marshall, he proceeded thus:

"*This, Sir, is my case!* It is the case, not merely of that humble Institution, it is the case of every College in our land. It is more. It is the case of every Eleemosynary Institution throughout our country—of all those great charities founded by the piety of our ancestry to alleviate human misery, and scatter blessing along the pathway of life. It is more! It is, in some sense, the case of every man among us who has property of which he may be stripped, for the question is simply this: 'Shall our State Legislatures be allowed to take *that* which is not their own, to turn it from its original use, and apply it to such ends or purposes as they, in their discretion, shall see fit?' Sir, you may destroy this little Institution; it is weak; it is in your hands! I know it is one of the lesser lights in the literary horizon of our country. You may put it out. But if you do so, you must carry through your work! You must extinguish, one after another, all those great lights of science which, for more than a century have thrown their radiance over our land! It is, Sir, as I have said, a small college. And yet *there are those who love it.*" Here the feelings which he had thus far succeeded in keeping down, broke forth. His lips quivered, his firm cheeks trembled with emotion; his eyes were filled with tears, his voice choked, and he seemed strugling to the utmost simply to gain that mastery over himself which might save him from an unmanly burst of feeling. I will not attempt to give you the few broken words of tenderness in which he went on to speak of his attachment to the College. The whole seemed to be mingled throughout with the recollections of father, mother, brother, and all the trials and preventions through which he had made his way into life. Every one saw that it was wholly unpremeditated, a pressure on his heart, which sought relief in words and tears.

The Court-room during these two or three minutes presented an extraordinary spectacle. Chief Justice Marshall, with his tall and gaunt figure bent over as if to catch the slightest whisper, the deep furrows of his cheek expanded with emotion, and eyes suffused with tears; Mr. Justice Washington at his side with his small and emaciated frame and a countenance more like marble than I ever saw on any other human being—leaning forward with an eager, troubled look; and the remainder of the Court, at the two extremities, pressing, as it were, toward a single point, while the audience below were wrapping themselves round in closer folds beneath the bench to catch each look, and every movement of the speaker's face. If a painter could give us the scene on canvas—those forms and countenances, and Daniel Webster as he then stood in the midst, it would be one of the most touching pictures in the history of eloquence. One thing it taught me, that the *pathetic* depends not merely on the words uttered, but still more on the estimate we put upon him who utters them. There was not one among the strong minded men of that assembly who could think it unmanly to weep when he saw standing before him the man who had made such an argument, melted into the tenderness of a child. Mr. Webster had now recovered his composure, and fixing his keen eye on the Chief Justice, said, in that deep tone with which he sometimes thrilled the heart of an audience: "Sir, I know not how others may feel," (glancing at the opponents of the College before him,) "but, for myself, when I see my alma mater surrounded, like Cæsar in the Senate House, by those who are reiterating stab upon stab, I would not, for this right hand, have her turn to me and say, '*Et tu quoque mi fili!*' " *And thou, too, my son!* He sat down. There was a deathlike stillness throughout the room for some moments; every one seemed to be slowly recovering himself, and coming gradually back to his ordinary range of thought and feeling.

Wendell Phillips' Visit to Hanover

SAMUEL R. BOND

❧ These recollections of Wendell Phillips in Hanover, written for the *Alumni Magazine* nearly 60 years after the event, have as much freshness as though written a few days after the Commencement of 1855. Samuel Bond taught school following college, read law, practiced in St. Paul, Minn., and later in Washington where he also lectured in the law department of Howard University.

THE *Dartmouth Alumni Magazine* for March, 1913, contains an interesting review . . . of the more notable graduates of Dartmouth, as well as those not alumni of the college, who have taken part in its commencement exercises. The omission from the latter class of the name of Wendell Phillips recalls to my mind some incidents connected with his addressing the United Literary Societies at the graduation of the class of 1855, of which I was a member. . . . The immemorial custom had been, and continued for a considerable period after 1855, that one of the addresses on commencement day should be delivered by some one selected by the two literary societies, the Social Friends and the United Fraternity which included the whole body of students. In 1855 I was made chairman of the joint committee appointed by those societies to select and invite the orator, as usual, and arrange for his attendance, etc. I conducted the correspondence requisite to the carrying out of that purpose, and recall that among those who were successively invited were Ralph Waldo Emerson, William H. Seward, Charles Sumner, Oliver Wendell Holmes and George S. Hilliard, all of whom declined. Dr. Holmes, in referring to his press of engagements, wrote that he was in the predicament of the patient who, when his physician prescribed a quart dose of some decoction, replied, "Why,

Wendell Phillips' Visit to Hanover

doctor, I don't hold but a pint," and Mr. Hilliard assigned his professional duties as the reason for his declination, adding that the law was a jealous mistress who demanded the undivided devotion of her votaries. Then, almost in despair, it was decided to extend the invitation to Wendell Phillips, [a leading Abolitionist]. This was done and a prompt acceptance received, whereby our minds were much relieved, and, as we supposed, free from any further cause of anxiety in the matter; but students sometimes propose and faculties dispose. In fact, when it had become known who had been invited as "our orator," I was requested to put in an appearance at President Lord's house at a designated time, and, construing such request as a command, I acted accordingly. Professor Sanborn met me in the ante-room, informed me that the faculty was in session, and, as its spokesman, said they had learned that the United Societies had invited Wendell Phillips as their orator for commencement day. I said yes, and that the invitation had been accepted, to which he replied that President Lord's consent had not been obtained. I asked if it had ever been required, or obtained on previous like occasions, and he replied perhaps not, but that he had the right of veto, and would not consent to Mr. Phillips delivering the proposed address; that, instead, it had been arranged for Professor Brown to address the alumni at the time and place usually occupied by the orator of the United Socities. Somewhat incensed and excited I said "Mr. Phillips has been invited, has accepted the invitation, and is going to speak." "But," he said, "we hold the key to the Church" (where Commencement exercises were then held). At this, overcome by my indignation, I arose from my chair and exclaimed, "But you haven't the key to the common," as we then called the campus, "and we will have Mr. Phillips speak there at the same time that Professor Brown addresses the alumni, and see which will draw the larger audience." Thereupon he said he hoped there would be no trouble which could be avoided, and asked me to sit down and wait until he had conferred with the faculty. In the course of some ten minutes he returned and said that, under the circumstances, Professor Brown declined to address the alumni, as had been arranged, and we might proceed with our arrangements as to Mr. Phillips; and when I was once outside the door and contemplated what I had said while within, I was astonished at my temerity in meeting the situation as I did, and at the result of my visit; for, as was well known, President Lord was a strong believer in slavery, an adherent, and also correspondent, it was said, of John C. Calhoun, and attempted to prove from the Bible and instill into our minds, with Calvinistic zeal, that it was a divine institution; so it goes without saying that an anti-slavery man like Wendell Phillips was to him emphatically *persona non grata*. So far as I was personally concerned, his efforts at conversion were like pouring water on a duck's back, and I loved him, nevertheless, for his zealous, fatherly interest in our welfare, and also held him in a kind of reverential awe as President.

But our troubles were not yet over. While the outer bulwarks of opposition had given away, no cordial welcome by the faculty was to greet Mr. Phillips' entrance to the conservative precincts of the college. It had been the custom for members of the faculty to entertain as guests at their homes those who were invited to deliver commencement addresses, but no one who would have been classed as a radical, except, perhaps, Ralph Waldo Emerson, had ever before strayed, or been brought, into the fold of a Dartmouth Commencement. Every room in the two then existing hotels of the village had been engaged, and I had received intimation that if I broached the subject of his entertainment to almost any member of the faculty I would be given the cold shoulder, so, as a last resort, I went to Professor Peaslee of the medical department, with whom I was best acquainted among the professors, and stated my dilemma. He came at once to my rescue, declaring that, while he differed as widely as any of the faculty from Mr. Phillips' views, he considered him one of the finest gentlemen of the land, and that it would be a reproach to Dartmouth College to ignore, or treat him with "scant courtesy," and that if there were a room in his own house which had not already been allotted to invited guests Mr. Phillips should have it. He then sallied out with me in search of quarters. We first called on Mr. Blaisdell, Treasurer of the College, who expressed to us his sympathy, but, saying, as Professor Peaslee had done, in regard to not having a spare room in his house, he suggested that we try at Professor Young's. We did so at once, saw Mrs. Young, a woman of fine intelligence, and, when we had stated the situation, her reply was prompt, and in the exact words which I vividly recall: "*Mr. Phillips shall have the best room in my house,*" which brought relief to my burdened mind. I well remember driving, as was then necessary, to Lebanon in a buggy, getting Mr. Phillips and, in due course, leaving him to be inducted into Mrs. Young's "best room," and, during his two days' stay in Hanover, as the faculty extended him no courtesies, I was with him during all his waking hours. I recall that while I was showing him about the college buildings and grounds, a messenger brought me the coveted red ribbon and notified me of my election as a Phi Beta Kappa and to appear at once for initiation, but I couldn't leave Mr. Phillips alone, and, unless my memory is at fault, I was never initiated, though I have since attended a meeting of the chapter.

Park Benjamin, of New York City, was poet and Mr. Phillips was orator at the commencement exercises and when these had closed, and the procession to the alumni dinner was about to form, Mr. Phillips was left standing on the platform where the exercises had taken place, and I went up the steps and took him in charge, and walked in the procession to the hotel where the dinner was to be served, but as we were about to enter, in looking about for some one of prominence who I thought would be willing to relieve me of my charge and give him a seat with the distinguished guests present, among whom I recall Salmon P. Chase and "Long John" Wentworth, my eye fell upon James Willis Patterson, who had just entered upon his professorship, and was afterward U. S. Senator, with whom I had slight acquaintance, and asked him if he would be kind enough to thus step in the gap, to which he readily assented, and for which I have always felt grateful to him.

With an exaggerated feeling of responsibility for my charge I kept closer to him than a brother until the time came for him to leave when I drove him to Lebanon where he was to take the train. I do not accurately recall the sum of money furnished me by the United Societies with which to pay Mr. Phillips, but when we reached the platform of the station, and I was taking out my pocketbook, he said very promptly, "Please put that right back, Mr. Bond," and when I told him I was about to apologize for the smallness of the amount which I had to offer him for his kindness and trouble in coming to address us, and urged him to let me at least pay his actual expenses, he declined to do so, and remarked: "You are a young man and may not readily believe it when I tell you that I regard the spontaneous invitation of the students of Dartmouth College, whose conservatism as an institution I know so well, to come and address them as the highest compliment which I have ever received."

In after years it was my fortune to hear, meet and talk with Mr. Phillips on several occasions on none of which did we fail to refer with interest to our intercourse and experiences at Hanover in 1855.

As to the subject, or full scope, of Mr. Phillips' address my recollection is not distinct, nor have I been able to find it among his published works, but its general purport was a comparison of radicalism and conservatism, how they were complemental to each other, both being necessary to the accomplishment of the highest purposes; and certainly it contained nothing rabid, or offensive.

As a Strong Bird on Pinions Free
WALT WHITMAN

By invitation of Dartmouth seniors, who apparently hoped to outrage the faculty with the poet's unconventionality, Walt Whitman came to Hanover in June 1872, to deliver the Commencement poem, "As a Strong Bird on Pinions Free." Whitman appeared on the platform of the White Church wearing "a flannel shirt, square-cut neck, disclosing a hirsute covering that would have done credit to a grizzly bear." His voice was so muffled that he was scarcely audible even to the audience in the front rows, and one listener grumbled that had he been able to hear, he probably would not have understood. While in Hanover Whitman stayed in the minister's house (it is now Choate House and relocated) on the north side of the Green, and from it he wrote to his friend Pete Doyle, the horse-car driver, the letter that herein follows the poem itself.

As a strong bird on pinions free,
    Joyous, the amplest spaces heavenward cleaving,
Such be the thought I'd think of thee America,
Such be the recitative I'd bring for thee.

The conceits of the poets of other lands I'd bring thee not,
Nor the compliments that have served their turn so long,
Nor rhyme, nor the classics, nor perfume of foreign court or
    indoor library;
But an odor I'd bring as from forests of pine in Maine, or breath
    of an Illinois prairie,
With open airs of Virginia or Georgia or Tennessee, or from Texas
    uplands, or Florida's glades,
Or the Saguenay's black stream, or the wide blue spread of Huron,
With presentment of Yellowstone's scenes, or Yosemite,

And murmuring under, pervading all, I'd bring the rustling sea-sound,
That endlessly sounds from the two Great Seas of the world.

And for thy subtler sense subtler refrains dread Mother,
Preludes of intellect tallying these and thee, mind-formulas fitted for thee, real and sane and large as these and thee,
Thou! mounting higher, diving deeper than we knew, thou transcendental Union!
By thee fact to be justified, blended with thought,
Thought of man justified, blended with God,
Through thy idea, lo, the immortal reality!
Through thy reality, lo, the immortal idea!

Brain of the New World, what a task is thine,
To formulate the Modern—out of the peerless grandeur of the modern,
Out of thyself, comprising science, to recast poems, churches, art,
(Recast, may-be discard them, end them—may-be their work is done, who knows?)
By vision, hand, conception, on the background of the mighty past, the dead,
To limn with absolute faith the mighty living present.

And yet thou living present brain, heir of the dead, the Old World brain,
Thou that lay folded like an unborn babe within its folds so long,
Thou carefully prepared by it so long—haply thou but unfoldest it, only maturest it,
It to eventuate in thee—the essence of the by-gone time contain'd in thee,
Its poems, churches, arts, unwitting to themselves, destined with reference to thee;
Thou but the apples, long, long, long a-growing,
The fruit of all the Old ripening to-day in thee.

As a Strong Bird on Pinions Free   139

Sail, sail thy best, ship of Democracy,
Of value is thy freight, 'tis not the Present only,
The Past is also stored in thee,
Thou holdest not the venture of thyself alone, not of the Western
    continent alone,
Earth's *résumé* entire floats on thy keel O ship, is steadied by thy
    spars,
With thee Time voyages in trust, the antecedent nations sink or
    swim with thee,
With all their ancient struggles, martyrs, heroes, epics, wars, thou
    bear'st the other continents,
Theirs, theirs as much as thine, the destination-port triumphant;
Steer then with good strong hand and wary eye O helmsman, thou
    carriest great companions,
Venerable priestly Asia sails this day with thee,
And royal feudal Europe sails with thee.

Beautiful world of new superber birth that rises to my eyes,
Like a limitless golden cloud filling the western sky,
Emblem of general maternity lifted above all,
Sacred shape of the bearer of daughters and sons,
Out of thy teeming womb thy giant babes in ceaseless procession
    issuing,
Acceding from such gestation, taking and giving continual strength
    and life,
World of the real—world of the twain in one,
World of the soul, born by the world of the real alone, led to
    identity, body, by it alone,
Yet in beginning only, incalculable masses of composite precious
    materials,
By history's cycles forwarded, by every nation, language, hither
    sent,
Ready, collected here, a freer, vast, electric world, to be
    constructed here,

(The true New World, the world of orbic science, morals,
    literatures to come,)
Thou wonder world yet undefined unform'd, neither do I define
    thee,
How can I pierce the impenetrable blank of the future? . . .

A Letter to Pete Doyle
WALT WHITMAN

Hanover, N. H., Thursday, June 27 [1872]. DEAR SON. I will write you just a line to show you I am here away north, and alive and kicking. I delivered my poem here before the College yesterday. All went off very well.—(It is rather provoking—after feeling unusually well this whole summer,—since Sunday last I have been about half sick and am so yet, by spells.) I am to go to Vermont for a couple of days, and then back to Brooklyn.—Pete I received your letter, that you had been taken off—write to me Saturday 30th, or Sunday—direct to usual address 107 Portland Ave., Brooklyn. I will send you the little book with my poem, (and others) when I get back to Brooklyn. Pete, did my poem appear in the Washington papers—I suppose Thursday or Friday—*Chronicle* or *Patriot*? If so send me one—(or one of each).—It is a curious scene here, as I write, a beautiful old New England village, 150 years old, large houses and gardens, great elms, plenty of hills—every thing comfortable, but very Yankee—*not an African to be seen all day*—not a grain of dust—not a car to be seen or heard—green grass everywhere—no smell of coal tar.—As I write a party are playing base ball on a large green in front of the house—the weather suits me first rate—cloudy but no rain. Your loving WALT.

EXTRA-CURRICULAR

Wearers of the Green
WILLIAM BYRON FORBUSH

≫ William Byron Forbush 1888 became a distinguished Congregational minister with churches in, among other places, Detroit and New York. He was a popular lecturer and was well known for his work among boys, for whom he organized the Knights of King Arthur, which at its height had nearly 200,000 members. His account of the Dartmouth-Williams baseball game in 1887 is taken from *Dartmouth Athletics*, edited by two members of the Class of 1894, John H. Bartlett and John Pearl Gifford (Concord, N.H., 1893).

IT WAS THE LAST GAME of the series, both colleges had beaten every opponent, and each had won a game from the other. This game decided the championship for the year. The game was to be played on the Wheelock college grounds. It was a sunny afternoon in early June. The graceful elms and maples that line the campus had put on their loyal college color of brightest green, and the sunlight sifted down through them upon a carpet of still brighter color. It is on such days as this, and at such a season, when the air is full of fragrance of flowers and songs of birds and lazily floating clouds, that the weary student is most tempted to leave his narrow study and wander up the hill behind the college halls and there let the afternoon drift away in dreams of the mysterious days to come. But none of the students were dreaming such dreams to-day. Even the hardest old 'plugger' in the institution had left his den this afternoon, and, coming out in the sunlight with a bewildered expression on his face, was hailed with cheers by his assembled classmates. The college halls were empty, except one room, where the base-ball nine, surrounded by their most devoted friends, were putting on their suits. Every one was on the campus, and this broad expanse, extending in front of the old halls, was bright with life and color.

The game was to be called at three, but before one the street around the campus was full of teams, and along the country roads for miles, could be seen vehicles of all descriptions, converging toward the great event. Before two o'clock the temporary grand stand was filled, mostly with ladies of the faculty and town, for the average college man is too restless during a ball game to be able to sit still. Upon the sidewalk under the trees was a continuously moving stream of people. Some were students, who strode gaily along, swinging their light canes, or puffing their short pipes. Some were nurse-girls or maids, who cast shy glances toward the students, which were for the most part cautiously returned.

Gradually the space in the campus was all this time filling with the boys, who were seated on light camp chairs and shaded by umbrellas. Everybody was ready long before the hands of the college clock pointed to three. It was singularly quiet, at least to what came after. The only sounds heard were the hum of conversation and the shrill cries of the little boys who went around yelling 'Score cards! Score cards!'

Suddenly there was a murmur of suppressed excitement among the students in the field. Several rose to their feet, and I heard one say, 'The Fem Sems have come!' It was the whole body of girls from a neighboring female seminary [Tilden], who had come up to watch the game—and the boys. Soon four great covered wagons, decked with ribbons, drew up to the campus, and they were immediately surrounded by students. But the joy of the occasion was marred by the fact that in every carriage, like an anxious hen brooding over a flock of restless chickens, was one of the lady teachers. This advent was the means of a strife between love and war, for the girls were not allowed to leave the wagons, and there was a very poor view of the game from this point, so that the student who saw the girls did not see the game. The girls were left a good deal alone that day.

At length I heard a desultory cheer from the lower part of the grand stand, which soon grew into a tempestuous roar, and looking down the field I saw that our boys were coming upon the ground. There they were, noble fellows, in their old white suits, which already bore the grass stains of many a victorious game. The boys ran lightly out to their respective positions, and the pitcher, standing by the home plate, batted the ball to each by turns. What a light little fellow he is! No one would think he could send the sphere whirling over the plate for two hours, but he is all nerve and sinew. Do you see that giant standing on the first base, with the great, clumsy gloves on his hands? You don't know how nimbly he will leap three feet in air when the careless third baseman sends the ball far above his head! He may not be a very good scholar, this giant, but he can play ball! Among the infielders who are picking up grounders, you notice the second baseman. The out-fielders are so far out you can hardly see their faces.

In about ten minutes the cheering breaks out again, but not as it did before. It is only perfunctory cheering this time. The Berkshire College nine are coming upon the field. The Wheelock men retire to give the others a chance to become familiar with the ground. Now every college man's eyes are wide open, for you can judge a nine pretty well by its practice work. It is evident that it is to be no one-sided contest to-day.

Finally a new sound breaks upon the ear. The college clock is striking three. The umpire steps out and beckons with his hand, all the players in the field run in, and all things are made ready. The Berkshire men have the toss and are at the bat. All of a sudden it is very quiet. The pitcher rolls the ball lovingly in his hands, then throws it like lightning over the base. Before the umpire has had time to cry out "One ball" there is a sharp *crack* in the air and the ball goes flying down the field. The batsman is at first in a second, and it is a hit. A feeble cheer rises from the region near the catcher. It is the manager and scorer of the Berkshire nine testifying their approval. It proves too soon to cheer, however, for the runner is cut out at second by the watchful Wheelock catcher and has to come in. The next two strike out, and half the inning is over. Now the Wheelock men are at bat, and as the centre-fielder, who is the first, comes out, he is hailed with an ovation. The Berkshire pitcher is a little nervous, and gives him his base on balls. The Wheelock captain runs down to first to coach him. "Now you're off, ste-ady, ma-ke him give you a good one, keep your eye on the ball he can't get one over the—*Go!*" this is what you hear in the silence of the game.

The next man strikes out. The third man makes a hit up in the air—a cheer is stopped by the running of the Berkshire third baseman to catch it. Some one starts to yell, but he is hissed down. "Give the man a chance!" some one says, angrily. Ah, he has caught it, and the inning is over. Nothing to nothing—not much to judge by yet, except that it is going to be a good game. And it was a good game, for so it went on for five innings and each side had made one score. Men began to move about uneasily. It was well to have it close; but, oh, if we were only one ahead!

It was the first half of the sixth inning, and Chandler, the great first baseman, was at bat. How much bigger he seemed to look than usual, as he stood there alone by the home plate! How that long club, wielded by those brawny arms, would send the ball, if they could but hit one corner of it. But Chandler was inclined to try too much for hard hits, and the pitcher, who had learned his weaknesses, gave him little, slow balls at which he struck so fiercely and so vainly that it seemed as if he would swing his arms off. But now his spunk was getting up, and this time, as he strode to his place, there was a look on his face which said, 'This time or never.' As he stepped up, somebody shouted 'A two-bagger this time, old fellow.'

He struck at the first ball. The club cracked, but held, and the ball went flying. It was one of those low, deceptive hits that don't look as if they were going very far. The short stop jumped up to catch it, but he couldn't quite reach it. The left fielder thought he had it, but he had moved too near, it was over his head. All the fielders started to get it. It reached the campus fence and bounded over, it passed the corner of one of the halls, and then was lost from sight, the fielders after it. Meanwhile, Chandler, in his slow and ponderous way, was making the rounds of the bases. He was so heavy he had to knock the ball farther than any one else to make any kind of a hit at all. The whole college was on its feet, the yells were deafening, umbrellas and hats were flying in air, and as the great fellow came staggering in home he was surrounded by a mob of apparent maniacs, who grasped his hand and nearly tore him to pieces. He had time to run around the bases twice before the fielders came back. They couldn't find the ball, they never found it. It was the longest hit ever made on the grounds. The fellows were never tired of telling of it. There even grew up legends about it; it was said that its velocity was so great that it cleared the world entirely and shot into space, and when some of the astronomical students the next year discovered what seemed to be a new star, it was at once christened Chandler's comet. Now the fun began. The next man made a two-base hit. The boys had already yelled themselves hoarse, and now they rested and yelled by detachments. I don't know that I have told you that the boys were seated by classes on the field, and that each class had its champion yeller, who started each cheer. By cheering in turn they could cheer all the time. There was one, the senior cheer-master, whose voice was noted. It wasn't so very loud in conversation or in recitation, but on the ball ground it was ear-piercing. He could outlast three other leaders, but even his powers were taxed to-day.

At the end of the inning the score was four to one. Every Wheelock man began to breathe freely. The next half hour was critical. The interest was such that men even forgot to cheer. It was three innings of sharp, perfect playing. Slowly but surely, and without any one great incident either, the tide turned. One by one the score ran up for the Berkshire men. The plucky scorer and manager had plenty of opportunities to cheer, and well they improved them. Wheelock was playing good ball, but the hits and brilliant plays did not seem to count. Berkshire did not make any long hits, but oh, they were so lucky! Neither side had made an error in the whole game so far.

It was the eighth inning, and the score was five to four. It was too close for comfort, surely. At length, amid great enthusiasm from the Wheelock men, it was nine innings and five to five.

I wish I could stop to give you every play that took place after this. I am sure such another game was never played before or since. Berkshire was at bat, their centre fielder made a hit, our short stop stopped it, fumbled it, then sent it speeding to second base. Ball and runner seemed to touch the second baseman at once. Both sent him flying, but he held to the ball. The runner declared that the ball did not touch him, the baseman declared it did. The umpire called the man safe. The crowd rose in a body and roared out their disapproval. Hundreds were ready to swear that they saw the ball touch him. The umpire remained firm, the crowd surged around him, and seemed ready to tear him limb from limb. The game stopped, the captains came up and excitedly argued the case. Time dragged on. The umpire reiterated his decision. The Wheelock captain seemed willing to forfeit the game, but the boys cried, 'Go on, we will beat them twice.' So the game went on. I suppose the point will never really be decided, but the fact that the umpire had once lived in the town of Berkshire made us believe that he was somewhat prejudiced. This man got in home, making the score six to five, and the next three men were put out, though one of them got as far as third base. Now it was Wheelock's last chance, and every man scanned his score card closely to see who was at bat. It was a gloomy prospect, for it was at the end of the batting list. Some gave up the game as lost, but none left the field. It was long after supper time, but nobody knew it. The field was growing a trifle dusky with shadows. The interest was now most intense, men told me afterward that they were as much exhausted as though they had undergone a fit of sickness. It was perfectly silent, save for the umpire's calls. 'One strike, two strikes,—three strikes, and out!' How discouraging! Every man held his breath now. 'One———out.' 'All is lost,' some one whispered. Artz, the catcher, was at bat. He was a silent, impassive fellow, who had stood calmly and quietly behind the bat during all the game, and had not let a ball, hardly, of any kind go past him. But he was a very poor batter. It seemed mere luck if he hit the ball. Two strikes, and he had not hit it. One ball more, and he just touched it enough to knock a slow grounder to short stop. Every man groaned. But the short stop missed it, and Artz was safe at first. A few relieved themselves by cheering. One more man at bat. But every one sighed when they saw him. It was the left fielder. He was only a passable player, and he had not made a hit all summer—I doubt if he ever had. 'One strike,' see the fellows cringe; 'two strikes,' numbers turned away their heads that they might not behold what followed. It seems hours before the next ball was pitched and centuries before it passed the plate. What is that? —a hit! Ranlett made a hit? But see, the field is all alive. The whole outfield is chasing the ball. Artz has gained second. Ranlett has gained first. Artz is at third and Ranlett at second, and now Artz is almost home and Ranlett is at his heels. The ball is coming in, too; but both are safe, and the college is closing in on the diamond. Safe home!—no need to ask the umpire,—and the game is won!

And now the diamond is full of maddened forms dancing up and down; some are yelling, some weeping, all are hatless. One great student seizes another, who is leaping in the air for joy, and, as he strains him in his arms, discovers that he is a professor. And now the victorious champions are lifted on a score of willing shoulders and carried to their rooms, the college bell is rung, and the great green pennant is raised to the belfry tower. After supper the celebration is begun by songs on the campus fence, and as soon as it is really dark a bonfire is built in the campus, and every man's unprotected woodpile is levied on for the purpose. The whole college is out again. Soon a procession is formed, with a band at the head of it, and the ball nine is dragged in a great chariot by three hundred pairs of hands around the diamond. The man who made the winning hit wears a new silk hat, just presented to him. Every player has to make a speech and be cheered, and everybody is happy. Then a line is formed again and marches through the principal streets. A stop is made at the house of every member of the faculty, and he must make a speech and be cheered also. At length the bonfire burns low, and the cheering ceases to silence, and it is the dead of night. That college cheer,—how much it brings back to me! Its savage 'wah-hoo-wah' rings in my ears, even as I heard it when last I gave it to bid my classmates farewell, in those days when college dreams were all there was of life and when BASE-BALL was its noblest conflict.

The First (and Only) College Balloon Race

JOHN PEARSON

➢➢ The Pearsons are a Dartmouth family. John Pearson's father (1881), two uncles, two brothers, a cousin, and a son were enrolled in the College, from which John Pearson was graduated in 1911. After years in investment banking and government service, he took up residence in Hanover, where among other activities he was associated with the famed Dartmouth Eye Institute. His reminiscence of the balloon race was printed in the *Alumni Magazine* in February 1952.

A YELLOWING CLIPPING from the *Boston Sunday Globe*, dated North Adams, Mass., June 3, 1911, reads: "College Men in Balloon Race; Dartmouth Airship Lands Early in Pelham; Pennsy and Williams Are Yet To Be Heard From." ...

The story starts on a frosty December night in 1910 when sixty undergraduates, seeking extracurricular relief from the tedium of classroom discipline and book-learning, and stimulated by aviator Glen Curtiss' winning the *New York Times* prize for a continuous flight from Albany to New York, gathered at College Hall and founded the Dartmouth Aero Club. Jay B. Benton '90, city editor of *The Boston Transcript*, had pepped up the meeting by inviting the two most productive members to join him on a balloon ascension in the spring. Membership was restricted, after "consultation with aeroplanists of Harvard, Cornell and Pennsylvania," to those who wanted to "experiment with a glider, or such men as are interested merely in the scientific study of aeronautics." ...

The Aero Club membership was quickly beguiled by the blandish-

The First (and Only) College Balloon Race 153

ments of magazine publishers and circulation builders. Weeks of soliciting subscriptions to *Aero* Magazine from the 1200 undergraduates of that period landed the grand subscription prize of a glider.

Consternation filled the ranks of the club membership when the glider was uncrated in the slush of March. It weighed a ton, it seemed. Housing was lacking for its forty-foot wing span. News that the nearest reliable glider soaring breeze was in far-away Elmira, New York, did not filter through until the twentieth reunion of the class of 1911.

Imagination was rife, however. Some club member, nettled by the prosperity of the Outing Club, suggested that the club president journey to the nearest steep hill and attempt glider flights on skis. To make the tale of back-breaking attempts short and snappy, the final try accomplished a record leap (for Grafton County, anyway) of 26 feet. The crash demolished the glider. What a break that was! I've often wondered about the outcome if the darn thing had really started soaring over forest-covered Mink Brook.

Blue skies of a lovely Hanover spring stimulated the club membership to fresh achievement. Plans for an intercollegiate balloon race were undertaken, with Harvard, Pennsylvania, Williams and Amherst. Mr. Jay Benton's balloon ascension invitation was recalled. The club president was unanimously elected as Mr. Benton's racing aide. Mr. Benton, ever loyal to Dartmouth's highest interests, promptly signed up his balloon *Boston*, all expenses paid. All efforts of the president to call a meeting and tender his resignation were rebuffed.

The Williams College Aero Club, hosts of the race, scheduled the take-off at the lee side of the nearest gas works. Prevailing winds were from the west; a rod or two to the east of the teeming city of North Adams, Hoosac Mountain reared its craggy head.

After a notably hospitable evening at Williams, designed to put the Icaruses of 1911 into a "higher than a kite" mood for the morrow, contestants were shooed over to North Adams on Saturday noon. Mr. Benton, with balloon, was waiting, checking his weather-eye with famed balloonist Leo Stevens, official starter. Mr. Stevens had declared to the assembled press: "This starts intercollegiate ballooning as the only air sport for colleges. Aeroplaning is killing a man a day.

The spherical balloon is the only safe instrument for those wishing sensible but exciting air rivalry and amusement."

Suddenly the gas man presented the writer, whose cash resources totaled $11, with a $45 gas bill and a document reading: "The undersigned releases the North Adams Gas Light Company from any expense, responsibility or damage, to us or others, directly or indirectly." Confusion reigned until Mr. Benton arrived with his pen and ampler wad.

The Harvard and Amherst entries failed to show up, but Professor David Todd of Amherst had telegraphed: "Hearty congratulations to all. Will watch. May the best bubble win." What do you mean, Professor, by "bubble," I thought to myself.

The Dartmouth entry, swelling with its 35,000 cubic feet of illuminating gas, tugged at its drag rope. A five-foot-square, four-foot-high wicker basket, decked with six bags of sand ballast, eighty pounds each, hung from the balloon. While waiting our turn to start, Mr. Benton chatted away and I chattered my response. He tried to reassure me: ballooning in New England was delightful; the chief danger was in being blown out over the Atlantic Ocean. "That calls for fast action with the gas rip-cord when the pilot sees the sea," said Mr. Benton....

How we vaulted into the basket is not clear to me today. Vivid, however, is the impression that the westerly wind had suddenly become quite "pert." And still vivid is Mr. Benton's strident call, "Heave in and untangle the ropes." He had spied high powered electric lines in the offing. Beyond were numerous chimney tops, just duck-pins for the drag-ropes which kinked into large balls.

"Heave it is," I thought, as I h'isted myself up the basket side, racing low over the house tops. I struggled with the ropes. Heaves! Whoops! and Burps! left me weakly "hanging on the ropes."

Suddenly Mr. Benton apprehended Hoosac Mountain rearing its forbidding boulders high above our path. "Dump sand," cried Mr. Benton, as he sensed the catastrophe of being dashed and/or bashed to death on the mountain. Still bushed from wrestling with the ropes, I balanced on the basket rim for a go at a sand bag. I still don't know whether it was the cookies I tossed or the sand I spilled that lightened

The First (and Only) College Balloon Race 155

the load enough for us to leap Hoosac Mountain, in the nick of time, with 3 ⅝ inches to spare.

So far, I thought to myself, isn't ballooning just ducky? I know of easier ways to "get up in the air." But once again, as an annal of history, stout heart and hidden strength had surmounted adversity and crisis. Soon the peace and quiet of ballooning dominated the scene as we soared into the empyrean to two miles above sea level. We scanned the heavens for our rivals. To the north the Williams balloon was bobbing about in the lightning flashes of a thunder storm. Closing my eyes, I mentally wafted thoughts of good-will and hope in their direction. To the east, over the sharply defined Vermont-Massachusetts boundary line, the Pennsylvania balloon sped on, way ahead.

Mr. Benton concluded that our dragging start had imposed a severe racing handicap on us. I have a hunch, also, that he enjoyed the sights of the Deerfield River Valley more than he did the constant chore of spilling sand, or releasing gas, in the search for the fastest moving air currents.

A cloud covered the sun. In the suddenly chilled air the balloon dropped. "How fast are we dropping?" I asked Mr. Benton. "Toss out some torn newspaper and guess," he replied. The sun emerged and up we soared. Soon the instruments showed a range in elevation from 10,000 to 3,000 feet with temperatures ranging from 110° to 38°.

The silent, hushed tranquillity of a balloon journey impressed me. Mr. Benton provided a lunch. As I drank my coffee, Mr. Benton constantly shifted his two-hundred-plus avoirdupois to drink in the scenery. How the wicker basket cracked and cracked! I wondered if the basket maker really took pride in his work when he tied the basket bottom to the sides.

"If you want to see some action," Mr. Benton said, "call out to the folks at the next farm house we pass over." I still hang my head with shame as I recall my sophomoric response: "Stop beating your wife!" I said in a firm tone to a couple sitting on their lawn. When last seen the couple were still running around, looking all over the place for the intruder. Not once, as I called out, time and time again, to engage folks in conversation, did anyone ever think to look heavenward.

The winner of a balloon race, dear reader, is the pilot who travels the longest distance in a straight line from the starting point. About 5 p.m., as we reached the Connecticut River above Northampton, a breeze from the north turned us down river. Beyond Springfield, a sea-turn zephyr sent us back up the river. In vain I scanned Mt. Holyoke's campus, looking for a wave of encouragement from my sister. At Greenfield, the down-river breeze took over again. For an hour we commuted, back and forth, up and down the Connecticut River Valley.

Shortly after 6 p.m. clouds darkened the sinking sun. At the time I didn't realize the effect of the sudden atmospheric change on the lifting power of the unspent gas. All I sensed was that suddenly we were plummeting landward, like a bat out of hell. The earth appeared to be swallowing us up. Let's get this over with, I thought, as I hoisted a leg over the basket edge for a leap to terra firma.

Zowie! It seems that the remaining gas more than balanced the ground-level atmosphere. The resulting bounce of hundreds of feet into the air left me bottom side up on the basket bottom. Mr. Benton knowingly clung to the basket side. "Pull the gas rip-cord," said Mr. Benton, "if you are in a hurry to get out." A whoosh of gas followed a yank at the cord. The next sensation was that of a leap from a third story window as the basket hit the ground with a thud. Mr. Benton remembered to note the time. It was 6:17 p.m.; the place—West Pelham, Mass.

Fortunately we had missed some woodlands and landed in a pasture. Twenty cows stood waiting to be called into the barn. It was milking time, in June. At our sudden intrusion, pandemonium—or whatever dumb animals experience—possessed the cows. They didn't give milk so good that night, we learned later.

Meanwhile a dying breeze lazily dragged the precious silk gas bag along a barbed-wire fence. The sound of the tearing and ripping silk was awful to hear. It was not music to Mr. Benton's ears.

A farmer loaded the torn bag and the basket into a cart for shipment back to Boston. Mr. Benton and I hopped an open trolley car to Amherst. I spent the evening at Mt. Holyoke imaginatively amplifying to

The First (and Only) College Balloon Race 157

my sister and friends the experiences of the afternoon. The next day, at my home in Concord, N. H., I learned that Father had sat out on the lawn all afternoon in case his son happened to blow by. "Every time a cloud darkened the sun," Mother said, "Father would rush into the house and call, 'Here comes John, Mother!'"

Oh yes—who did win the race? Dartmouth's entry started last and finished last. Somehow that makes sense. Due to the right-angle southward detour we took at Northampton, we never did catch our "second wind." The sashaying we did up and down the river scored us only 41 miles travel credit from the starting point. Our time in flight was three hours and fifteen minutes.

The Williams balloonists, H. P. Shearman and aide Kenneth T. Price, finished second, landing at Paxton, Mass., at 7:45 p.m. with a flight credit of 66 miles in five hours. Reporting an exciting trip, they claimed they "narrowly escaped freezing to death, caught in a whirlwind that rushed them to a height of 12,000 feet at a rapid rate!"

The winners, Arthur T. Atherholt and aide George A. Richardson, Pennsylvania, credited with 110 air miles, stayed aloft seven hours and landed in West Peabody, Mass., six miles from the Atlantic Coast. "The flashing Baker Island lighthouse, off Salem, caused me to drop my balloon through the darkness and a drenching thunder storm into some woods," Pilot Atherholt reported. Their basket sheltered them for the rest of the night.

"What contribution did the Dartmouth Aero Club make to aviation?" someone may well ask. Who knows but what a country lad, residing in the Deerfield River Valley, the Charles Lindbergh or Eddie Rickenbacker of tomorrow, had glimpsed the Dartmouth balloon floating majestically overhead? Who knows, as the lad fell asleep on the night of June 3, 1911, but what he resolved that he too would some day sail the great blue yonder and make aviation history? Who knows?

Cattle Boat
CHARLES HAYWOOD

🙢 Working one's way to Europe by cattle boat was an experience of many a Dartmouth man in the 1920s, an experience recalled by Charles Haywood 1925 in this account that first appeared in the *Alumni Magazine* in February 1956. After college he became a Boston attorney by vocation, a sometime novelist by avocation.

A BIG GANG of us left Hanover that June evening and headed for White River Junction to catch the night mail to Montreal. Some had gone on ahead, others would follow, but every one of us had a letter from the Dartmouth Outing Club directed to a man named John Storen down on St. Antoine Street, near the riverfront. We were the cattlemen; extra crew for the ships that carried wild steers raised in the Canadian Northwest across the ocean to England.

That first night was a rough one. To save money we purchased one berth for each two men and when the northbound night mail came chuffing into the Junction in the small hours, with two Moguls on the head end, we stowed ourselves away and tried to go to sleep. In my half of an upper berth I squirmed around and cursed Ed [Edward Ruth 1927] and Ed cursed me and we asked each other what time it was, and where the train was now, and why we had paid money for this miserable little shelf. However, we slept some as the train rumbled up the White River Valley of Vermont, dozing to the rhythm of wheels clacking over the rail joints and the steady beat of the steam locomotives horsing the heavy train over the grades.

The night ended; in the dawn the train raced across the French Flats toward the St. Lawrence, while we gratefully dressed. By breakfast time we were trooping out of St. Bonaventure Station, headed for the

Cattle Boat 159

Hotel Windsor to set up our base and reconnoitre. At the hotel we managed to save some more money. Two of us hired a large room, and with well-placed tips the chambermaids were persuaded to show us where spare cots and blankets were kept. By careful conserving of space and a couple of extra mattresses on the floor, the room accommodated eight of us.

Our headquarters set up, we held a short conference in the Windsor Tap Room, before starting for the harbor front to find out from John Storen where our ship was and when we sailed. There we had bad news.

Three of us were to ship aboard the Alan Line's *Devonian*, due to sail at mid-morning of the next day and three more were to join White Star's *Cornishman*, which was to depart by noon at the latest. They were all ordered to report at the Quai Alexandria immediately after breakfast. As for Ed and me, we were assigned to Anchor-Donaldson's *Salacia*, time of departure unknown. "Just keep in close touch with me," said John Storen, leaning on the counter of his little waterfront shop and scribbling in his big ledger.

Early next morning our room at the Windsor was in an uproar. The lucky six who were to be sailing down the St. Lawrence by dinner time packed their street clothes carefully away and hauled out their ski outfits, which for Dartmouth men of 1925 were mostly clothing purchased from firms that supplied lumber camps. Dressed for the cold voyage across the North Atlantic, they picked up their bags and tramped down to the lobby, and a hard-looking lot they were.

Ed and I dashed after them, rode with them in their taxi to the waterfront and watched them go aboard. Both vessels had taken on their cattle in the early morning hours and were ready to sail, whistles blew, lines were cast off and the ships backed out into the river, headed downstream and were off for England.

Staring until they were out of sight, we stood on the pier wondering how many days we must hang around waiting for our ship to sail. Idly we drifted from one wharf to another, watching the work of the waterfront and at noon we again reported to John Storen's office. He shouted at us as we crossed his threshold.

"Get your gear and get aboard the *Salacia*," he roared. "Cattle will start running at one o'clock. Hurry, boys, hurry."

We raced back to the Windsor in a taxi and changed into our seagoing outfits. Again the clerk stared wide-eyed at two hard-looking tickets checking out of his hotel, but we tarried for no explanations. We paid and ran, and in another taxi we headed for the Quai Alexandria, shouting at the driver for more speed.

We need not have hurried. Alongside the pier lay the *Salacia*, deserted, no smoke rising from her single stack, no cattle, no crewmen except a big stoker viewing a huge pile of coal on deck and vehemently expressing himself with obscene British participles. The vessel had no railings. The upright stanchions were in place, but the steel cable that should have been rove through the eyes lay snaking about the deck in rusty confusion. Odd pieces of lumber lay scattered about; flies buzzed around a heap of garbage beside the galley door; her sides and superstructure were marked with big patches of rust like the map of a group of unlovely islands. This was the British Merchant Marine, and we were horrified.

We had not stood long gazing upon this miserable and apparently abandoned tramp steamer when a little gray-headed man with a red nose, a lush mustache and a hatchet came stumping down the pier.

"Are you boys cattlemen?" he queried, when he spied us.

"Yes," I said. "When do we—"

"Follow me," he ordered, "and hurry."

Hurry? Why? It certainly looked as if tomorrow or next day would be soon enough. But we followed him, along the pier, up a narrow flight of stairs, into a room crowded with men and over to a counter where a clerk presided over a big ledger.

"Ordinary seamen," grunted the little man with the hatchet to the man with the ledger. "These coves are the last two. I've a crew now."

We scratched our names in the big book, rounding out a list of twenty men signed on as extra crew to feed the cattle on the long voyage to the British Isles. The little red nosed man waved his hatchet at the roomful of men.

"Listen. I'm Shorty McConville, cattle foreman. You've signed up for hard work and a free passage to the old country. Only one thing to remember and don't ever forget it. England this day expects every man to do his duty. Now get down to the ship. Cattle will be running any minute now."

Down the deserted pier we tramped with our luggage, aboard the dingy tramp, along the cluttered deck to the stern, where cattlemen stay, a ship's length from the regular crew in the forecastle. While we scrambled for bunks and stowed our dunnage the old *Salacia* began to come to life. She trembled, the staccato beat of a steam donkey engine on deck boomed through the empty 'tween decks like a bass drum; over and above the hollow rumbling rose the voice of Shorty McConville.

"Lay on deck. Tumble out. The cattle are running. 'England this day expects every man'...."

The rest of it was drowned out by the deep-throated whistle of a freight locomotive on the pier not twenty feet from the cabin porthole and the rush of men "tumbling out." We surged through the door of the cabin, clambered up the stern companionway and poured out onto the after deck. Seamen were reeving the wire cables through the eyes of the stanchions so that the ship had railings. From the stack billowed thick black smoke and from the fire room below came the metallic clang of shovels and slicing bars and slamming furnace doors as the black gang hurried to build up a head of steam. At a 45-degree angle from the foremast hung a boom, a seaman sat at a steam winch and snatched great sling-loads of boxed 90-pound Canadian cheeses from the pier and lowered them into the forward hatch. From the mainmast another boom reached out toward the wharf, another seaman worked the levers, the winch chattered as it swung cargo aboard. Wide metal pipes led from the grain elevator down into the ship; from them came the whispering, rustling, rushing sound of wheat pouring into the hold.

Yet all this activity was background—taken in with a glance. The cattle trains on the pier alongside were our business; long strings of cars loaded with bellowing steers from the plains. Dozens of stevedores—little Frenchmen—manhandled a big gangplank to the door of the first car; they fitted together sections of fence to enclose the narrow cleated runways that led all the way to the lower deck. Then the door of the car slid open, the Frenchmen yelled and poked at the beasts with broomsticks sharpened to a fine point; the steers bellowed some more and began to trot down the gangplank, slipping, sliding, stumbling. Any who hesitated were goaded by men posted along the fence-ways; harried and prodded until they moved on into the darkness below decks.

When the last steer in the car had been rounded up by the shouting stevedores and chased down the gangplank, the yard locomotive gave a few puffs and the long line of cattle cars moved ahead a little. Another car door slid open, more wild yelling from the drovers and forty more steers trotted and slid and stumbled down into the *Salacia's* cattle pens.

Peering through the open hatch at the stream of cattle pouring down the runway, we saw Shorty McConville. And Shorty saw Ed and me.

"You two school boys lay below and git to work," he shouted. "What the bloody hell do you think this is? An excursion boat?"

Suddenly we realized we were alone on deck. While we had watched, fascinated, the other men had gone to work below. Britishers, Scots and Irishmen taking this opportunity for a free summer visit home, they were men of Canada accustomed to such scenes. Without an order, they had turned to the work of tying up the animals, leaving us on deck, staring. We hurried down the companionway into the maelstrom below. Shorty glared at us, waving us toward a pen where Ellis and Paddy struggled with thirty steers milling around inside.

The pens were like horse stalls varying in capacity from an enclosure of a size to hold a single beast to some three times as big as the largest box stall in a millionaire's barn. The pens ranged down the B deck from bow to stern; most of them along the sides of the ship, but some in the center to use advantageously the space not taken up by the fore and after hatchways and the engine and smokestack spaces. Cattle boats were ordinary small ocean-going cargo carriers of five thousand tons and upwards with the conventional forecastle, forward well deck, amidships structure with pilot house, bridge, officers' quarters and radio shack, then an after well deck and poop or stern castle.

Between the forecastle and the amidships, the well deck was covered with a temporary wooden housing to provide more room for cattle pens. The after well deck was covered over in the same way, so that every spare foot of deck space in the ship was used for cattle.

Every part of both decks was an uproar of shouting men and bellowing steers as the Canadian drovers prodded the stream of cattle into the pens. When each enclosure was full, they slammed the gate, rearranged the fencing and guided the animals into the next empty space. We had no time to watch them; nothing concerned us except the steers milling around in this pen.

Each one had a length of half inch rope about four feet long tied around the base of his horns. Who fastened the ropes to these wild beasts of the plains I never knew, nor did that concern us. Our duty was to catch the loose end dangling between the steer's fore legs, slip it through a hole bored in the horizontal plank across the front of the pen and tie a knot. When we had done this thirty times, we would be ready to move on to the next pen.

The four of us leaned on the belly-high plank gazing at the huddled animals. Paddy turned to me and grinned.

"Well, boy, want to go in there and bring one o' them beasties up front here so I can grab the rope an' tie him up?"

I stared at the long-horned steers huddled at the back of the pen. It seemed to me that every one of the thirty were glaring at us, hostile, malevolent, ready, the instant a man ventured anywhere near, to give one quick swing of the head and plunge a two-foot-long, needle-sharp horn into his vitals. Those horns fascinated me. Their whole spread was over four feet, they were like none I had ever seen around New England; more like the horns on some trophy on the wall of a banquet hall. Again I wondered how any mortal man had ever managed to tie a rope around them.

"I'm not blaming you school boys for not doing this," observed Paddy, slipping under the horizontal head plank. "This you can learn from no book."

With a quick motion he had one of the steers by the nose, fingers up both nostrils. With his right hand he had the beast's tail and he commenced to wind it with a crank-like motion. With tremendous bellows the animal edged to the front of the pen, with Paddy's iron grip on the nose guiding him and his strong tail twisting furnishing the motive power.

Reaching under the head board, I seized the dangling rope, slipped it through the hole and tied a knot. This steer was secure. Then Paddy reached for another animal, and Ellis, who had lived for years in Alberta, started working at the other end of the pen, bringing them up to the head board so Ed could reach the rope and tie the knot.

This sort of thing went on and on. Up and down the decks our team ranged, with Paddy and Ellis doing the tail twisting, while Ed and I tied them up. Sometimes we saw other groups near us; but often we seemed to be alone in these murky decks, endlessly struggling with steers, always looking ahead and more to be done.

And then we suddenly discovered it was accomplished; 635 beeves were securely fastened in their pens. During it all, Shorty McConville was up and down the decks, exhorting, advising, occasionally laying down his hatchet to assist with a difficult one. When he saw all his cattle safely in place, he produced a half a dozen hatchets from a bag and with appropriate remarks as to what England this day expected, he conferred them upon the six most likely looking of his men. This made them foremen of a particular section of the deck and the rest of us were briefly instructed as to the proper attitude toward our superiors.

The hatchets were to chop the wires on the bales of hay, as well as serving as the insignia of office. We gave the cattle plenty of hay and a measure of grain, we watered them and bedded them down with straw. Somewhere along in here we heard shouting on deck, and short bursts of action from the steam winches. The ship trembled and shook, from amidships we heard the slow rhythmic beat of the reciprocating steam engine—a three-cylinder triple expansion job. Moving further aft we could feel the motion of the propeller shaft and the steady muffled thump of the *Salacia's* single screw. We were under way; we had not been on deck to witness the scene of departure. But it did not matter. There had been no one on the pier to wave to us.

When at last all the cattle were fed we were allowed to go on deck and look around. Far astern, silhouetted against the June sunset, lay the skyline of Montreal, the Sun Life Building, the church spires, the rectangular bulk of the grain elevators along the river front, all very small in the distance. We were in the middle of the broad St. Lawrence; the distant banks were verdant green, dotted here and there by white farmhouses and occasionally one of the villages of French Canada with its big church looming above the close clustered buildings.

We sent two men to the galley amidships and before long they returned with two buckets containing our supper and a big kettle of tea. In the dusk we sat on the poop deck eating from the tin plates issued to us, watching the St. Lawrence widen into Lac St. Pierre. Seamen rigged hoses, the ship's pumps started filling the huge tanks with enough lake water to last over six hundred cattle for ten days to two weeks. For a while we watched the foaming wake of the ship; a line in the placid waters of the lake reaching far astern toward the last glow of the setting sun. Then we lay below and turned in.

The Anchor-Donaldson Line, in conformity with British Merchant Marine regulations, did well by us. The bunks were boxes, coffin size, a bit more shallow, and, of course, no lid. A mattress of fresh straw in clean new gunny sacking lay neatly fitted into each bunk. These mattresses, we learned, were burned after one round-trip to Britain; a measure which greatly reduced the normal vermin population of a ship's cabin. A few of us were fortunate enough to have small straw pillows and we each drew two blankets apiece, redolent with carbolic acid odor, but clean. So we took off our hats and our shoes and tumbled in. Beyond the cabin door lay the first of a long line of steers that reached to the bow, beneath us the steady beat of the propeller, and a rushing, churning sound as the blades bit deep into the waters of the St. Lawrence. We soon slept.

In the gray dawn we were awakened by Smittie, a little Cockney selected from our group to be night watchman. Through the hours of darkness he had trudged up and down the dimly lit aisles between the pens of sleeping steers. His orders were to turn out the cattle crew if anything went wrong, and at 4:30 to get a kettle of coffee from the galley and rout the men out of their bunks.

Smittie executed his orders. Nothing wrong during the night out among the pens, so he had to bother no one. As for waking up the cattle crew, he could have done it in the immemorial usage of the sea with wild shouts, lush profanity and tremendous poundings on the bulkheads. But Smittie had put in years in the employ of a fine London hotel.

"Time to get up, sir." I felt some one gently shaking my arm.

"Coffee's 'ot and on the tyble, sir."

As soon as I sat up and yawned, he moved on to the next bunk to wake up the next gentleman. By the time we had put on our hats and our shoes and gathered around the cabin table with our tin cups we heard Shorty McConville descending the after companionway, shouting as he came.

"Up, you beggars. Tumble out. Hit the deck. Rise and shine. There's cattle to be fed."

He barged through the cabin door, flourishing his hatchet.

"Swill that bloody coffee and get out there on the decks. This ain't no excursion steamer. England this day expects. . . ."

In the gray dawn light every man did his duty; we forked hay and lugged water until all 600-odd animals were fed. Then we sent a man to the galley to bring back our breakfast—a two-course affair; oatmeal in one bucket, pancakes in the other. The *Salacia* was passing Quebec as we ate, sitting on the after hatch. Above us loomed the great steel bridge over the river and we stared at that awful middle span that fell so many years ago as they were trying to fasten it into place and carried a whole construction crew to death in the waters a hundred feet below.

The morning we spent hoisting bales of hay from the forward hatch with a block and tackle and manpower; no steam winch for this job. After that we fed the cattle again and ate our dinner and cleaned the aisles between the pens and lugged water and fed the beasts their supper and got our supper from the galley and ate all of it that was fit to eat and hove the rest over the side. The shores of the great river ever widened as the *Salacia's* engine steadily beat out her thirteen knots, black smoke poured from the stack and cinders were gritty under foot on the after deck. A long wake trailed astern; ahead the eastern sky darkened—sundown was not far away.

At dawn we had been off Quebec—the head of tidewater. We had steamed down river through all the hours of daylight of a long June day and now we made ready to drop the pilot. The engines stopped, the ship waited for the little pilot-boat making out from Father Point. When he had gone over the side and his boat had cleared away, the *Salacia's* engine again started its slow beat, the thump of the screw made our cabin tremble and shake, but it was a rhythm to help tired men sleep. We tumbled into our bunks; soon we were snoring, but in the few minutes before I dropped off I could feel under me the long heave of the ocean swells as the ship headed out into the Gulf of St. Lawrence.

The next day was straight seafaring out of sight of land; pitching, rolling, spray over the bows and a wildly racing, vibrating, screw as she put her nose into it; then, as the stern settled and the bow pointed upward, the slow steady stroke of a propeller biting water, thrusting ahead. In this seaway men were sick and beasts were sick. The men had the better of it; they need only be sure it was the lee rail they leaned over. But beef creatures are not made so they may quickly be rid of whatever sets heavy on the stomach. They lay moaning, eating nothing, too miserable to eat or drink or move.

The day we crossed the Gulf of St. Lawrence, the ship was full of rumor and speculation. Were we to go south of Newfoundland, through the Cabot Strait, leaving Nova Scotia's Cape Breton starboard? Or had the ice cleared sufficiently from the Strait of Belle Isle so the *Salacia* might take this narrow passage between the Labrador and the northernmost reaches of Newfoundland? For less than three months in summer this route, saving a day, is available to shipping. The rest of the year it is choked with ice floes and bergs, unsafe for any vessel but an ice-breaker or a government cutter.

We went to bed still guessing, but by the time Smittie brought the morning coffee and waked us, we knew.

"We're in Belle Isle," he whispered. We tumbled out and raced up the companionway for a look. We saw nothing; the fog walled us in, thick white, cold and clammy—so heavy we could not see the bow and the smokestack amidships was but a dim and vague shape. The tempo of the steadily thumping propeller slowed down now to the cautious, timid beat of half-speed; every man of us felt as if we were shuffling through a dark room, feeling ahead lest we slam into a solid object. The *Salacia's* whistle sounded; then, from far away in the fog came the bass tones of another vessel's whistle, and, from a different quarter a third ship's warning, and then a fourth, from ahead.

By noon the fog was burning off, the sky lightened, through the mist the sun showed vaguely, no brighter than an old tin plate. In minutes the fog was gone; miles to the northward lay the bold shores of the Labrador—bleak, cold and forbidding. To the south lay Newfoundland's northern shore, a pleasant place of green fields and little white houses shining in the sun.

It was cold in Belle Isle. When we turned in, not long after eight, some of the old hands said we were near an iceberg. From the deck we had not been able to see it, but a numbing chill penetrated everything. The two thin blankets Anchor-Donaldson had issued to us were not enough, even though we lay in our bunks fully clothed, with our hats on.

"I've had a bloody 'nuff of this," announced old Timmins, swinging his legs out of his bunk. "I'm going to see the bleedin' engineer and get some steam."

The engineer, too, must have felt the nearby presence of the bergs, for he made no argument and the steam pipes in our cabin were snapping and sizzling before Timmins returned. Cozily warm, we fell asleep to the beat of the ship's propeller thumping steadily beneath us. By the dawn, when we were turned out to commence feeding our cattle, we were in open sea.

Now every day was like every other day; an unbroken expanse of water, far horizons and near-at-hand problems. The work was hard and monotonous; an endless purveying of hay, grain and water to the steers. . . .

After taking our departure from Labrador's dark rocky coast, at Belle Isle, we were seven days on the high seas. The sameness of the days made us feel as if we had been at sea as long as we could remember; feeding cattle, hoisting hay from the hold, cutting baling wire with our hatchets, eating, sleeping, looking forward to the day we had plum duff.

I was physician for the cattlemen. My uncle, a doctor, had presented me with a little leather case containing medicines and I had added to my supply in Montreal. For a cold, I dispensed aconite pills, for *mal de mer* I handed out Mother Sill's Seasick Remedy and I did some bandaging of cuts, using my iodine bottle freely. I had a small box of licorice powder, a good old remedy for what today is known as a torpid colon and the patients who came to me for this complaint were the most appreciative of all. Before the end of the passage my little box was empty and so, too, were the grateful patients.

"The Irish pilots," said Timmins one night, pointing at the gulls circling about the ship. "We'll see land in the morning."

Land in the morning; the entire cattle crew brightened up and commenced babbling about what they planned to do ashore, as if they were aboard a whaler returning from a year's voyage. And Timmins' prediction was accurate. When Smittie routed us out in the dawn, instead of yawning and grousing over our coffee, we raced up the stern companionway to see where we were. There it was: Ireland—low green hills to starboard.

All morning we followed the Irish coastline and by noontime we sighted, dead ahead, a strange little island with sheer rock sides and a green tufted cap of verdure on top. Paddy's Milestone, this is, standing at the mouth of the Firth of Clyde, the last land the Irish immigrant sees as he sails out of Glasgow, bound for the New World.

Now the big cargo booms were unshipped, steam hissed in the pipes leading to the winches, and crewmen took their places at the control levers. A cattle owner is allowed free carriage of a fourteen days' supply of hay and grain for his steers and we had made it in ten, so up from the hold came the surplus. This time we did not mind the work; steam did the hoisting and all we had to do was roll the bales along the decks and leave them where they could easily be unloaded in port.

The Firth narrowed, we were nearing the river itself, a narrow stream carrying a tremendous water-borne commerce. Two little paddle-wheel tugs came out to meet us; one took a line ahead, the other a line astern to keep the *Salacia* steady so she would not swing into one of the nearby muddy banks. Throughout the late afternoon, at half speed, the vessel felt its way up river, past farms and fishing villages, then towns and shipyards and the outskirts of Glasgow itself. It was ten o'clock and the long Scottish twilight was fading when at last the laboring, splashing tugs eased our ship up to Brumelagh Pier.

A crowd of fellows in long white butchers' coats swarmed aboard, untied our cattle and drove them out on to the pier, the whole business taking a surprisingly short time. Or perhaps it was only that it seemed short to us, for now we were only spectators. Leaning on the ship's rail we idly gazed at these men who now had the responsibility of herding over six hundred wild steers to their next destination. It was nothing to us, our work was done; if one of them got loose or gored a man, it would not be our man who was carried off on a litter. Yet these big Scotsmen did not have half the trouble the little Frenchmen had loading the cattle at Montreal, or that we had tying them up as the ship sailed down the St. Lawrence. These steers were tamer now, chastened by ten days in the pens of the *Salacia*—the ordeal of trying to keep their feet on a ship that pitched and rolled to the swells of the North Atlantic. Their legs were weak from ten days with little use and they had been seasick. They trotted meekly off and that was the last we saw of them.

The tugs shifted us to a nearby pier and we slept in a strangely quiet ship; no beat of the propeller beneath us, no creaking of cabin timbers in a seaway; no bellow of steers from the cattle decks; no yelps from

Shorty McConville, our foreman. In the dawn we were still slumbering, Smittie, the night watchman in his bunk, too, for a patrol of the pens was no longer necessary. We arose at a gentleman's hour and enjoyed a leisurely breakfast, sitting around the table and discussing our plans.

Then a new uproar commenced.

A hundred men carrying shovels and hoes and brooms came tramping up the gang plank, every one of them wearing a curious arrangement of gunnysacking tied with crisscross thongs to protect his legs from the knee down. This they needed for their mission was Operation Manure. The cranes on the pier alongside lowered enormous iron buckets, six feet in diameter, and into these went everything. They dumped the huge buckets into a dozen coal cars of the Caledonian Railway, the four-wheel, ten-ton-capacity type.

By mid-morning the ship was clean, the cars were on their way to Anchor-Donaldson's farm and the hundred Scotsmen had departed, leaving us alone with the beady-eyed British Immigration officer who was examining our papers. When it came my turn I had trouble signing, so stiff were my fingers from ten days with pitchforks and hatchets and hauling on ropes. He compared the signature on my entry permit with that on my passport, sighed deeply, studied the photograph, scrutinized my features, and at last committed His Majesty's Government to letting me wander about Britain for a while, although plainly he was uneasy about it.

So we were ashore with a pocketful of money, not a large pocketful, but enough to do the grand tour of Europe if we did everything the economical way. Scorning any guide book, we did Britain and the Continent with only a ten-cent map and our own recollection of what we had heard one should see. The place is well posted, we found, and we missed little.

In that summer midway through what people now call the Roaring Twenties, the boulevards of Europe's capitals were like the main street of one's home town in that one might expect to meet a friend at any time. In Bruxelles we met three more Dartmouth men and spent the day sauntering through museums and palaces, pausing after each visit at a sidewalk café to discuss what we had learned. In Paris, walking down the Boulevard des Italiens, of an evening, we met several groups of fellow students. When we inspected Harry's New York Bar, The Moulin Rouge and the Folies Bergeres, others from Hanover were there, absorbing atmosphere.

By mid-August we had seen it all, or thought we had. In quaint little hotels and pensions from Scotland to the Alps we had eaten queer food, talked with odd proprietors and fought an occasional unsuccessful battle with bedbugs. Now if anyone talked about the Rhine or the Venus de Milo or Oxford University, we could immediately join in the conversation. We were full of sight-seeing, tired and broke; so we whirled through England on the Bristol Express of the Great Western, to get our free ride home on a Montreal-bound cattle steamer.

We came back on the *Parthenia*, a sister of the *Salacia*. The cabin was full of returning cattlemen, but none of the *Salacia's* men were aboard. This ship seemed dead. It was the cattle we missed, the life and vitality of the two decks loaded with beasts which ate and drank and slept and bellowed and smelled and needed our attention. The empty pens did not seem right; the vessel was not a day from port before we wished we once more were pitching hay and lugging grain. But there was no cargo needing attention. The *Parthenia* carried Welsh coal and a hundred tons of English crockery—enough, we figured, to put an appropriate receptacle under every farmer's bed from Toronto to Saskatoon.

So we read and played cards and talked with the other homeward bound cattlemen. After tedious days, we awoke one morning to the long, deep, musical notes of the whistle of a Canadian Pacific steam locomotive working a freight drag along the river bank. A man's engine, this; so different from any little European peanut stand with its shrill piping whistle. It sounded mighty good to us.

A Hero's Uniform
JOHN R. SCOTFORD, JR.

≫ John Scotford 1938, football ambitions far behind, is a graphic artist and Assistant Director of the Hopkins Center at Dartmouth. The reminiscence, from which the following excerpt is taken, was printed in *Sports Illustrated*, November 14, 1966.

MAN AND BOY, ever since I was old enough to leave the house self-propelled, my mother has never failed to greet my return with some reference to a fancied loss of weight. She says, "John, you look thinner." I entered Dartmouth in 1934 depressing the scales at a robust 135 pounds. Why I did not put on 20 pounds during my freshman year at college still baffles nutritional experts. All first-year men were required to eat at the Commons. The fare served up by Mr. Sweet and his caloric cohorts was the type one would expect to find at a well-run southern penal institution, and I loved it. I guess it appealed to my American-heartland background. (I was contemplated in Arkansas, conceived in Oklahoma, born in Texas and raised in Illinois and Ohio.) One of my favorites was the Sunday morning fried mush with maple syrup. My more sophisticated classmates found its charms limited and were glad to give me their servings. I often stumbled out of College Hall with a couple of quarts of cornmeal as ballast. But to no avail—I was graduated at 135 pounds net weight. It is true that though once during the intervening three decades I did get up to 145, the effort drained me and my present fighting weight is 140. Of course, as in the case of most aging athletes, my 135 pounds in 1934 were all muscle and sinew, but the 140 pounds of 1966 are all fat.

So it is not surprising that when I make a passing reference to my college football career over a tray of hors d'oeuvres, some overweight skeptic asks for a fuller explanation.

In the fall of 1934 Dartmouth was on the verge of the football era developed and sustained by Coach Earl (Red) Blaik and his talented assistants, Andy Gustafson, Harry Ellinger and Joe Donchess. There were a lot of football prospects in college that year. Even though it was before the advent of platoon football, the varsity squad had 51 players on the roster, and there were 31 listed for the junior varsity. Red Blaik had cranked up his recruiting machinery, and 143 men turned out for the freshman football team. I cite these population figures not to give the impression that everyone at Dartmouth played football. Far from it. Just a favored few, on a percentage basis. I mention these statistics to give you some idea of the equipment inventory the Dartmouth College Athletic Council had to maintain, which is an important part of my story.

One of the highlights of the freshman-orientation period was the presentation of Recreational Opportunities. All freshmen and sophomores had to take Rec in the fall, winter and spring. And we had to sign up for the sport of our choice right away. To help us make an educated decision, Robert J. Delahanty, Physical Education Department chairman, gathered all the members of the Amazing Class of 1938 (we had not earned the adjective "*amazing*" yet, but that is another story) in Webster Hall. One by one an upper-class advocate of each sport would paint a vivid picture of the glories and satisfactions that would be ours if we signed up with him.

I had just about decided to go out for track with Bob Chickering, my roommate, since my preparation for college had not included tennis, golf, soccer, lacrosse or crew. Where I grew up there were just three organized sports—football, basketball and baseball. As I said, I was about to opt for following Chick around the cinders when one of the assistant managers of football got up on the rostrum. He knew we were aware, he said, that most of the experienced football players in the class already had been signed up and even as he spoke were trampling one another into the turf on their way up from the D, C and B squads to the A squad, or down in reverse order. However, he pointed out, it was possible at Dartmouth to elect Rec football. The Rec squad didn't have a very impressive game schedule, but they had a lot of fun fooling around with the football and scrimmaging among themselves.

And (this was where my ears snapped to attention) the college would furnish each man who signed up with a complete uniform!

Now I had played football in the yard behind the Glenville Congregational Church with the 123rd Street Musketeers in Cleveland (I was quarterback on that team due to my blinding speed and the fact that my father was the pastor), and I also had played with the Eddy Road Ramblers in the vacant lot by the Willard Storage Battery office. I had even played two years in the annual Stage Crew vs. Score Board Squad Classic at Mount Vernon High in New York on a real football field. But I had never played in a game with a stitch, strap or lace of honest-to-goodness football equipment between me and my opponent, and often there was nothing between me and the cold hard ground but my kid brother, David.

It was at this moment that I knew I had chosen my college wisely and well. Dartmouth would issue me That Which Would Make the Big Difference.

As we filed out of Webster, I could understand why my football skills were still among the world's greatest underdeveloped areas. They had never been given a chance. With cleats I could zig, zag and dance away from any tackler. With a stout helmet and shoulder pads I could blast my way through a wall of human flesh with a disdainful laugh. With hip pads and thigh guards to protect my heretofore visible skeleton I could snag and bring down any opposing back foolhardy enough to wander around to my end of the line.

I signed up.

The next day I said casually to my roommate, "I guess I'll go over to the field house and pick up my gear." As I have noted, there were 225 men out for intercollegiate football that fall at Dartmouth. Coach Blaik had gotten the best and latest equipment for his boys. That is, for Captain Hill, Don Hagerman, Bill Clark, Eddie Chamberlain, Mutt Ray, Dave Camerer and the rest of the first team. The second string would naturally use last year's set of uniforms. And, of course, those on the third string would get uniforms two years old, the scrub team the 1931 issue, the three jayvee teams what was left of the 1930 inventory. And then the 12 freshman teams would get their pick of the remaining rummage-sale material. This normal and understandable progression, or rather retrogression, did not occur to me until I stood in front of the counter.

I indicated my desire, as a member of the Rec football squad, for a complete uniform. Art Thibodeau, . . . DCAC Supervisor of Equipment, graciously and swiftly filled my arms with an extraordinarily fragrant collection of antique armor.

I tottered back to my locker reeling under the weight and the fumes. It was the work of the better part of an hour to sort it out and try it on. The shoulder pads were not bad—that is, the right shoulder pad. Its mate had lost most of its stuffing. . . .

The Dartmouth undergraduate is resourceful. I counted on doing most of my blocking and tackling to the right.

I can still remember every detail of the construction of the pants. The fabric was khaki canvas with the drape and stretch of a salt-encrusted tarpaulin. They laced at what was once the fly. Zippers had been invented by then, but were not considered trustworthy for critical applications. In those days the hip pads were not a separate part of the uniform as they are today. They were built right into the pants. I wrapped these great thick wads of felt around my svelte waist, overlapping them at the navel both in the interests of a snug fit and to make the absence of laces in the fly academic. The hip pads were in good shape—they matched. What was missing from the right also had been chewed away from the left; thus I was assured that I would suffer no asymmetrical damage below the rib cage. But some Sam had made the pants too long. This disproportion caused the built-in knee pads of reprocessed excelsior to reach the tops of my shoes. But the pants did keep my legs warm since I was issued no stockings. In those days, or rather in the days when the pants were built, the gladiator's thighs were protected by a series of wooden dowels sewn into the front and sides of the pant legs. This vertical alignment of the rods made the pants bendable around the circumference of the thighs like a rolltop desk on edge, but not flexible up and down. Luckily all the dowels had been broken at some point in their length, so that even though the pants came way below my knees the fractured sticks allowed my legs to bend enough to walk without goose-stepping.

I admired the hard knit of the dark-green jersey and the petrified condition of the leather strips that decorated the front. I raised it over my head and let it slide down over my arms and shoulders. My foresight in donning the pants first was rewarded. If I hadn't had that great leather-and-felt girdle around my waist, the jersey would have descended to my feet unimpeded. The neck was quite large. But the gentle swish of the knitted shirt past my nose was rewarded. It was then I knew how precious was this humble-looking raiment. As the wool mesh passed before my face my nostrils were alerted to the most rewarding aroma a Dartmouth freshman's nostrils ever got rewarded with.

My mind quickly calculated the passage of the years, the rate of attrition and the roster of the teams of yesteryear. Sure, the smell smelled like all the unventilated YMCA locker rooms in the mid-Atlantic states. It smelled of distilled liniment with a dash of rubbing alcohol and mellow adhesive, a touch of Plough Boy Rough Cut and an awful lot of sweat. I knew that scent was greater than the sum of its parts. I knew that bouquet belonged to titans. I knew who had worn that rag to glory. I, 135 pounds of Johnny Scotford, was at the end of a dynasty of football greats that had been born when its first owner back in 1925 put on that shirt and carried Dartmouth to its first undefeated, untied season. *I was wearing the jersey that Swede Oberlander, '26 All-America, had inaugurated!*

The condition of the remaining parts of my ensemble did not bother me then. I was still caught up with my vision of the Great Succession. Eddie Dooley, I was sure, had worn these shoes. Bill Cunningham had stretched his legs into these pants. And the helmet could have—must have—covered the head of Gus Sonnenburg!

I arrayed myself in these artifacts and made my way out of the locker room and across to Chase Field. It wasn't easy.

Eddie's shoes were my size but had seen a lot of football. The cleats under the balls of my feet and at the heels were worn down to mere nubs. The soles had lost their flexibility. This combination of age and erosion caused me to walk at a slight back slant, since the forward cleats were still at full height. Balance could only be maintained by excessive vorlage from the waist.

I have a very small head. Six and three quarters. Any time I want to get a cheap laugh I just put on someone else's hat. I have never clapped one on that didn't go over my ears. Instant hilarity. Gus's helmet was a beauty—a monument to the art of tanning. It was leather, well stitched and deep in the crown. All I needed was a couple of cow horns on each side and Flagstad would have clutched me to her bosom. But it, too, had seen many years of combat. Use, abuse and time had rendered it as soft as a fielder's glove. And since it was size 8+, whenever I turned too quickly I found myself sighting my course through the hole in the earflap.

I didn't impress the coach much that first day, since I couldn't see very well under the helmet, block to my left, or crouch without digging the shattered ends of the dowels into my upper legs. My gait resembled Jacques Tati at 36 frames per second.

My teammates were not much better off, except that they were bigger. What they got issued fit them better. And I guess they were more socially secure, for they left off those items that were worn beyond repair.

I was there because of the uniform, and I needed the disguise to prove that I was a football player. But during the succeeding days of practice I gradually discarded the most confining parts of my wardrobe. First the shoes, then the shoulder pads, then the helmet. I kept the jersey from sliding to half-mast by sewing up the neck opening on both sides. And so, in my jersey and pants I rattled my way across South Park Street to scrimmage. For a while after every tackle or pile-up I would ask for timeout to remove the woody fibers from my perforated lap and shins. I looked for a tribe of carpenter ants and prayed for an infestation of termites, but eventually the dowels got broken up into short sections or split into supple splinters.

I didn't get to suit-up for the Rec squad's big game that year with the Hanover High School B team. The week before the game, Doc Pollard thought he heard a murmur in my heart. I am sure it was nothing more than the creak of a deciduous sliver in my bloodstream as it rounded the turn into the left ventricle. But my diagnosis was too late.

The murmur subsided, but by that time the season was over. I discovered the joys of the horizontal bar while taking special gym with Curly Sadler the week I was banned from football. I went out for the gym team and never got back to football.

My only regret is that I was too honest. I turned all that historic, redolent equipment back to Art Thibodeau. I should have kept the shirt a few years and then given it to the Football Hall of Fame. I can see it now—"Jersey worn by Swede Oberlander, Dartmouth '26, All-America '25. Donated by subsequent wearer, John R. Scotford Jr., Dartmouth '38, Rec Squad '34."

The Presidents in the Grant
EDWARD WEEKS

>>> Edward Weeks, for many years editor of *The Atlantic Monthly*, is not only a man of letters but a man of the outdoors, a fisherman, a nature lover. "The Presidents in the Grant" is an essay in his collection *Fresh Waters* (Boston, 1968).

IN JUNE 1950, and in company with other worthies I received an honorary degree from the hands of President John Dickey of Dartmouth. The Commencement exercises were held in a natural amphitheater, the Bema, and on the platform I found myself seated beside a fellow editor, Harold Ross of the *New Yorker*. Ross sat with his mortarboard on his knees studying the program. "It says here," he remarked, "that I'm to be a Doctor of Humane Letters and that you're to be a Doctor of Literature. Must mean that I am a kinder man." "The hell it does," I exclaimed. "You turned me down for my first job the summer of 1923." At that moment Ross's name was called and he jammed the mortarboard on the back of his head and went forward to receive his citation.

When the ceremonies were over, we crossed the green-and-white elm-shaded campus to the President's house and in an aside during the buffet President Dickey gave me a tempting description of the Dartmouth Grant, the forest bounded by the Diamond River and just under the Canadian border, with which the state had initially endowed the College. "I'd like you to come up there and fish with me," said John—and that proved to be as happy an invitation as I have ever had.

One of the unpremeditated purposes of the Dartmouth Grant is to cool off the President after the rigor and festivities of Commencement. All Dartmouth Presidents are anglers—I assume it is a qualification for the job—but the two I have known should be classified as addicts. I never had the delight of fishing with President Hopkins, though we talked it whenever we met. But John Dickey has taken me up to the Grant for many a June and my love for the place and for the man has increased with each outing.

My anticipation begins to rise with the plane bearing me to West Lebanon, and as we taxi up to the gate of the little airport there is John looming above the waiting passengers with his rusty felt hat on the back of his head. I grin at the other members of the expedition, store my gear in the heavily laden beachwagon with the President's long green canoe strapped to the roof; John takes the wheel and we head north. John gives so much of himself to the double-barreled Commencement—first the seniors and parents, then the alumni—that it is no wonder if he is a little absent at the outset, like a house without its host. But this is the most beautiful drive in New England; we pass through the gleaming white hamlet of Orford, conjecture about the early days in those red brick mansions at Haverhill; catch water vistas such as that of the Connecticut at the Oxbow, and before we have reached the Salmon Pool on the Ammonoosuc, John's spirit has returned and the talk is flowing. On one of my early trips Dr. Jay Gile was with us, and his account of the buggy and sleigh rides he had made with his doctor-father through these same valleys half a century earlier peopled the road with a romance I have never forgotten.

We drive straight through with only a single stop to buy our licenses and the shadows are lengthening as we make the long run through the Thirteen Mile Woods with the pools and the white water of the Androscoggin showing through the spruce and hemlock. In our thoughts each man is already mounting his rod and trying to decide which fly, wet or dry, to begin with. But first there are two formalities: we make our politesse as we pass through the gate into the Grant. And then when at last we have reached the Management Center to be greeted by Bob Monahan [1929, the College Forester], there is the succulent business of unloading. Mrs. Dickey never quite trusts our ability to net enough fish and so here in case of need are steaks the size of a catcher's mitt, homemade bread, a cherry pie, a tin of cookies, and a crock of fresh stewed rhubarb. Once they have been put in the icebox and the bunks dealt out, the President says in that drawl of his, "Well,

I guess we might as well put up our rods and go to work." In his fishing shirt, rusty hat and waders, John at six feet four inches is a towering figure; he likes to wade and with his periscope advantage one can understand why. The Half Mile Falls have always challenged him, and after placing his guests on milder waters, this is probably where he will go.

For those who have never seen it, the Grant is a forest of 27,000 acres enclosed within the two spreading branches of the Diamond River, the Swift Diamond to the west, the Dead to the north. Eleven miles below Hell's Gate the streams flow together just before entering a roaring precipitous gorge. Along those eleven miles lives the forest which the College has been cutting and cultivating since 1807, an undetermined population of deer, bear, and varmints, and the wildest trout it has been my privilege to know. By preference we fish the Dead Diamond because it is the more navigable and because in its winding, wooded course it throws up sandy crescents with delectable pools at either end. The sand bears the footprints of wildlife but not a beer can, nor the chassis of an old Ford.

Those who have seen it will agree that the Grant is never the same. I have been there when it was so cold that my heavies and the layers of sweaters and windbreak were insufficient and other years when it was so hot that good fishing was confined to dusk and dawn. The hotter it gets the better the fishing and there never seems to be any shortage of black flies, mosquitoes, and no-see-ums. We fish in pairs, carrying a sandwich (mine always gets wet) and a chocolate bar. These we shove in with a handscoop of river water somewhere past the midpoint downstream, often at Slue Gundy, a deep pool still half in shadow at high noon. On one occasion when John and I were working the upper stream and Sid Hayward [1926, and then Secretary of the College] and Paul Sample [1920, and Artist in Residence at Dartmouth] the lower, the wind came strong in our face as we approached the Slue. John, wading on ahead of me, put the full power of his right arm back of a dry fly oblivious to the fact that his back cast was already latched to an alder. The shock shivered his rod's middle joint but when I splashed in he had already improvised a splint made firm with adhesive

The Presidents in the Grant 183

tape and manila strands from the canoe's painter. With this contraption he hooked and was netting another trout, a scene which Paul has preserved in a watercolor.

Faces come out of the past. Sam, the Norwegian fire warden in his conical red hat, never removed, who fed the deer at his door in the dead of winter and who prefaced every one of his Paul Bunyan stories with "Pijesus, I vant to tell you . . ." Sid with his slow smile. Young John, now an able geologist but still in the Grant an appetizing and cheerful cook. John senior working away with a hammer and screwdriver to free the wedge of hamburg which he had stacked away in the ice compartment and had frozen solid. Dexter Keezer, the former president of Reed College, a master of the wet fly, bringing a sulking big fish to the surface; Dave McCord waxing poetic over a mug of rum; Beth Webster cooking scrambled eggs in the big skillet; George Harrar, president of the Rockefeller Foundation, reflectively wiping the dishes; Ralph Hill, the Vermont editor, discussing his plans for the new Dartmouth history, *The College on the Hill*.

And Sinclair Weeks, Secretary of Commerce under President Eisenhower. Sinclair is as staunch a Republican as I am a Democrat, and our trip in the tippiest of all canoes was conducted on a bipartisan policy until at the end we approached the logging bridge which crosses the stream just above the Upper Farm landing. John was on the bridge awaiting our arrival. I was in the bow in my waders, Sinclair in the stern; the current was stronger than either of us suspected, and as we neared the high bank the canoe began to broach. "You can make it," said Sinny, and I did, with a backward thrust of my left boot strong enough to turn the canoe half over. "OH, NO!" cried John. But Sinclair was more explicit. When we had got him back to camp and dried him off, he denied that there were any politics involved, but added, "You'd be a hell of a man on the bridge of the *Queen Elizabeth*!"

Historically, the high point was President Eisenhower's visit to the Grant in the spring of 1955. He had been visiting Sinclair Weeks in New Hampshire, and after delivering himself of half a dozen speeches, was on his way to spend a fishing weekend at the Parmachanee Club in Maine. John invited him to take lunch at the Grant on his way east and with him came a retinue of senators, congressmen, Secret Service men, and reporters. We who were there to fish spent the day before the great event scouring the river for a mess of trout. Sid Hayward and I made an all-day foray on the Dead and with presidential privilege each went beyond his limit, for we figured that we would need a minimum of forty trout for those in the President's party. It was warm work and the bugs were fierce. One moose fly got me on the right temple when I was tied into a strong fish and the welts there and behind both ears invited scratching for several nights. Sam the fire warden, whose skin was impervious to any insect, went his own way downstream to the breakwater which checks the united river just before it enters the gorge. Here with worms he derricked up a perfect beauty, quite the largest, which was designated as "Ike's fish."

That Saturday there wasn't a cloud in the sky, and I remember that just after the gatehouse had telephoned to say that the cavalcade was coming in, a golden eagle, which had been nesting on the high cliffs across the valley, swung off and came drifting toward us riding the air currents, so John's greeting was, "Mr. President, there is an eagle up there which just came out to make you welcome," and as we all looked up, there he was.

As host that day John was perfection. Members of the Outing Club had come to camp the night before to cook a great pit of baked beans and to serve the trout. John presented every one of them individually to the great man, as he did Sam and the other wardens. It was an occasion when dignity and friendliness walked hand in hand.

The trout, all forty of them, were cooked on a bed of charcoal, so that they were done in an instant. But not "Ike's Fish." "That's not the way I want mine," he said. He asked for some chef's foil, rubbed down the beauty with a piece of bacon, added a touch of butter, then folded it in the foil and put it on the coals to bake. When it was unfolded he insisted that we each take a bite of it, and there was no question that it was the juiciest fish of the lot.

The President had no thought of fishing the Grant with a delegation from Congress and a score of reporters watching him from the bank, and in the early afternoon he moved on to Maine. Later that same evening after we had supped, a lumber truck pulled up in the yard and in came a stocky French Canadian reeking with liquor. We will call him Henri Ledur. He had been logging in the Grant and living there in a tarpaper cabin, drinking hard, impervious to Bob Monahan's warning, and when his jags were on him, beating his spunky little Indian wife. There and then in ten minutes of downright masculinity, John put him on the carpet, reducing him—temporarily—to repentance and sobriety. That man-to-man talk in the half-light was something to have heard; it too is part of the history. . . .

TRIBUTES

The End of the Quest
JOHN MOFFATT MECKLIN

⋙ "In my day," Budd Schulberg 1936 once wrote, "there was little doubt that Professor Mecklin's sociology courses were the most popular on the campus, or that he was one of the college's most vivid and lovable characters." For twenty years, until his retirement in 1941, he was one of the great Dartmouth teachers. The passages below are from his memoir, *My Quest for Freedom* (New York, 1945).

SOON AFTER my arrival at Dartmouth in 1920 I was asked to address the Freshman class on the great steel strike that was still fresh in the minds of all. The question at once arose in my mind as to whether I could tell the bald truth as I had experienced it without arousing criticism and perhaps prejudicing my work in Dartmouth. I was assured, however, that I could talk frankly. . . . That was the Dartmouth way.

This experience was to me more or less of an acid test of Dartmouth liberalism. It did have its effect upon this class who long looked upon me as a "radical" but, so far as I could see, it did not affect in the slightest my standing on the campus. I now had convincing proof that for the first time in my teaching career I had complete academic freedom. This filled me with profound satisfaction. Yet as time passed the old, old problem took on new phases and presented difficulties of which, heretofore, I had not even faintly dreamed.

Before I came to Dartmouth I had sought freedom in the traditional pioneer sense of *laissez faire*. Freedom had been for me largely negative for the simple reason that I had never enjoyed enough of it to force me to ask whether its intelligent and creative use did not involve a measure of restraint. I believed with my whole soul in intellectual *laissez faire*. It had never been necessary for me to raise the question as to the difference between freedom as a wholesome factor in our lives and as a menace to character and social ethics. I now had to ask, does freedom alone *assure* the good life? Stated in other terms, does not its enjoyment also entail certain responsibilities? What is the price we must pay for it? I had already put this question to myself in a crude way in Pittsburgh. It was born of my conviction of the end of *laissez faire*. To say the least, it was intriguing. I was soon forced to seek an answer to this query by events on the Dartmouth campus.

At Dartmouth freedom seemed to be taken for granted. It was more or less of a tradition or convention, much like the cut of one's coat or the norms of correct speech. Both students and faculty seemed to react to it as they did to the pure air they breathed or the clean food they ate. Shortly after my arrival I dubbed a group of good-natured and courteous loafers "intellectual flappers." They insisted that I define the term. I replied that "flapper" is a colloquialism for a young woman who has more liberties than she knows what to do with. The reference to the other sex naturally intrigued them but they questioned the moral analogy. This led to a most interesting discussion as to the ethical phases of intellectual freedom. Does intellectual freedom lead necessarily to laxity in the mental life? Is ethical latitudinarianism the inevitable accompaniment of intellectual latitudinarianism? I found these queries raised problems to them that were new and strange. They had never had occasion to ask the question: What price freedom?

The problem of freedom at Dartmouth I found quite baffling in its complexities. Were the freedoms I found embedded in student mores and practiced in the classroom the logical development of the earlier traditions of the college? How were these freedoms related to President Tucker, the creator of modern Dartmouth? How was the freedom of the classroom related to that of the campus? After all, were these freedoms essentially different from the negative *laissez faire* freedom of our capitalistic society that I had rejected?

All these varied queries, clamoring for answer, tended to narrow down to one ultimate question: *Are there moral responsibilities that go along with freedom and if so what?* Are these moral responsibilities purely individual or are they corporate? How is the individual phase of free-

The End of the Quest 191

dom related to the corporate and institutional? Can the individual sense of responsibility be effective without institutional sanctions? It is obvious that these queries can not be answered intelligently without a word on the history of Dartmouth liberalism.

I once asked a Dartmouth graduate, my own son, what a liberal education meant to him. He replied, "A liberal education means the ability to understand and to judge without bias." Coming from a more or less typical Dartmouth product, this reply seemed to me rather suggestive. It fell in with my favorite historical point of approach. It led me to ask this question: Could it be possible that the liberal college, such as Dartmouth, is the last logical refinement of the sacrosanct right of private judgment that inspired the Protestant Reformation? Immediately a mass of historical material seemed to marshal itself in support of this thesis.

Was not New England founded by middle-class dissenting Englishmen who fled to the wilderness to preserve the right of private judgment in religion? Did not Eleazar Wheelock get his inspiration for the founding of Dartmouth College from the famous Separatist movement with its insistence upon the primacy of the individual religious experience of conversion? Did not Nathan Lord, one of Dartmouth's most famous presidents, put the dictates of conscience above everything else and resign the presidency because of his proslavery convictions? Did not Dr. Tucker, Dartmouth's greatest president, bring to the college convictions as to the right of private judgment, matured during eight long years of theological controversy as professor in Andover Seminary, and make them the very core and inspiration of his educational philosophy? Finally, was it not possible that the delightful freedom that has characterized the administration of President Hopkins was influenced to some extent by the liberalism of his father, a Baptist minister and graduate of Harvard, who embodied "the dissidence of dissent" of a group who revolted against the New England establishments in the interest of the sacrosanct right of private judgment in matters of religion?

Herbert Spencer has remarked somewhere that many a beautiful theory has been murdered by a gang of brutal facts. As I delved deeper into the facts of Dartmouth's history I became convinced that any historical connection between Dartmouth liberalism and the early Protestant emphasis upon the right of private judgment is exceedingly remote, if not entirely absent. In spite of the assertion that the charter of 1769 was "the most liberal charter in America," Dartmouth was not then and did not become until one hundred and twenty-five years later a liberal college in the modern sense of that term. To be sure, the New England colleges of the eighteenth century were called "liberal arts colleges" but the connotations of "liberal" were mediaeval rather than modern. The *artes liberales* were the studies pursued by a small group who occupied a privileged position in society. Who, then, is the author of Dartmouth liberalism?

It has been frequently remarked that Dartmouth College has had three founders. The first in time, and for that reason perhaps the most important, was Eleazar Wheelock with his zeal for the salvation of the poor Indian. Only in his spirit of adventurousness can it be said that Wheelock anticipated Dartmouth liberalism. Daniel Webster contributed only indirectly and unwittingly to Dartmouth liberalism. By his persuasive eloquence he induced the Federalist John Marshall to make his famous decision which placed underneath the college and all similar institutions, as well as business corporations, the legal fiction of an inviolate charter. This assured the college corporate security and independence and made possible the accumulation of millions of endowment without which the freedom of the great Eastern colleges was hardly possible. President Tucker built upon the material foundations laid by his predecessors and gave to the institution a new birth of freedom. He created "the New Dartmouth" which has made the college the pride of all its sons and the admiration of the educational world.

It has been said that the spirit and ideals of Thomas Jefferson pervade the campus of the University of Virginia to a degree that is almost palpable. I feel that the heritage of freedom left by President Tucker is Dartmouth's most precious possession in spite of the fact that this is hardly realized by students and faculty. To be sure, the parallel between Jefferson and Tucker can not be pushed too far. Jefferson created his university out of whole cloth and in it his personality and ideals found concrete institutional embodiment. Tucker inherited the Dartmouth of the past and yet he molded this heritage to give expression to his ideal. Dartmouth liberalism apart from Tucker's work is meaningless. Tucker's liberalism was deeply, almost mystically, religious while Jefferson's was naturalistic. Jefferson made religion the handmaid of reason. Tucker was inclined to make reason the handmaid of religion. Eighteenth century rationalism spoke the last word in Jefferson's liberalism. The ethical idealism born of the New England conscience spoke the last word in the liberalism of Tucker. Yet, strange to say, a creative freedom, mediated by the institution and made dynamic in the individual, was the goal both of Jefferson and Tucker. For this reason the liberal college, as Tucker visualized it, perhaps more than any other American institution, embodies the spirit of Jeffersonian democracy.

To me there was a distinct challenge in the trilogy that formed the foundation of Tucker's educational ideal, namely, freedom, humanism and religion. In the sense that freedom implemented the educational process it came first. "Personal freedom," he said, "is the keynote of college life. Paternalism will destroy the moral power of any college. Where it saves one, it weakens and demoralizes the whole body." The emphasis of personal freedom in Dartmouth liberalism as interpreted by Tucker explains the courage and the virility that are the outstanding traits of the typical Dartmouth man.

As an educator and lover of freedom I admired Tucker as the archenemy of all forms of intellectual tyranny. Bitter experience has taught me that intellectual freedom is the basis of all other freedoms. I found myself in thorough sympathy with him, therefore, when he said, "Humanity has suffered more from the tyranny of theories which were believed to be right or, if wrong, inexorable, than from any other one source. The history of economic progress, as of political progress, has been the history of deliverance from the fetish of so-called laws, laws of supply and demand and the like." I admire his wisdom and tact, his broad humanism and his tolerance. But towering above all his many fine qualities the one thing about this great educator that fills me with the profoundest respect is that his love of freedom was implemented by an indomitable moral and spiritual courage.

In 1919, the year before my arrival, Dr. Tucker, then in his eightieth year, was invited to take part in the Dartmouth Dinner of the Boston Alumni Association. Being unable, because of great age, to accept the invitation, he wrote a letter urging them to "keep the faith" as Dartmouth men and used as his theme the title of Richard Hovey's ode to the nation during the Spanish war, "Unmanifest Destiny." The true test of loyalty to Dartmouth liberalism is not found, says Tucker, in any "manifest destiny" whether laid down in some predestined scheme of a Calvinistic god, whether assured by the "inalienable rights" of Locke and Jefferson or assumed in the traditional optimism of the American people. The true test of Dartmouth liberalism is found in the unpredictable and hence "unmanifest destiny" which, as a matter of history, faced Dartmouth from the very beginning and still faces her sons, bewildered and confused by the chaos of the present.

There is something particularly impressive in the spectacle of this octogenarian still clinging to the faith he strove to build into the very walls of Dartmouth—"the faith, that is, of the open, the courageous, the undistorted, the unconfused mind in the presence of great issues as they arise. This is the power as I apprehend, perhaps the greatest gift of our inheritance as it is the greatest discipline of our citizenship, through which we as the sons of Dartmouth and as loyal citizens of the state are to strive to fulfill the 'unmanifest destiny' whether of the college or the nation."

This is Tucker's last word on freedom. It is the same old courageous note that has dominated the college since its birth. It is the most precious legacy of all Dartmouth's sons. It is a *creative freedom* which an "unmanifest destiny" has left uncharted and to a large extent autonomous in the chaos of two world wars. . . .

My teaching in Dartmouth took its point of departure from the ideal of a creative freedom. I felt that the vital function of the liberal college in the democratic tradition was endangered by the negative tough-minded liberalism that dominated the campus. My experience

The End of the Quest 195

at Pittsburgh had given me a most vivid impression of the menace of an individualistic *laissez faire* capitalism to the democratic tradition. At Dartmouth I detected a similar menace to the moral and spiritual integrity of the student in an individualistic, *laissez faire* educational philosophy. It was natural, of course, that boys who came very largely from capitalistic homes should carry over the negative individualistic freedom of the counting house and the factory and apply it to the intellectual life. The result was that freedom was interpreted to mean the right to the unenlightened and dogmatic assertion of individual beliefs whether in religion, politics or business. The exceedingly popular Dartmouth "bull sessions" were often prolonged and excited intellectual encounters lacking in intelligent and sympathetic insight and the spirit of compromise that is the very life blood of democracy. The dogmatic individualist was living in a dark room and repeating the slogans dimly inscribed on its walls by family, party, church or business. In spite of the intellectual "dope" absorbed in laboratory and classroom a regnant tough-minded freedom was keeping men in the dark.

Here was indeed a paradoxical situation. The student who comes to a great liberal college apparently to become intellectually emancipated and wedded to those universal human values supposed to underlie our democracy finds a situation in which his traditional dogmatic individualism is encouraged rather than overcome. All unconsciously this negative individual freedom plays into the hands of his ingrained class consciousness of home and business and community. The liberal college, which is supposed to be the one democratic institution that is our best safeguard against undemocratic class consciousness, preaches a freedom which unwittingly strengthens class consciousness. The knowledge and mental training instilled by all the machinery of the liberal college thus merely provides an equipment to be utilized in the defense of an entrenched position of privilege in a capitalistic society. A negative individualistic freedom inevitably stultifies itself. It invalidates the democracy that gave it birth. It was this that made me realize more than anything else that the first step towards a liberal education is a measure of *disillusionment*. To be liberally educated one must first acquire the habit of seeing in the dark. This conclusion I had long reached as a result of my experiences with men in the ordinary walks of life.

I was exceedingly fortunate in that President Hopkins gave me entire freedom in following my bent. When he asked me where my interests lay I said, "I am particularly interested in the origin of fictions and stereotypes and the rôle they play in shaping belief and action in groups and individuals." "Why not teach that?" he said. "We will make a place for you." The result was a course that was highly unorthodox, academically speaking, and sprawled in various directions trenching upon the fields of history, psychology, economics, political science and, of course, religion. I was constantly being sternly reminded of the traditional departmental sign, "Keep off the grass." In time I became painfully aware of the fact that anarchistic departmental *laissez faire* passed for freedom in the liberal college just as did economic *laissez faire* in business. As a result of this negative notion of freedom the glow of departmental enthusiasms and loyalties tended to throw other disciplines into the shadow. There was need here also for the ability to see in the dark. There was lacking any method or whole point of view that would help illuminate the landscape and dissipate these shadows. For some time I was made to feel that I had pitched my tent in a "No Man's Land" inhabited only by academic Ishmaelites. In time, however, the free spirit of Dartmouth made a place for me and I became part of the academic landscape.

My point of departure I found in a famous allegory of Plato. During my stay in Greece I had studied the cave of Vari on the slope of Hymettus where Plato played as a boy. He made use of almost every detail of this cave in his famous allegory in the seventh book of his *Republic*. The allegory is the high point of this, his masterpiece, which has been called the political Bible of the Western world. The race is like men, says Plato, who live in a cave. "They have been here from their childhood and have their legs and necks chained so that they can not move and can only see before them; for the chains are arranged in such a manner as to prevent them from turning around their heads." Behind is a lighted fire and between the fire and the chained prisoners there is

The End of the Quest   197

a raised way [this is all in the cave at Vari] and everything that passes along the raised way of course casts its shadow on the wall.

Now, says Plato, would it not be perfectly natural for the man who had lived his whole life in a cave and had seen only the shadows of things cast upon the wall to imagine that the shadows were the reality? If, however, he be "compelled suddenly to go up and turn his neck and walk and look at the light will he not suffer sharp pains? Will not the glare distress him?" But suppose we take him out of the cave into the sunlight [I am not concerned with the difficulty of the details of the allegory] and let him look first at the shape of things reflected in water, then at their shadows in the sunlight until finally he is able to gaze upon the sun itself "who gives the seasons and the years and is the guardian of all that is in the visible world." Would not this be a still more marvelous revelation to the cave dweller?

Plato thus fits the allegory into his philosophy: "The prison is the world of sight, the light of the fire is the sun, the ascent and vision of the things above you may truly regard as the upward progress of the soul into the intellectual world." He then enforces the practical implication of the allegory for his hearers in the following immortal words which I cannot refrain from quoting in full, for they are just as true today as twenty-five centuries ago. They are particularly pertinent to the intellectual responsibilities of the student in a liberal college.

"Now the wild plant which owes culture to nobody has nothing to pay for culture; but we have brought you into the world expressly for this purpose, that you may be rulers of the hive, kings of yourselves and of other citizens. And you have been educated far better and more perfectly and are better able to share in the double duty. And, therefore, each of you when his turn comes must go down to the general underground abode and *get the habit of seeing in the dark* [italics mine]; for all is habit; and when you are accustomed you will see ten thousand times better than those in the den, and you will know what the images are and of what they are images, because you have seen the beautiful and just and good in their truth. And thus the order of our state will be a waking reality, and not a dream, as is commonly the manner of states; in most of them men are *fighting with one another about shadows and are distracted in the struggle for power* [italics mine], which in their eyes is a great good. But the truth is that the state in which the rulers are the most reluctant to govern is the best and most quietly governed and that in which they are the most willing, the worst." (Jowett's translation.)

In all my teaching at Dartmouth my task, as I conceived it, was to give my students "the habit of seeing in the dark."

It followed from this, of course, that my first challenge to the student was one of critical disillusionment. I pointed out that what interested us was not primarily the philosophical meaning of the allegory. In the mind of Plato things are but the pale and shadowy reflections of eternal archetypal ideas that form the structure of the universe. The allegory interested us because it fits quite as well the realm of the fictions, stereotypes, or social myths, that shape the thinking of our daily lives and mold the destinies of nations. The insidious weakness of them all, from the family, neighborhood, church, or party stereotypes up to the larger national or cultural social myths, is that men are inclined to take these traditional ingrained patterns of thought as eternally true. Fundamentalism, I insisted, is not confined to the "Bible belt" of the South and West but is found everywhere and is as old as the heart of the race.

My sophisticated reader will doubtless pronounce this a trite principle to make the basis of a philosophy of a liberal education. Yet I was astonished to find that it was something entirely new and even revolutionary to the upperclassmen of Dartmouth, who are a selected group, coming from cultured homes and trained in the best secondary schools of the land. I was forced to spend weeks illustrating the meaning and implications of the allegory for their daily lives, for their communities, the nation and the world. My thesis was received by some with scepticism, by others with numerous criticisms but by none with complete intellectual indifference, which for me was the most important thing. One serious-minded student sat with a frown, partly of scepticism, partly of bewilderment and partly, doubtless, of genuine mental discomfort during the lectures. After days of vigorous mental bombardment his serious and rather strong face was suddenly covered

The End of the Quest 199

with a broad grin and he upset the dignity of instructor and class by blurting out, "Gosh, this leads all over the place."

It is interesting in this connection to note how this point of view clashed with the dominant tough-minded liberalism of the Dartmouth campus. After several weeks of lectures I once held an hour examination to get the mental precipitate of our discussion of the allegory. An able student, a vigorous individualist, who came from a privileged and well-to-do home, closed his paper with these tough-minded remarks: "I confess, professor, that this cave business has me worried. I now see that I have lived in a cave all my life, a sort of high capitalistic cave, and I am determined to get out of this cave and find out what the rest of the world is thinking. But, if ever I do get out, I refuse to follow Plato's advice and go back into the cave. As for the rest of those in the cave they can go to hell as far as I am concerned." His interest apparently was purely intellectual and personal and there was no sense of social responsibility. It is an interesting question as to how far this mental attitude is characteristic of many of the best minds of the privileged group that pass from the liberal college campus into the world of business or politics. It is one thing to understand; it is something quite different to accept whole-heartedly the responsibilities that come with the acquisition of the ability to see in the dark. . . .

John Moffatt Mecklin

A. J. LIEBLING

>>> "We used to nail the window shut in the fall and keep it that way until spring," A. J. Liebling 1924 wrote of the Dartmouth winter. His journalistic career began on *The New York Times* as a sports writer, but ended abruptly when he named a referee of a basketball game "Ignoto" (Unknown). For nearly thirty years until his death in 1964 he was a writer and sometime foreign correspondent for *The New Yorker*. Among his many books was *The Wayward Pressman* (New York, 1947), which supplied the following recollections of Hanover.

A NEWSPAPER gives the reader the impression of being closer to life than a book, and he is likely to confuse what he has read in it with actual experiences he has not had.

"You should have seen Charlie White," a middle-aged bore may say to me in a bar. "*He* had a left hook."

I too know White had a left hook, because I read about it so often, but it is no more or less likely that the fellow talking saw him than that I saw Ty Cobb, about whose base-running I talk with the same knowing ease. I don't think I ever did see Cobb, personally, but I do know I saw Hans Wagner and Christy Mathewson in a game between the Pirates and Giants when I was small, and I can't remember what either of them looked like on that particular day or what he did. What I *know* about them, like what I know about Cobb, is simply the cumulative product of newspaper stories and newspaper photographs, and in that way I know as much about Cobb as I do about either.

In the same way, the first President I actually saw was Warren Gamaliel Harding, but he is a paler memory to me than the first Roosevelt, or Taft or Wilson. And it is incredible to me even now that I never saw Franklin D. Roosevelt, who was nearly as much of a personal experience as my own father.

I cite these examples of the suggestive power of newsprint because the principle applies also to ideas. You read a thesis set forth as a fact in the newspapers a certain number of times and you begin to think you have figured it out for yourself or at least had it at first hand from what the press would call an authoritative source.

A book has a less treacherous effect. Even its least wary reader is strongly conscious that there is a *man* at the other end of the process, telling him something. The studied impersonality of the newspaper, its simulation of photography in words, all soften the outline of the printed phrase as it blurs against the background of reality.

So when I went up to Dartmouth in the fall of 1920, lacking a month of being sixteen, I took it for granted that William Jennings Bryan was a crackpot and Nicholas Murray Butler a profound scholar, that the Reds in Europe were ravening beasts and Socialists here a bit touched in the head. I believed that all Allied failures in the then recent war had been well-conceived and ably conducted enterprises, doomed by circumstances beyond human control, and that the country would be forever prosperous if we let prosperous-looking people run it. All these notions I erroneously thought were the result of my own ratiocinations. . . .

Most of my 623 classmates at Dartmouth were older than I, but I never heard one of them make any criticism of newspapers except that the Boston ones devoted a disproportionate amount of space to Harvard and Boston College football. The college was liberal; there was an exemplary freedom of thought and speech, but we never bothered to think or say anything more than "Hi" or "Howdy." Professor John Moffatt Mecklin told one of his classes that they were intellectual flappers, they had more freedom than they knew what to do with.

We weren't reactionary; the word wasn't even part of the current vocabulary. We were just indifferent. A certain number of students had served in the war, but they must have been convinced of its episodic quality. That was the autumn of Harding's presidential campaign for a "return to normalcy," and the concept seemed reasonable to our parents and us, although the English department sneered at the bastard word. We had not yet even arrived at the era of the campus aesthete, which was to be followed by that of the campus radical.

F. Scott Fitzgerald, who had just published "This Side of Paradise," was the most heterodox prophet we listened to. If I go into this seemingly superfluous detail it is because I want to reconstruct for myself as well as for you the portrait of the paragon of newspaper readers I then was. I was as avid, unquestioning, and respectable as a piece of blotting paper with the name of the Guaranty Trust Company printed on the reverse side. . . .

Professor Mecklin's arrival at Hanover had coincided with that of the class of 1924, to which I belonged. Journalism was not his subject; as I shall illustrate later, a course in journalism is the last place in which to look for journalistic education. Mecklin, who was then fifty years old, had left the chair of philosophy at the University of Pittsburgh as a fairly direct consequence of his sentiments and speeches in the great steel strike of 1919. He had come to Dartmouth as a professor of sociology. I didn't know anything about him or his past when, in the week between the Penn and Brown games—that was the way we measured time—I was summoned along with all my class to a lecture he was to deliver. This lecture was part of a survey and orientation course in the social sciences, which all freshmen had to take. I cannot remember anything else that happened in any other session of this course. This is an example of the charming grab-bag quality of a liberal-arts college education—the items that will prove of subsequent value turn up in the most unexpected places. The lecture was a great event in Mecklin's life as well as mine, although I didn't learn this until much later, when I read the old man's autobiography, "My Quest for Freedom," published in 1945. . . .

"Soon after my arrival at Dartmouth in 1920 I was asked to address the freshman class on the great steel strike," he wrote. . . . "I faced several hundred freshmen who had already been lectured into a state of incipient revolt. They were restless and noisy, but I had provided a map of the steel mills and as I began to state frankly the treatment of the workers by the 'Cossacks' they began to listen. Within thirty minutes I had close attention. At the end, to make things concrete, I drew a parallel between the military methods of the steel barons and the militarism of Germany and stated that the strike was merely a

John Moffatt Mecklin 203

crude effort by the strikers to do for the steel industry what Wilson sought to do in his struggle to 'make the world safe for democracy.' At the close a dozen or more rushed to the platform and insisted that I was talking 'socialism.' One boy with a white and tense face said that his father was in the steel business and he knew that what I said was false...."

The part of Professor Mecklin's test-case talk that affected me most was not about the company police, whom he called Cossacks. It concerned newspapers. He has written, "The press in particular became utterly untrustworthy. We had to get the news as to what was going on in Pittsburgh from the Philadelphia and New York papers." But what he said was that of even the New York papers, the *World* was the only one that told the truth about the strike. After I heard him there was only one paper in the country I would have considered working on. That was the *World*.

The impact of the Mecklin lecture on me, . . . must have been directly connected with the nature of the man himself, although I never sought out his acquaintance afterward. . . . He had begun his life with a struggle against the Calvinism in which he had been reared as the son of a backwoods Presbyterian clergyman in Mississippi. Educated for the ministry himself, he had quit it after one year of self-torment in a small town in Georgia. He had made his definite break with Calvin after a controversy with the president of Lafayette College which had resulted in the resignation of both of them, in 1913, when Mecklin was forty-four. The Pittsburgh episode had followed. He had been a man all his life desperately trying to live at peace with authority, first spiritual and then temporal. But he had always been impelled in the end to speak out by the terrible Calvinist conscience he had inherited along with the God Who oppressed him. He was a most reluctant rebel, and I think this is what made him so convincing. . . .

The newspaper world is full of alumni of schools of journalism, but they seldom admit it until their interrogator thrusts hot needles under their fingernails. I got to be one primarily because I was thrown out of Dartmouth twice for absenting myself from chapel on cold mornings. Every morning from October to May is cold in New Hampshire. I could not believe, even after I had been sent down for one semester, that the college could be serious about maintaining such an absurd vestige of its missionary days. It was easy to make up the points lost during a semester by attendance at summer school, and I returned to college and stayed away from chapel some more. So they threw me out definitively. Dartmouth, realizing its loss, or so I have surmised without being told in so many words, abolished compulsory chapel a couple of years later. Professor Mecklin records: "The abolition of required chapel was received with great satisfaction." But then it was too late.

Like Stephen Burroughs, another great misunderstood Dartmouth man who found himself in a similar situation in 1784, "I began to look about me, to see what was to be done in my situation, to what business I could turn my attention." Burroughs temporarily solved his difficulty by hiring out as a minister, having thoughtfully stolen a set of his father's old sermons as a provision against such an emergency. He later became a counterfeiter. My misfortune determined me to become a newspaperman, a decision which I might have reached in due course anyway, but which I would have postponed as long as possible, like every other I have ever had to make. In deciding to go to the Pulitzer School of Journalism at Columbia, I was influenced equally by my reluctance to go straight to work and by a feeling that to attend another undergraduate school after Dartmouth would be anticlimactic. The name of Joseph Pulitzer of the *World* may have had some influence upon me too.

The inspiration of Dr. Mecklin's lecture had been reinforced by the assurances of all my English teachers except one obvious fool that I was a hell of a writer. My secret plan was to write fiction combining the macabre qualities of Bierce with the naturalism of the Ecole de Medan, but I did not feel ready to fulfill myself. I had told a Barnard girl during the summer holiday of 1922 that I did not think I would write anything great until I was twenty-five. In the meantime I determined to conquer journalism.

There is an underestimation of the potentialities of the journalistic medium inherent in this attitude, but I am convinced that it has brought into the current newspaper game whatever writing talent is at present engaged in it. Thousands of youngsters going into journalism dream of writing the great American novel, but few think of building a great American newspaper. You don't need to have ten million dollars to start a novel.

Campus Liberal
EDWARD LAMB

≫ After the undergraduate success as a money-maker that Edward Lamb 1924 recounts in his memoirs *No Lamb for Slaughter* (New York, 1963), it is not surprising that he went on to a highly successful and varied career as a businessman and lawyer. The selections from his memoirs supplement A. J. Liebling's account of Dartmouth and student life in the twenties.

I ENTERED DARTMOUTH in the fall of 1920. I immediately found that my ability to type was a great asset. Professors who were writing books and theses provided me with a constant source of income. I got sixty cents an hour—good wages in those days.

Then, in my second year, I conceived of a much easier way of making money. I decided to put on intercollegiate dances in New York City during the holiday periods. I sent out notices to all the Eastern colleges. The response was good, so I engaged one of the largest ballrooms in New York—the Grand Crystal Hall at the Pennsylvania Hotel. The $600 rental had to be paid in advance, but most of it wasn't due until just before the dance began and the tickets had been paid for. Then I wrote to Paul Whiteman to hire his famous dance band. For his band and a "personal appearance," though it meant that he need appear for only five minutes, the charge was $1,500. But, again, I didn't have to pay all of the huge fee until just before the dance began. As it turned out, I had more than enough cash in hand before the evening arrived to pay for the posters, the hall, the band, and Paul Whiteman. Tickets at the door sold like hotcakes; and Whiteman had so much fun that he stayed till the party was over. I ended up with a profit of $3,000, even after I had paid for the breakage of furniture and light bulbs, which was extensive because of the exuberance of the overflow crowd.

I put on twelve more intercollegiate dances before I got out of college. By that time, I must say, the idea had worn a little thin. However, when I left Hanover, I had $7,500 tucked away in the bank to take me to Harvard Law School. . . .

At Dartmouth my grades were average, perhaps because I spent so much time in extracurricular activities. Aside from my business operations, I went in heavily for sports, especially skiing. I was on the fencing, track, and ski teams, in varying degrees of unimportance. In addition, I became the business manager of the *Jack O'Lantern*, the humor magazine. This also brought in money because, by custom and general agreement, the three top members of the magazine's staff simply pocketed whatever was left of the advertising and circulation revenues after the bills for printing and other services were paid. Faculty control did not come until later. Our abuses may have brought about reform, though I have heard that students who get into positions of responsibility on college publications still do well.

I was full of curiosity about the world, and at the end of my first year at college, I got a job on a cattle boat bound for Europe. It was easy then for a husky young fellow to get such jobs. Once abroad, he could jump ship, and, after traveling about, call at the nearest American embassy and obtain help in getting back home. That first summer, I managed to make my way through Poland, Italy, and Germany. The next summer, I got a job on a freighter that went to Central and South America. The year after that, I saw Scandinavia and some of the Mediterranean countries. Finding a ship that would get me back to the States before college opened was not always easy. Twice I got back late and had to do some fast talking to get readmitted. . . .

Dartmouth in those years boasted of its alliance with the tradition of liberalism. Although the trustees of the college were everywhere referred to as "telephone-company men"—many of them were directors of the giant Bell system—students were encouraged to test out ideas. We had the repeated assurance of our president, Dr. Ernest Martin Hopkins, that we were expected to develop inquiring minds, and we were taught that intellectual freedom included access to the writings and speeches of "radicals." H. L. Mencken and Sinclair Lewis were kidding our undergraduate generation about its orthodoxy, but radical publications like the *Daily Worker* were on the shelves of Wilson Library. So was *Das Kapital*. And the students read them.

When I first went to Dartmouth, I wasn't much interested in political matters. I did belong to the Christian Association, which was rather like the YMCA. Eventually I joined the Liberal Club. It was in my third year, I think, when I was president, that the club put on an event that marked one of the high points in the cultivation of intellectual freedom at Dartmouth. We invited William Z. Foster, who had led the unsuccessful steel strike of 1919 and had been one of the chief organizers of the Communist party of America, to make an address. The announcement of his appearance caused a sensation not only in Hanover but elsewhere. The Hearst newspapers all over the country took it up; and some of Boston's more reactionary sheets, always out for circulation builders, tried to get a witch hunt started at Dartmouth.

Dr. Hopkins was on the spot with his trustees, but in view of his eloquent speeches in chapel about our historic freedoms, he could hardly forbid us to hear Foster. The student body rallied to the idea of listening to a leader of the Communist party... and part of the faculty also went along. It was a time when disillusionment was growing because of what had happened since the end of World War I—the war to end wars and make the world safe for democracy. To our minds it seemed that Woodrow Wilson's lofty war aims had been sullied and defeated by high-powered European politicians. And hadn't England and France grabbed Germany's colonies? Even at that time there were rumblings of war profiteering, and scandals in the manufacture of munitions.

The campus and the town were in a state of excitement when Foster arrived in Hanover. The members of the Liberal Club were worried, because the day before Foster had made a speech at Clark University in Worcester, Massachusetts, and had been physically attacked. In the midst of his speech, he told us, the lights in the university hall were "officially" disconnected and then "all hell broke loose."

A few students and faculty members who were at the railroad

station to meet him formed a "guard of honor" to watch over him during his stay in Hanover. Some of us considered him an "atheistic anarchist," whatever we meant by that, but we still thought he had a right to speak.

Probably some members of the faculty knew what had gone on during the steel strike of 1919, but I doubt that many of the students did—it was too far in their short past. They found out when Foster made his speech that night in the packed hall. He told us what had happened when the steelworkers struck for a working day of less than twelve hours. The United States Steel Company had demanded immediate cash payment for debts to company stores, where prices were far higher than in ordinary stores; local utilities had cut off services; doctors had refused to provide medical care. Many of the workers and their families had been evicted from their company-owned homes. What was even worse, the forces of law and order had been ranged against the strikers. Officers of the law had prevented picketing and broken up meetings. Injunctions had been granted without the formality of a hearing. Other court orders committed workers to jail for contempt of unpublicized and secret decrees, and thousands of men were clapped into jail, often without being formally charged. They were denied bail, and were not even allowed to have counsel. . . .

At Dartmouth the reaction to Foster's speech was mixed. Some students were really shocked to learn that such things could have happened in the United States. Others shrugged off the revelations as something not too important. And I daresay some students wondered whether the jobs they were counting on in industry might be jeopardized by this show of "radicalism" at Dartmouth.

Foster had originally planned to leave Hanover the morning after his speech. I was delegated to take him to breakfast and put him on the train. But when I called for him, he told me that he had decided to stay in Hanover for the next three days. A weekend was coming up, and he had no speaking engagements and no place else to go. It was late in May, the weather was fine, and I decided that the best thing to do was to take him to one of the outing cabins—there was a chain of them through the White Mountains to accommodate skiers and other outdoor enthusiasts. He was most agreeable. I asked various faculty members and students to join us, but by this time the "liberals" were in retirement, or for other reasons unavailable. Only a German exchange student would, or could, accompany Foster and me. The three of us hiked out to the cabin and spent three days there.

We found our guest friendly and witty as well as dedicated. He relished the new experience of "going to college" by walking, swimming, canoeing, and camping. We swam in the nude, of course, and the German student took a photograph of Foster and me coming out of the water. For a while he refused to give me the negative of that picture and kidded me by telling me he might have a use for it someday. It didn't worry me much then. There came a time, however, ... when I was glad that the German had finally given me the film. I can just imagine a picture of William Z. Foster and Edward Lamb in the nude spread across the front pages of the Hearst press!

Our discussions at the cabin were not particularly profound. Foster expressed his views on the nature of capitalism, and the Marxist theory of the struggle American workers were going through to get a little security and a "legitimate" standard of living. Of course, he tried to paint socialism, the common ownership of the means of production, in the most glowing terms. I must say that I was shocked most by his description of the role of the church in the "class struggle." I was also impressed, I remember, by his extensive knowledge of religious history and dogma. Foster, like Robert Ingersoll, Clarence Darrow, and other nonbelievers, held that opponents of religion should know as much about the Bible and the religions of the world as the people they were combating.

Foster didn't try to convert us. On the contrary, he seemed to respect our religious attachments. He was even tolerant of our assertions that Soviet Russia had "nationalized" women (after all, we had read about these things in the Hearst press) and unloosed a "Red terror." His attitude was "Take what I say or leave it," with the result that instead of antagonizing us he stirred our curiosity. We were particularly interested in his talk about personalities in the labor movement, about American Socialists like Adolph Goermer and Norman Thomas, American labor leaders from Samuel Gompers to John L. Lewis, and the social democrats in Europe. He told us, too, of other Americans who had become crusaders for the cause—the political cartoonist Robert Minor, the writer John Reed, the organizer Earl Browder, and others. He gave us vivid glimpses of the intensity of the struggle, not only between employers and labor, but also between rivals and factions in the left-wing movement.

Foster's health, like that of so many leaders of the radical movement, was bad. Long hours of work, hazardous living conditions, bad food, late meetings, all took their toll. Foster was an anemic-looking, exhausted man when he came to Hanover. If the weekend in the sun and air refreshed him, it gave me my first exhilarating experience with "dangerous thoughts." Frankly, I didn't understand much of what he talked about, and I certainly didn't agree with his conclusions. But I realized for the first time that there were great and burning problems to be solved. There still are, and I hope I never stop searching for solutions.

David Lambuth
BUDD SCHULBERG

≫ Some years ago a handbook *On Writing*, which Professor David Lambuth and his colleagues in the Dartmouth English Department had published in 1923, was reissued as *The Golden Book on Writing* (New York, 1964). The foreword to the new edition was contributed by one of Lambuth's students: Budd Schulberg 1936, the author of novels (*What Makes Sammy Run, The Disenchanted*) and prize-winning screen plays (*Waterfront, A Face in the Crowd*). Here is the foreword.

IT WAS AN EXPERIENCE, knowing Professor David Lambuth at Dartmouth College thirty years ago. On the outside, Davidlambuth—as his Alice-in-Wonderland wife always called him—was the answer to a freshman's dream of what a college English professor should look like. (This sentence ends with a preposition on good authority—Professor Lambuth's. He was precise but not fussy. He was not a grammarian's grammarian. He was a literary pragmatist. What *worked* was right.) Like his *Golden Book*, Lambuth asked that our writing be clear, vivid, moving. He was a big verb man. He knew the power of our language flowed from verbs that were "busy doing or making something." To think clearly, to think forcefully on paper, he taught us to use active verbs. A classic Lambuthism: Not "When Elizabeth was queen," but "When Elizabeth *reigned*." It is said, with good reason, that no one can teach anyone else how to write. Well, if Lambuth cannot make you drink, at least he turns you in the general direction of the water.

The look of Lambuth, and his eccentricity, hardly prepared you for his uncompromising rejection of pompous sentence structures and prolix paragraphs. He affected pince-nez, a white professorial beard, a rakish black beret, white "Mark Twain" suit and white shoes, a black opera cape, and a white Packard. The white Packard was not an affectation. It was the professor's way of accommodating Mrs. Lambuth's absent-mindedness. It was Mrs. Lambuth's custom to shop along the small Main Street of our college town and drop her purchases in any vehicle that happened to be handy. Professor Lambuth thought a white Packard would stand out among the less spectacular autos parked alongside it. But Mrs. Lambuth had a genius for absent-mindedness. Leaving Tanzi's Grocery Store with an armful of bundles, she deposited them confidently on the front seat of a white milk-wagon. When the driver found them he knew exactly where to deliver them. In fact it became a custom for the milkman to deliver the Lambuth groceries. My first meeting with her still shines in my memory. I had been invited to dinner, and with undergraduate enthusiasm for this rare privilege I was the first guest to arrive. I had visions of sitting near the fire with the learned, pipe-smoking professor to discuss Conrad and Stevenson. Instead an animated lady met me at the door in a long apron over her dinner dress. She handed me a large bowlful of raw string beans. "Since you've come so early, I hope you're good at stringing beans," she said in welcome.

For nearly half an hour I extracted strings from string beans. And this brings me back to this fine little book. For all his flamboyance and theatricality, Professor Lambuth commands our devotion and deserves this republication because he was a bear for pulling the strings—the stringy, unnecessary, indigestible fibers and excesses—from the English sentence, the English paragraph, the sturdy Anglo-Saxon English language. Lambuth was an uncommon man who taught that good writing began with common sense. He was a Flaubertian stickler for the right word. He loved English with a nice passion. Can any other language fuel such a raging bonfire with so few sticks? At its best it provides heat and light, a maximum of thought and emotion, with a minimum of syllables. Shakespeare knew this. Twain and Hemingway. And Frost. Our Davidlambuth was able to put it down in a book short on pages but long on insights. When you write, he said, make a picture with the nouns. And make that picture move with the verbs.

Professor Lambuth rode a white Packard like a white charger into battle against the hordes of bad writing flying the enemy flags of pretension and verbosity. His flag was the deceptively simple *Golden*

Book on Writing. Now we pick it up and carry it forward. No extra flourishes, please. No circumlocution curlicues, no rhetorical ringlets. Give it to me straight, says the Lambuth flag. If I may paraphrase another Lambuthism, he had a nail to hit, and in this welcome little bible of a book he practices his preach and hits it on the head.

Lew Stilwell

RICHARD BARBER

≫ Richard Barber 1962, a writer, and editor in a New York publishing house, sets down here his warm recollections of Lewis Dayton Stilwell, for more than 40 years a shaker of the Dartmouth mind.

D ARKNESS COMES EARLY in northern New England in midwinter, and by five-thirty the lights of the college buildings were halos in the falling snow. Hunched figures in parkas and fur-lined boots made their way across the campus, bent over against the swirling flakes. Some had come straight from athletic practice and were missing dinner. Some had left warm fraternity houses and unfinished kegs of beer. Some were cutting their own assigned classes, drawn instead to this weekly ritual. Like the spokes of a wheel, footprints from all directions moved steadily toward the hub, converging on Reed Hall.

The small lecture room on the first floor was already crowded with students. Steamy parkas were piled high on radiators, and every available chair had been commandeered. Others who could find no seats squatted on their coats in the aisle and across the front of the room. Latecomers packed the hall outside, hoping to find room to squeeze in. Only the platform remained empty.

Precisely at six o'clock, as the campus chimes started ringing, there was a stir of voices in the hall, and a figure strode through the doorway. He was wearing a World War I "Dough-boy" uniform, the jacket tugging at the buttons, the pants straining a little at the seams, the puttees wound smartly around his shanks. Under the broad brim of his campaign hat, his face was stern and military, and his eyes did not betray the pleasure he derived from the affectionate laughter and applause which greeted him. The old soldier snapped to attention, marched to the platform, executed a sharp left face, saluted. His right foot moved out and he stood at parade rest. The crowd silenced. Slowly his eyes moved over the class and then fixed themselves on an invisible spot in empty space just above their heads, a habit he always had when he addressed his class.

"Gentlemen, tonight we join the American Expeditionary Forces for the Meuse-Argonne Offensive, September 26 to November 11, 1918. More commonly known as the forty-six day battle won by General John J. Pershing and Private Lewis D. Stilwell."

Lew joined Dartmouth's history department in 1916 and almost immediately became a tradition. He was the campus iconoclast pricking the balloons of cherished beliefs and middle-class prejudices. Always a favorite at class and fraternity smokers, Lew would stand before a quieting gathering and announce, "When I was a senior at Amherst, I was voted 'Most Likely to Succeed.'—Look at me now."

During the early 20's, Lew taught a course in the western expansion of the United States (the "cowboy" course, as it was known) that was recalled long after by his students as the most stimulating thing they had experienced as undergraduates. Later he organized and directed a required freshman course in the History of Citizenship. After a paradoxical "Cit" lecture, the students would rush to his desk demanding a fuller explanation, but with a mischievous laugh, he would depart, leaving them to reason their way out of the dilemma.

Lew was preeminently a teacher, and his classes were provocative and incisive, filled with collegiate wit and earthy analogies—never dull. He expressed his teaching philosophy with characteristic brevity. "The college is a classroom. In that classroom you must talk plain, honest English, and you must know a whale of a lot."

He did not recite, he excited. We would sit in class determined to take down his every word. But I can remember days when scarcely a pencil moved as history came to life before our eyes. His strong enunciated voice was like that of a professional Shakespearean actor soliloquizing without note or reminder. He enjoyed telling stories on himself about his lecturing. "One time," he said, "after I had had too many beers at a fraternity-faculty gathering, I came back to my classroom late at night. I turned on all of the lights, and delivered a complete lecture to the empty seats. This is the final proof of one of the things that I most like about teaching—merely the chance to hear my own words."

"A Battle a Day," as we students colloquially dubbed his most popular course, became, after Lew's retirement, a series of evening lectures he called "Battle Nights." They were so much in demand that Lew was induced to repeat his talk a second hour to accommodate all those who wished to hear him. Each was "a drama with five acts," he told me once. "First, a description of the setting, second, the presentation of the opposing forces or characters, third, the fight, and then the climax, and the denouement."

At heart Lew was a pacifist in the sense that he abhorred war. "I think that war should be used in the way that a surgeon performs an operation. A surgeon sheds blood and risks human life, but he usually has a definite and limited objective. Most wars have been conducted with no such intelligence or restraint. We often simply try to destroy whole enemy peoples, which is outrageous." His purpose in teaching military history was to help students understand war, for "without understanding it, there is no hope of preventing it." Getting them interested is easy, he said. "War is the greatest of outdoor sport from the standpoint of the spectators." But, soberly, he would reflect: "We learn from history that we never learn from history."

I think I remember Lew best when he was discoursing in this way with students. He liked definite opinions and he loved argument. His office hours were crowded with students eager for a probing "bull-session with Lew," and these sessions continued on the street, and in fraternity houses, and in the drug store where he ate. "I am a teacher, not an administrator," he used to say. "As a matter of fact, I would rather spend my time with the students than with my colleagues. They are generally more stimulating, and besides, they are paying my salary."

Lew believed very deeply in the classic Socratic method of teaching. Standing in the midst of a cluster of students in a fraternity bar, dressed in old chinos, sweat socks, worn cordovans, and his favorite tweed jacket, a cigarette pinched between his fingers, a glass of beer in his hand, he would adopt some unorthodox position and hold forth. Then as the heated counter-argument started, eyes sparkling, he would cut through the surface and expose our fraudulent logic and rationalizations. An awkward silence would be shattered by his booming laugh, and a quick bon mot would relax the tension and we would be back on the path of analysis. He was an iconoclast in the sense that he wanted us to understand why we gave credence to certain ideals. The conclusions that he helped us to find might not be his conclusions, but that did not disturb him. Life would have been too boring for him if we had always agreed. He liked what he called "a healthy resistance to education."

Second only to teaching was Lew's love of the out-of-doors. The Connecticut River Valley was his "Walden," and he spent many happy hours walking beside the river and paddling his canoe into its backwaters. He bought an island in the middle of the river, and on it built himself a cabin to the exact dimensions recorded by Henry David Thoreau. Life on Stilwell's Landing gave Lew the simple richness he sought. There he bathed in the sun, swam, fished, cut wood, and thought. Often he would share this joy with a close friend or two. In many cases it was one of his students whom he met on the street, and whose problems or arguments needed more attention.

But Lew enjoyed the hours he spent alone. A great walker always, he would set out late of an evening, coatless and hatless, for a ten or fifteen mile jaunt. Often he would make use of this time to polish a lecture that he was soon to deliver. In his pocket would be a flashlight and notes, and his course was marked like that of a restless firefly over the hills and along the back roads of his beloved valley.

Once I urged Lew to set down his "Battle Nights" for publication, but he laughed, that explosive snort that ended in the hacking cough of a chain smoker. "Oh, maybe I will one of these days—after I have been retired for a while. Right now I am working on a new lecture I think the guys will enjoy."

Hopkins of Dartmouth
STEARNS MORSE

➳ Stearns Morse wrote his tribute to President Hopkins out of the knowledge accumulated from long membership on the Dartmouth faculty and in the Hanover community. He came to Dartmouth in 1923 to join the English department; from 1946 to 1956 he was dean of freshman. His essay appeared originally in *The American Scholar* in 1966.

Ernest Martin Hopkins' consuming interest was in people; he was consequently wary of tags like "liberal" or "conservative." Nevertheless I first became aware of his existence from a reference in the *New Republic* in June, 1921, shortly after I had accepted a position in a small private school in northern New Jersey.

A year or so before I had worked for a brief time in a humble capacity for this liberal journal of opinion. This was the era of the postwar Bolshevik scare and the minions of A. Mitchell Palmer were scurrying about looking for revolutionaries in their hidden lairs. At this point the *New Republic* was considered a radical rather than a liberal journal and a raid by the Department of Justice was not unlooked for; indeed it was only hoped that, if this should occur, it might be on a Wednesday, when the weekly editorial luncheon was taking place with Thomas Lamont of the Morgan firm likely to be one of the guests.

The New Jersey school, I discovered, was scarcely sympathetic to radical ideas. Indeed I soon learned that one of the masters had recently been fired because of alleged radical tendencies. (He went on to a distinguished career in New England private schools.) The head of the board of trustees of the school was Grinnell Willis, son of N. P. Willis, the poet and critic; he was, in his eighties, the principal owner of textile mills in Scotland. At the culmination of the episode the rather awesome Mr. Willis had addressed an assembly of the school and demanded that all the masters take an oath to support the Constitution of the United States.

The headmaster rose to this challenge. His chief distinction at Harvard he had won as a member of the crew. In his middle fifties, broad-shouldered, at least six feet tall, with iron gray hair, a crisp iron gray mustache and a ruddy countenance, he was truly a gentleman of distinction. On this occasion he lived up to his appearance. In rather bumbling but no less decisive phrases he allowed that since an ancestor had been one of the first to fall at the battle of Lexington he would consider it an insult to take any such oath or ask any of his masters to do so. Truer to their common Harvard heritage than his principal trustee, he thus put an end to the affair.

It was in this context that I came across the reference to Ernest Martin Hopkins: a quotation from the commencement address he had given in June (of 1921) at the University of Pennsylvania in which he deplored the reluctance, after the war, "with which there is returned to an ancient people the ancient right of access to knowledge of the truth, the right of free assembly and the right of freedom of speech." And in the fall of 1922 I read (again in the *New Republic*) an account of the convocation address in which Hopkins startled people with the statement that "too many men are going to college"; deprecated the use of the college to define an aristocracy of birth or wealth; and called for an "aristocracy of brains."

In the spring of my second year at the New Jersey school I walked down the corridor to the headmaster's office, glancing amusedly at the suit of armor on the stair landing, the helmet of which years before the young John Reed had crowned with a chamber pot. For my carefree mood was somewhat akin to his: I was going to tell the headmaster that I had accepted a position in the English department at Dartmouth. But before I had a chance to break my news he began, rather shamefacedly and with a certain amount of hemming and hawing to tell me that he had neglected to say, as he was supposed to earlier, that the trustees had voted a prohibition of such organs as the *Nation* and the *New Republic* in the classroom; he had not done so, he went on, because he trusted my discretion. I did not bother to confess that I had in fact used the latter journal once or twice since I was full of my own news, which I then proceeded to tell him with emphasis on my admiration for Dartmouth's president.

He listened rather glumly. There is an unconscious parochialism about some Harvard men that is rather endearing—a parochialism, of course, by no means peculiar to Harvard; one meets it in graduates of other institutions, Oxford and Cambridge, for example. And it is endearing, I say—like Queen Victoria's habit of sitting down without looking behind her in the certainty that someone would provide a chair. One would have supposed that a headmaster would have had at least a dim awareness of other college presidents than the presidents of Harvard, Yale and Princeton. But such was not the case. "Is he a Harvard man?" he blurted out. "No," I admitted. He said nothing but looked a little as Queen Victoria might have looked if the chair had not been there.

Insular complacency was scarcely a mark of Ernest Martin Hopkins, but he appreciated it in others. When I told him about the episode he at once matched it with a remark his father had made to him when he announced in his last year at Worcester Academy that he was going to Dartmouth. The Reverend Adoniram Judson Hopkins, a Baptist clergyman, who had gone to Harvard, looked at him in amazement. "What makes you think you couldn't get into Harvard?" he asked.

This exchange occurred after I had been several years at Dartmouth. As a young instructor I had little occasion for personal contact with the president. Not that he held himself aloof from younger members of the faculty. In fact my friend Artemas Packard, who came as an instructor also the year after I came, was in close touch with Mr. Hopkins almost from the first. This arose from the fact that Packard had fresh ideas about the teaching of art that corresponded to the radical ideas of Mr. Hopkins' good friend Adelbert Ames, then pursuing his researches in optics and psychology. After a year or so in the English department Packard was asked by the president to revitalize the art department—it was he who induced Mr. Hopkins to invite Orozco to paint the frescoes in Baker Library in the thirties.

During these early years, then, it was largely through Packard's relationship to him that I formed my impressions of his thinking and his methods of administration. But one did not need to be in intimate touch with Ernest Martin Hopkins to assess his particular quality. I used occasionally to watch him from my living room—I lived for two years in Choate House, the last remaining house on the campus—as he went by from his house on College Street to his office in Parkhurst Hall. He had a distinctive walk, which I can best describe as a sloping walk, throwing in leisurely fashion his weight from one foot to the other.

The immediate impression was one of dignity and reserve—dignity without stuffiness. ("He is the first college president I have ever met," a friend of Czech extraction once wrote me from Lincoln, Nebraska, "who is not a stuffed shirt.") In his way, too, he was a "gentleman of distinction," although not of the superficial photogenic quality that readily lends itself to the advertising of whiskey. He was scarcely the back-slapping type, yet he could casually throw an arm about your shoulder. In conversation he looked at you directly from deep brown eyes—not of the piercing sort, they were too friendly for that, but they took you in and sized you up without seeming to, for he was always as interested in what you had to say to him as in what he had to say to you. He spoke always easily, and laughter came easily to him; but a certain slight trembling of the lips and what seemed, but was not, a hesitancy in speech and a nervous habit of rubbing his hands betrayed, beneath the dignity and reserve, shyness and an emotional capacity always kept under control.

All that I became aware of later. At this time I knew him only as he presided at faculty meetings or spoke on official occasions. I am inclined to think that during these years of the twenties his pronouncements were quoted in the metropolitan press more often than those of any other college president. Yet his public speech—at least on official occasions—was somewhat involved and labored. I suspect this sprang partly from self-consciousness, the realization that a prominent "educator" was always in the public eye. Perhaps, too, it was the result of the contemptuous comment of a member of the faculty after his inaugural address: "Sounds just like a business man." (He was, in fact, one of the first men to come from the world of business to head a major college.) After that, I think, he resolved (perhaps subconsciously) that he would "talk like a professor." This was unfortunate, for in extemporaneous speech, as in his letters, he expressed himself simply and vigorously.

He had been president since 1916, with time out for war service under Newton D. Baker, one of his admirations, when I came to Dartmouth in 1923. I remember my surprise at a dinner in my first year when the Dartmouth librarian expressed regret that both members of the faculty and undergraduates saw so little of him. Of course, like most college presidents he was busy about money-raising (in this he was preeminently successful, although seldom, I believe, did he ask a potential donor outright) and in talking to the alumni. "Whatever do you say to your alumni?" President Lowell once asked him. "Why, I talk about education." The librarian's remark surprised me for even though I had been there less than a year I had been impressed by the warmth of admiration and affection expressed by both students and members of the faculty—even by those who had, I knew, as little contact with him as I.

The point is that he had the rare faculty of establishing, despite his reserve, an immediate personal relationship with one. He had come to Dartmouth after six years of personnel work with Western Electric, Filene's Department Store in Boston, the Curtis Publishing Company, and New England Telephone. For this he was preeminently fitted, for he possessed a sixth sense about people. Of course, he was not infallible in his appraisals of them, but his intuition seldom led him astray: when it did it was from a generous impulsiveness rather than from a lack of judgment. A striking example of this sixth sense I happened on years later in a memo in the files of the Dean of the Faculty. Dean Bill had recommended a senior for an important assistantship. The president's note expressed doubt as to the advisability of taking a man fresh out of college; and went on to say: "What about John Dickey, '29—do you know him?" Yet, President Dickey has told me—he was still in the Harvard Law School, I think, at the time of this memo—he had seen Mr. Hopkins only once or twice in his entire college career and then only briefly. The important role Mr. Hopkins played in the choice of his successor is quite clear.

Although he was all too frequently absent from Hanover, one felt, nevertheless, the pervasiveness of his influence; in fact his frequent absence was paradoxically a mark of his influence: he trusted his faculty and his students; one was not being watched. The result was a complete freedom from inhibition in the classroom. The Freshman English course, for instance, made use in the twenties of a collection of "Essays toward Truth" compiled by three of the staff, which consisted of highly controversial and often quite opposite views on a variety of subjects, with the aim of stimulating untrammeled discussion among students who often came from very conventional and unsophisticated homes. One cannot, of course, adequately teach Shakespeare without shocking someone's sensibilities or preconceived ideas.

Controversial speakers were invited to the campus; more important, the choice of these speakers was generally left to various student organizations. Raymond Robbins came, with his intimate glimpses of Lenin and Trotsky after the "Ten Days that Shook the World." Bertrand Russell came, although forbidden to speak on other campuses; his wife Dora filled Webster Hall with a talk on sex. Scott Nearing told Mr. Hopkins that he was the first college president to have shaken his hand in years. Mr. Hopkins himself introduced his good friend Alexander Meiklejohn, who had recently been ousted from the presidency of Amherst.

Meiklejohn and Hopkins were an interesting contrast. Meiklejohn was the academic, the theorist, the intellectual; Hopkins the man of affairs. The one was the man who played tennis, the other the man who played golf; in temperament Meiklejohn was like a nimble terrier, Hopkins like the ranging Scotch deerhound he once owned. Meiklejohn was a master of incisive Socratic dialectic; Hopkins more earthy and pragmatic. Meiklejohn, during his brief term as president of Amherst (to say nothing of his later years in various positions) exercised an extraordinary influence, of which the number of his "boys" still teaching on college faculties throughout the country is a reflection. Hopkins' influence was more diffuse; he left it to others (his faculty, men like John Mecklin, for instance, whom he brought to Dartmouth after harrowing experiences at Lafayette and Pittsburgh) to stimulate intellectual activity. Meiklejohn was ousted from Amherst. Hopkins, by virtue of his experience among men of business and also by virtue of his personality, was able to weather attacks from critics of his administration. . . .

During the twenties my relations with him were limited and incidental: an exchange of views on the baneful effects of prohibition, for instance; and a few small social occasions at his house in which the tone set by Mr. Hopkins and his wife was easy and informal. In the thirties our contacts became more frequent.

This was partly because in the latter part of that decade committee assignments brought me more often to his office, but mainly because we were both incurably political animals and the politics of that period became increasingly intense. In the days before World War I we had both been Bull Moosers. It was just a few years ago that we were recalling those days at a luncheon where we were guests along with Robert Frost, who had just returned from his visit to the Soviet Union and his talk with Kruschev. That Grover Cleveland (but also Kennedy) Democrat listened with amusement as we recounted our enthusiasm for T. R. Suddenly we discovered that we had both been present at a rally in the Boston Arena in 1912—in fact E. M. H. had climbed up on the platform where T. R. was about to speak. I was then an undergraduate, but E. M. H. was a young businessman. As such it required more courage to be for Roosevelt. ("Don't walk with me," T. R. had called out in his falsetto voice across the street to Dean Briggs as they were both walking down to the Porcellian Club in Cambridge shortly after he had thrown his hat in the ring, "don't walk with me, you'll lose your standing!")

We both called ourselves independent Republicans, although I was more independent than Republican. Mr. Hopkins was an admirer of Woodrow Wilson as well as of Baker; if Baker had ever been a Presidential candidate I think he would have voted for him. But I'm sure he voted for Hoover in 1928, even though Henry B. Thayer, Chairman of the Board of American Telephone and Telegraph, startled him and the other Dartmouth trustees by expressing a preference for Smith over Hoover on the ground that Smith was a master of people, more important for a President than to be a master of materials.

After the 1929 debacle and the deepening of the depression Mr. Hopkins' neighbor and friend, Adelbert Ames, approached his Wall Street friends who were high in the councils of the Republican party with a view to promoting the Dartmouth president as a candidate for the Vice-Presidency. Nothing came of this and on election morning in 1932 E. M. H. met Mr. Ames in the Corner Bookstore in Hanover. "Well, Mr. Politician," he said, "I've thrown a wrench into your machinations. I've just voted for Franklin Roosevelt."

Mr. Hopkins never became a convert to Keynesian economics. As time went on he became more and more disturbed about the fiscal policies—or lack of them—of the New Deal and about what the increasing centralization of affairs in Washington might do to the private colleges. Consequently in 1936 he came out for Landon with an article in the *Atlantic*. On election night he listened to the returns with a few friends, among them Professor James P. Richardson of the political science department. In 1927 Richardson had aroused the ire of many alumni by writing a letter to Governor Fuller in which he, albeit reluctantly, quoted the remark Judge Thayer had made to him about those "anarchistic bastards," Sacco and Vanzetti. One alumnus had offered a substantial sum to the college if Richardson were fired. Mr. Hopkins reported the offer to his friend: "I'll take him up," he said, "and we'll split the money between us." Richardson was not amused. Neither was he amused on this evening. As the vote for Roosevelt mounted, his face grew longer and longer. Finally he turned to the president: "Hop, it looks to me as if your article didn't do a goddam bit of good."

Sometime a sober historian will supplement the rollicking caricature of these years drawn by the late Senator McCarthy. The picture so far as the colleges are concerned will not be without its comic components: it will contain somewhere a portrait of a charming young girl seriously but naïvely discussing "historical materialism" and the "dialectic"; of an ebullient youth crossing a college campus wearing a flaming red blazer, with a copy of the *Daily Worker* under his arm; of the slim intense son of a stock broker, gone broke in the depression, leading a Marxist study group. As to Marx my own education in college had been limited to the *Communist Manifesto*, so that when a group of young radicals asked me to organize a seminar to read *Das Kapital* I blithely consented. A junior—he later became a writer on the staff of *Fortune*—made a brilliant analysis of several chapters until the project palled; a young member of the political science department, I recall, suggested that the views of Karl Mannheim had greater relevance to our contemporary situation.

The American Student Union and the American League Against War and Fascism organized peace strikes and meetings on all sorts of issues. It later appeared that there was a cell of the Young Communist League on the campus, although I knew only one student at this time who openly avowed membership in the Communist Party. Nevertheless the A.S.U. and the American League, of which I was the local chairman, were manifestly Communist fronts. It should be said that most of the "fellow-travelers" were essentially either dissenters, good Jeffersonian democrats, or philosophical anarchists rather than Communists: in the remote contingency of a Communist revolution they would have been among the first to face a firing squad....

It was inevitable that *The Dartmouth*—"America's oldest college newspaper," as it liked to call itself—during these years should engage in crusades that, equally inevitably, could be acutely embarrassing to the college. Of course, Mr. Hopkins could have cut the Gordian knot of this problem, not by suppressing the paper (which would have been difficult to do, since it had an independent corporate entity) but by expelling the editors. This would have gone against his grain. He met each critical situation coolly, on occasion sitting down to talk with the editor, but seldom unless the editor requested an interview.

I happened to be in his office one morning—this was in 1935, Budd Schulberg was then the editor—after *The Dartmouth* had come to the defense of striking granite workers in the Rutland, Vermont, quarries belonging to the Proctor family. Mr. Hopkins picked up the paper and remarked ruefully that for some time the college had been working on the Proctors for a substantial gift. "We'll have to lay off that project now, I guess," he said, and recited with wry amusement other occasions when *The Dartmouth* had spiked the wheels. He tossed the paper onto his desk. "But we've lived with and shall keep on living with it." Censorship was unthinkable, for once the college exercised a veto it would be held officially responsible for every view the student editors expressed.

With the purges in the Soviet Union and with the Nazi-Soviet pact in 1939 radical agitation on college campuses waned, to be succeeded by a wave of neutrality in the days of the "phoney" war. It was Mr. Hopkins' conviction, as well as that of most of the faculty, that sooner or later the United States would have to stand up to the Nazi menace. The editor of *The Dartmouth* stoutly upheld a neutralist, not to say a pacifist, position. Again Mr. Hopkins kept hands off. Not many years later the editor, then in the O.S.S., parachuted into occupied France; after the war he returned to Dartmouth as an instructor and one day asked E. M. H. why he had not been fired from college. Mr. Hopkins merely smiled. Today he is a trustee of the college.

During these years, partly because of a period of ill health, Mr. Hopkins had moods of disillusionment about the cause of liberal education to which he had devoted his life. Was the college too sheltered in a world that put a premium on action, too often violent action? Was the American undergraduate too pleasure-loving, too undisciplined, by contrast, for example, with Fascist and Communist youth? He often spoke wistfully of the Chinese students of the famous "long march" into the interior. When Leopold of Belgium surrendered to the Nazis, he said, with a touch of bitterness: "He must have gone to a liberal college." Like many other people, as their years advance, he would sometimes refer to the softness of the younger generation, recalling his year as a timekeeper in a granite quarry to earn money in order to go to college, and the country lads, like Henry B. Thayer, who walked to and from college for their vacations. . . .

Despite a shrewdly realistic view of human nature, he was a born

Hopkins of Dartmouth 229

hero-worshiper. Some of his critics said, indeed, that he was unduly impressed by men of great wealth. This was unjust, for although, by virtue of his position, he was constantly thrown with leaders of the American plutocracy and admired many of them, he was as acutely aware of their limitations as of their virtues, as he was also aware of the limitations of the academic and theoretical mind. The man who most profoundly influenced his life was President Tucker, whose memory he never ceased to venerate. I have already mentioned his admiration for such different people as T. R. and Newton Baker. Although, rather curiously, I cannot recall that he and I ever later mentioned Winston Churchill in conversation other than casually, I am sure that he, as well as I, recognized in him the greatest statesman of our time.

So I suspect that it was approximately at the moment when Churchill assumed the dynamic leadership of the Western world that Mr. Hopkins—he would be sixty-five in 1942 and would already have served as president for twenty-five years—resolved to see the college through the emergency, ill health or no. In fact, in the following strenuous years he brought renewed vigor and imagination to the crowding problems of the college; not only that, but he assumed important responsibilities in Washington. Then, in 1945, he turned over to his successor the administration of the college. . . .

A distinguished historian once said to me: "Of course Hopkins was not an educator." It may be so. But he was a great person; an amateur, if you will, in the best sense of the word. His influence upon thousands of persons who came into contact with him directly and indirectly is, of course, intangible, immeasurable. He had the wisdom that is something more than mere knowledge. He used to suggest that it was not a mere waste of time for a boy in college "to lie in the sun." One of his traits, which along with his mental alertness endured until his death in his eighty-seventh year, was a controlled ebullience, a quiet gaiety. A favorite quotation of his was from Stevenson's "The Lantern Bearers": "He who misses the joy misses all." And in a letter he sent me in the last full summer of his life he wrote: "Robert Frost once said to me, 'I hear so many college presidents bewailing their sad lots! You like it, don't you?' The answer of course was 'Yes.' " Frost, I am sure, never thought of himself as a teacher. Neither did Hopkins. Their views of life were too wide to concentrate upon pigeonholes. Nevertheless Hopkins, like Frost, was a great teacher.

ROUND THE GIRDLED EARTH

The Death of Captain Cook

JOHN LEDYARD

⇒ The adventures of John Ledyard did not end with the canoe trip down the Connecticut in 1773. They had only begun. That same year he shipped from New London, Conn., as a sailor bound for the Mediterranean, returned, then went to London where he was just in time to sign on for Capt. James Cook's third voyage of exploration that sailed for the Pacific in July 1776. Ledyard's recollections of the voyage and of the death of Captain Cook were published in 1783 as *A Journal of Captain Cook's Last Voyage to the Pacific Ocean* (Hartford, 1783).

WE HAD NOW BEEN 19 days in the bay Kireekakooa, in the Island of Owyhee, we had repaired our ships, had regaled and refreshed our people, and had lain in a supply of pork that would probably support us 6 months; the only article we wanted in particular was water, which was here very brackish and bad. In order therefore to procure a supply of this necessary article, we determined to visit the island of Mauwee, where we were informed by the natives we might get plenty of it, and that there was a good harbor.

On the 6th of February we unmoored and came to sail standing along the south side of Owyhee, intending to visit Mauwee and water our ships.

On the 7th we had a hard gale of wind, and being close in with the southern and western shore of Owyhee, which being high land occasioned the wind that came partly off the land to come in irregular and most terrible gusts, such as we had never seen.

On the 8th the gale became not only more violent but more irregular and embarrassing, and before night was improved into a mere hurricane; we wrenched the head of our foremast, and sprung it about 9 feet below the hounds, and also made a great deal of water. During this severe night the Discovery [Cook's ship] had lost us.

On the 9th the violence of the gale or rather the tornado ceased, but the excessive mutability of the wind, and the irregular sea, was such as demanded our best skill and unremitted attention to keep the ship under any kind of command.

On the 10th the weather became tolerably settled, and hauling off the land we saw the Discovery in the S.E. quarter, and before night spoke her all well. We informed her of our situation, and that in consequence of the misfortune, it was determined to return again to our old harbour at Kireekakooa.

On the 11th of February we again entered Kireekakooa bay, and moored both ships in their old berths.

On the 12th we got the foremast out and sent it on shore with the carpenters, we also sent our two observatories on shore, and a markee for a guard of marines.

Our return to this bay was as disagreeable to us as it was to the inhabitants, for we were reciprocally tired of each other. They had been oppressed and were weary of our prostituted alliance, and we were aggrieved by the consideration of wanting the provisions and refreshments of the country, which we had every reason to suppose from their behavior antecedent to our departure would now be withheld from us or brought in such small quantities as to be worse than none. What we anticipated was true. When we entered the bay where before we had the shouts of thousands to welcome our arrival, we had the mortification not to see a single canoe, and hardly any inhabitants in the towns. Cook was chagrined and his people were soured. Towards night however the canoes came in, but the provisions both in quantity and quality plainly informed us that times were altered, and what was very remarkable was the exorbitant price they asked; and the particular fancy they all at once took to iron daggers or dirks, which was the only article that was any ways current, with the chiefs at least. It was also equally evident from the looks of the natives as well as every other appearance that our former friendship was at an end, and that we had nothing to do but to hasten our departure to some different island where our vices were not known, and where our extrinsic virtues might gain us another short space of being wondered

The Death of Captain Cook 235

at, and doing as we pleased, or as our tars expressed it of being happy by the month.

Nor was their passive appearance of disgust all we had to fear, nor did it continue long: before dark a canoe with a number of armed chiefs came alongside of us without provisions and indeed without any perceptible design, after staying a short time only they went to the Discovery where they went on board a part of them.... These men ... came with a determination of mischief, and effected it. After they were returned to the canoe all but one they got their paddles and every thing ready for a start. Those in the canoes observing the sentry to be watchful took off his attention by some conversation that they knew would be pleasing to him, and by this means favored the designs of the man on board, who watching his opportunity snatched two pair of tongs, and other iron tools that they lay close by the armourers at work at the forge, and mounting the gangway-rail, with one leap threw himself and his goods into the canoe, that was then upon the movement, and taking up his paddle joined the others and standing directly for the shore, they were out of our reach almost instantaneously; even before a musket could be had from the armed chest to fire at them.... When Cook heard of this he went armed himself in person to the guard on shore, took a file of marines and went through the whole town demanding restitution, and threatening the delinquents and their abettors with the severest punishments, but not being able to effect any thing, came off just at sun-set highly displeased and not a little concerned at the bad appearance of things. But even this was nothing to what followed.

On the 13th at night the Discovery's large cutter which was at her usual moorings at the bower buoy was taken away.

On the 14th the captains met to consult what should be done on this alarming occasion, and the issue of their opinions was that one of the two captains should land with armed boats and a guard of marines at Kiverua and attempt to persuade Kireeaboo who was then at his house in that town to come on board upon a visit, and that when he was on board he should be kept prisoner until his subjects should release him by a restitution of the cutter, and if it was afterwards thought proper, he or some of the family who might accompany him should be kept as perpetual hostages for the good behavior of the people, during the remaining part of our continuance at Kireekakooa, and this plan was the more approved of by Cook as he had so repeatedly on former occasions to the southward employed it with success. . . .

Cook in his pennace with six private marines: a corporal, serjeant and two lieutenants of marines went ahead followed by the launch with other marines and seamen on one quarter, and the small cutter on the other with only the crew on board. This part of the guard rowed for Kireekakooa. Our large cutter and two boats from the Discovery had orders to proceed to the mouth of the bay, form at equal distances across, and prevent any communication by water from any other part of the island to the towns within the bay, or from them without. Cook landed at Kiverua about nine o'clock in the morning with the marines in the pennace, and went by a circuitous march to the house of Kireeaboo in order to evade the suspicion of any design. This route led them through a considerable part of the town which discovered every symptom of mischief, though Cook blinded by some fatal cause could not perceive it, or too self-confident would not regard it.

The town was evacuated by the women and children, who had retired to the circumadjacent hills, and appeared almost destitute of men, but there were at that time 200 chiefs and more than twice that number of other men detached and secreted in different parts of the houses nearest to Kireeaboo exclusive of unknown numbers without the skirts of the town, and those that were seen were dressed many of them in black. When the guard reached Kireeaboo's house, Cook ordered the lieutenant of marines to go in and see if he was at home, and if he was to bring him out; the lieutenant went in and found the old man sitting with two or three old women of distinction, and when he gave Kireeaboo to understand that Cook was without and wanted to see him he discovered the greatest marks of uneasiness, but arose and accompanied the lieutenant out, holding his hand; when he came before Cook he squatted down upon his hams as a mark of humiliation,

The Death of Captain Cook 237

and Cook took him by the hand from the lieutenant, and conversed with him.

The appearance of our parade both by water and on shore, though conducted with the utmost silence and with as little ostentation as possible, had alarmed the towns on both sides of the bay, but particularly Kiverua, who were in complete order for an onset otherwise it would have been a matter of surprise, that though Cook did not see 20 men go passing through the town, yet before he had conversed 10 minutes with Kireeaboo he was surrounded by three or four hundred people, and about half of them chiefs. Cook grew uneasy when he observed this, and was the more urgent in his persuasions with Kireeaboo to go on board, and actually persuaded the old man to go at length, and led him within a rod or two of the shore, but the just fears and conjectures of the chiefs at last interposed. They held the old man back, and one of the chiefs threatened Cook when he attempted to make them quit Kireeaboo. Some of the croud now cried out that Cook was going to take their king from them and kill him, and there was one in particular that advanced towards Cook in an attitude that alarmed one of the guard, who presented his bayonet and opposed him: Acquainting Cook in the mean time of the danger of his situation, and that the Indians in a few minutes would attack him, that he had overheard the man whom he had just stopped from rushing in upon him say that our boats which were out in the harbour had just killed his brother, and he would be revenged. Cook attended to what this man said, and desired him to show him the Indian that had dared to attempt a combat with him, and as soon as he was pointed out Cook fired at him with a blank. The Indian perceiving he received no damage from the fire rushed from without the croud a second time, and threatened any one that should oppose him. Cook perceiving this fired a ball, which entering the Indian's groin he fell and was drawn off by the rest. Cook perceiving the people determined to oppose his designs, and that he should not succeed without further bloodshed ordered the lieutenant of marines (Mr. Phillips) to withdraw his men and get them into the boats, which were then laying ready to receive them. This was effected by the serjeant, but the instant they began to retreat Cook was hit with a stone, and perceiving the man who hove, shot him dead: The officer in the boats perceiving the guard retreating, and hearing this third discharge ordered the boats to fire, this occasioned the guard to face about and fire, and then the attack became general, Cook and Mr. Phillips were together a few paces in the rear of the guard, and perceiving a general fire without orders quitted Kireeaboo, and ran to the shore to put a stop to it, but not being able to make themselves heard, and being close pressed upon by the chiefs they joined the guard and fired as they retreated. Cook having at length reached the margin of the water between the fire of the boats waved with his hat to cease firing and come in, and while he was doing this a chief from behind stabed him with one of our iron daggers just under the shoulder-blade, and passed quite through his body. Cook fell with his face in the water and immediately expired. Mr. Phillips ... drew his sword and engaging the chief who he saw kill Cook soon dispatched him, his guard in the meantime were all killed but two, and they had plunged into the water and were swimming to the boats, he stood thus for some time the butt of all their force, and being as complete in the use of his sword as he was accomplished: his noble achievements struck the barbarians with awe, but being wounded and growing faint from loss of blood, and excessive action, he plunged into the sea with his sword in his hand and swam to the boats, where however he was scarcely taken on board before somebody saw one of the marines that had swam from the shore laying flat upon the bottom. Phillips hearing this run aft, threw himself in after him and brought him up with him to the surface of the water and both were taken in. ...

After dark the sentries upon the gangways saw a canoe approaching the ship in a very silent and hasty manner, and when she got within call the officer of the deck hailed her, but the Indians returning no answer the sentry fired at her, and shot one of the Indians through the leg, upon which he bawled out tutee tutee, that is Cook. Clarke was acquainted with the matter and came upon deck and ordered her alongside and the Indians on board: there were only three of them, and one had Cook's hat on his head which he gave us to understand he had brought at the hazard of his life: the man that was

The Death of Captain Cook

wounded was taken to the surgeon and had his wound dressed. But we were extremely affected and disgusted when the other Indian produced from a bundle he had under his arm a part of Cook's thigh wrapped up in clean cloth which he said he saw himself cut from the bone in the manner we saw it, and when we enquired what had become of the remaining part of him, he gnashed his teeth and said it was to be eaten that night. As soon as the wound of the Indian that was shot was dressed, they departed with a promise if they could to bring the remainder of Cook's body the next night.

The prospect of recovering Cook's body though by pieces afforded some satisfaction, and we therefore suspended the further prosecution of business on shore for the next day. In the evening about the same time he appeared before, we saw the same Indian with other parts of Cook's body, to wit, the upper part of his head and both his hands, which he said he had been at infinite pains to procure, and that the other parts could not be obtained, especially the flesh which was mostly eat up: the head was scalped and all the brains taken out: the hands were scored and salted: these fragments of the body of the unfortunate Cook were put into a box and preserved in hopes of getting more of them: the Indians who brought them were well satisfied with presents, and returned again to the shore the same night, and though they assured us they could not procure any more of those remains: we yet waited another day but saw no more of the Indian.

Desert March
WILLIAM EATON

⇶ Of all the romantic stories concerning Dartmouth men, none compares with that of William Eaton's march across the northern Sahara in 1805. Soon after his graduation in 1790 he obtained a captaincy in the United States Army, the first step in a career that led to his becoming consul in Tunis in 1798, where with the American diplomatic agent he carried out successful negotiations with the piratical Bey. In 1801 the Barbary state of Tripoli, whose pasha had usurped his brother's throne, declared war against the United States. Eaton, as a means of countering, proposed that with American aid the deposed brother be restored, and when that scheme received some support in Washington, he proceeded to carry out the idea, having meanwhile been named Navy agent to the Barbary States. The deposed pasha had sought refuge in Egypt, where Eaton caught up with him, raised a motley army and marched across the desert to capture the Tripolitan town of Derne, a major move in the war against Tripoli. At that victorious moment Eaton learned that the United States was negotiating with the reigning pasha, that in a sense his expedition had been repudiated. Eaton's account of the march, from which extracts have been taken, is incorporated in Charles Prentiss's *Life of the Late Gen. William Eaton* (Brookfield, Mass., 1813).

WHATEVER EVENTS may take place to regulate its government, and ameliorate the situation of its inhabitants, Egypt, like Carthage and Syracuse, will no more see its ancient splendor. It was the commerce of India and the borders of the red sea, flowing through these plains, more than inherent resources, which gave wealth and grandeur to ancient Egypt: these sources having found new channels, wealth and grandeur have flown with them. I can see nothing therefore on the celebrated Nile which the Ohio, Mississippi, Altamaha, Savannah, and Chesapeake, do not offer us: even her crocodiles and her *cajal* would have nothing to boast side and side by our allegators and catfish; they are precisely the same; and her *half grown mice* of geography can certainly be nothing more than abor-

Desert March 241

tions. But when I contrast the pure currents, healthful margins, and delightsome landscapes of our Susquehannah, Delaware, Hudson, and Connecticut, with the muddy waters, miry or parched banks and eternal desarts of this river; and the intelligence, freedom and felicity of the citizens there, with the stupid ignorance, riveted vassalage and hopeless misery of the peasants here, I almost lose the sensibility of pity in the glad reflection that I am a citizen of the United States.

Ruined temples, pyramids, and catacombs, monuments of the superstition, pride and folly of their founders, disgust my sight; for with their magnificence I cannot but couple the idea of the slaves who must have groaned under the oppressive folly of their fabrication. . . .

Sunday, March 3d. [1805] Left Alexandria, and joined Hamet Bashaw. . . . We had been several days delayed by the delinquency of Richard Farquhar, to whom I had intrusted the commissary's and quartermaster's department, and to whom from time to time I advanced a sum of $1350, which he chiefly embezzled or misapplied. In consequence of which I discharged him; and was obliged to make myself the provisions for our passage through the desert. . . .

March 5th. Freighted a caravan of 190 camels, as I supposed for the passage, at $11 per head. The Chiek il Taiib raised fresh demands for cash; and seemed determined to retard the march until his pretensions were satisfied. Pacified him with promises.

March 6th. Broke up camp and marched to Arab's tower, forty miles from Alexandria, leaving part of our baggage behind. This tower is an immense ruin . . about three hundred feet square, the walls five feet thick and thirty two high, with bastions at the angles, and battlements on the curtains. In its vicinity are catacombs and other excavations in the ridge of a freestone mountain upon which it stands, and which divides the sea shore from the barren plains in the rear. From Alexandria to this post is a desert. The tower is not Arabian architecture but Greek. . . .

March 8th. Arranged our caravan and organised our force; which now consisted of nine Americans, including Lieut. O'Bannon and Mr. Peck, a non-commissioned officer and six private marines; a company of twenty five cannoniers, commanded by Selim Comb, and Lieut.

Connant and Roco, and a company of thirty eight Greeks, commanded by Capt. Luco Ulovix and Lieut. Constantine. The Bashaw's suit consisted of about ninety men.... These, together with a party of Arab cavalry under the orders of the Cheik *il Taiib*, and Mahamet, and including the footmen and camel drivers, made our whole number about four hundred. Our caravan consisted of one hundred and seven camels and a few asses.

Marched at 11, A.M. fifteen miles. Camped on an elevated bluff upon the sea board. Good water near the shore.

March 9th. Remained in camp, some difficulties with the owners of the camels and horses hired for the passage. They demanded advanced pay. It was not safe to do it. They became mutinous.

March 10th. The camel drivers and footmen who followed the horses revolted and made a stand. The Cheik il Taiib had insinuated a suspicion among them that if they performed their services before being paid, the Christians would be apt to defraud them. The Bashaw seemed irresolute and despondent. Money, more money was the only stimulus which could give motion to the camp. The forenoon was consumed, and no appearances of a disposition to proceed ahead. I ordered the Christians under arms and feinted a countermarch; threatening to abandon the expedition and their Bashaw, unless the march in advance proceeded immediately. This project took effect; the mutiny was suppressed; and we marched twelve miles....

March 13th. Marched twenty five miles. These three days we have passed low sand valleys and rocky, desert plains. Few vestiges of ruins except a castle fifty miles from Arab's tower, which has all the appearance of Grecian architecture. About 2 o'clock, P.M. this day, a courier met the Bashaw, from Derne; informed him that the province was armed in his defence, and the Governor shut within the walls of his castle, (which we afterwards found to be false.) In consequence of this good news feats of horsemanship and a feu de joie were exhibited in front of the Bashaw, by his people. Our foot Arabs, who were in the rear with the baggage, hearing the firing, and apprehending that we were attacked by the wild Arabs of the desert, attempted to disarm and put to death the Christians who escorted the caravan. They were

Desert March 243

prevented by an Arab of some consideration among them, who insisted that prudence dictated they should suspend their execution till the cause of the firing should be known. . . .

March 17th. Morning rainy. Our Arabs refused to proceed farther without money. Reconciled them with promises. Marched twelve miles—camped in a deep ravine: some small brush and good rain water.

March 18th. . . . I now learned, for the first time, that our caravan was freighted by the Bashaw only to this place, and that the owners had received no part of their pay. No persuasion could prevail on them to proceed to Bomba, nor to wait our arrival thither for their pay. They alleged that they had fulfilled their engagement with the Bashaw, and would now return to their families in Behara, for whose safety they had serious apprehensions from the Kerchief of Demanhour. The Cheik il Taiib favored their pretensions.

I promised to procure the cash for their payment on condition that they would proceed two days further, where we expected to find Arab tribes and hire another caravan. This they engaged to do. I reduced my stock of cash to three Venetian sequins, and, with a hundred and forty dollars borrowed of the Christian officers and men, passed into the hands of the Bashaw, *six hundred and seventy three dollars*; which sum, together with what he raised among his own people, enabled him to meet the claims of these chiefs of the caravan.

March 19th. The Bashaw paid off his caravan, who promised to proceed two days march ahead. But, the same night, all except forty of them drew off for Egypt; and the others refused to proceed, leaving us in a perplexed and embarrassed situation; as it was impossible to move without the caravan, and uncertain whether we could procure them to start from this place. . . .

March 20th. Last night the rest of the camels left us, to return to Egypt. I now discovered a complot between the Cheik il Taiib and sundry other chiefs, at which I thought the Bashaw connived, purporting a resolution to proceed no further until they should have assurance of the arrival of our vessels at Bomba. . . .

We have marched a distance of two hundred miles, through an inhospitable waste of world without seeing the habitation of an animated being, or the tracks of man, except where superstition has marked her lonely steps over burning sands and rocky mountains, whence the revelation of one of her most hypocritical fanatics trains her wretched victims a tedious pilgrimage to pay their devotion at his shrine. But while we reproach the impostor we cannot but ascribe some good to the effect of the imposition: it has here and there opened a water source to its votaries, which now allays the thirst of pilgrims, bound across this gloomy desert on pursuits vastly different from those which lead to Mecca; the liberation of three hundred Americans from the chains of Barbarism, and a manly peace.

March 21st. . . . Fifty camels were prevailed on to return to us, and go on two days further. We marched at 11, A.M. and proceeded to an elevated stony plain barren, about 13 miles, where we found good cistern water. . . .

March 30th. . . . From Alexandria to this place, we have experienced continual altercations, contentions and delays among the Arabs. They have no sense of patriotism, truth nor honor; and no attachment where they have no prospect of gain, except to their religion, to which they are enthusiasts. Poverty makes them thieves, and practice renders them adroit in stealing. The instant the eye of vigilance is turned from an object on which they have fixed a desire, it is no more to be found. Arms, ammunition and provisions, most engage their furtive speculations; but sundry of our people have been robbed of their clothes and other articles. With all their depravity of morals they possess a savage independence of soul, an incorrigible obstinacy to discipline, a sacred adherence to the laws of hospitality, and a scrupulous pertinacity to their religious faith and ceremonies. Day before yesterday I was admitted, as a mark of special distinction, within the walls of their castle. Curiosity brought every Arab about me who belonged to the tribe. They examined the lace of my hat, epaulettes, buttons, spurs, and mounting of my arms. These they took to be all gold and silver. They were astonished *that God should permit people to possess such riches who followed the religion of the devil!*

Desert March 245

My interpreter explained that the religion of the Americans was different from that of all other nations who wore *hats*; (the *hat* and *turban* are distinguishing marks of *Christian* and *Turk*:) that we believed in God and respected all his revelations; that we made no distinction in our respect to people of different creeds; all were free with us to worship God as their consciences dictated; and that all honest men were equally respected in America....

The Bashaw fears desertions in case of approaching Derne without provisions. We have only three days half rations of rice, and no other supplies whatever: and, what renders our situation truly alarming, we can get no information of any vessels having appeared off the coast; as we now plainly perceive their arrival alone will prevent a revolt among our Arabs, who will undoubtedly take any side which will give them the best fare.

Seven o'clock, P.M. An officer came to my tent and informed me that mutiny was organized in the company of canoniers, and that they were about to embody and demand their full ration of provisions before this tent. I told him to endeavor by gentle means to suppress the mutiny; and, if he found this method impossible, to caution them on pain of death, not to appear in arms to make any remonstrances with me. At the same time sent for the issuing commissary to be informed of the exact quantity of rice on hand. I mentioned the disagreeable situation of affairs to no one but Mr. O'Bannon. Before any thing serious took place, about half past seven in the evening, the courier which had been dispatched to Bomba arrived with intelligence of our vessels being off that place and Derne. In an instant the face of every thing changed from pensive gloom to enthusiastic gladness. Nothing more heard of the mutiny. The Arabs resumed confidence. And the Bashaw promised to force the residue of our march to Bomba.

Nine in the evening. The Bashaw attacked by spasms and vomiting; continued the greater part of the night.

April 11th. Marched at 6, A.M. gained five miles a head, and camped. The Bashaw's indisposition rendered a halt indispensable. No water. Discovered a singular commerce between our soldiers and the Arab women. They exchanged their buttons, which they cut from their clothes, for dates. The women strung them as ornaments about their necks. Six, P.M. The Bashaw recovers.

April 12th. Marched twenty five miles; the first part of the day in the continuation of the valley mentioned the tenth; but camped on an eminence where there was neither water nor fuel. The residue of our rice issued to day; but the troops were obliged to eat it without cooking. Such of the Arab tribes as moved with their families camped five miles in the rear; being unable to come up, exhausted by fatigue and hunger.

April 13th. Marched seven and a half miles. Hunger and fatigue rendered the foot soldiers and Bedouin families unable to pursue the march. The Bashaw killed and issued one of his camels of burthen, and exchanged another with the Arabs for sheep; which together gave a full ration to our troops, but they were without bread or salt.

April 14th. Marched fifteen miles. Camped in a pleasant valley of rich strong land, but totally uncultivated. Good and abundance of feed for our horses, and sundry cisterns excavated in the ridges on the borders of the valley contained excellent rain water; but we were totally destitute of provisions. Near these cisterns and in the valleys are ruins of ancient architecture and visible marks of former cultivation; but now all is waste.

April 15th. Marched at seven in the morning. Our people this day scattered throughout all the plain in search of roots and vegetable substances to appease the cravings of hunger. A species of wild fennel and sorrel which we found in the small ravines contributed something to our support. At 4 o'clock P.M. we reached Bomba. But what was my astonishment to find at this celebrated port not the foot trace of a human being, nor a drop of water. And what my mortification to find no vessels here. We had this day taken up three Arabs who gave me positive declarations that they had seen two vessels. . . .

April 23d. Cold, high winds with rain. Marched ten miles over a mountainous rocky country, and camped in a ravine, within a mile from a natural source of water, springing from the top of a mountain of freestone, near cape Razatine. This is the first natural spring we have found since leaving Egypt. We are approaching cultivated fields. A herald cries through the camp—"he who fears God and feels attachment to Hamet Bashaw will be careful to destroy nothing. Let no one touch the growing harvest. He who transgresses this injunction shall lose his right hand!"

April 24th. Marched fifteen miles over mountainous and broken ground, covered with herbage and very large and beautiful red cedars: the first resemblance of a forest tree we have seen during a march of nearly six hundred miles. Camped in a pleasant valley, by a natural rivulet bordered with delightsome verdure and fields of barley, about five hours march from Derne. Certain information came to us here that the Governor of the country had fortified himself and was determined to defend the city against our approach. The same courier confirmed the intelligence which had frequently before been stated to us that the army of Joseph Bashaw, which he had sent out for the defence of the province, were near Derne, and would probably, by a forced march arrive before us; especially if we waited the return of our vessels to the coast, which had been blown off in the gale of the 23d. Alarm and consternation seized the Arab chiefs; and despondency the Bashaw. The night was passed in consultations among them at which I was not admitted.

April 25th. At six in the morning beat the general and gave orders for marching. The Arabs mutinized. The Cheiks il Taiib and Mahamet at the head of the Arab cavalry took up a retrograde march, and the Bedouins refused to strike their tents. After much persuasion, some reproach, and a promise of two thousand dollars to be shared among the chiefs, they were prevailed on to advance: and at two o'clock, P.M. we camped on an eminence which overlooks Derne . . . .

Derne, April 29th, 1805.

Sir,*

. . . I did not leave Alexandria till the third of last month. The host of Arabs, who accompanied the Bashaw from that place and joined him

---

* To James Barron, commander-in-chief of the U. S. forces in the Mediterranean.

on the rout, moving chiefly with their families and flocks, rendered our progress through the desert slow and painful; add to this the ungovernable temper of this marauding militia, and the frequent fits of despondency, amounting sometimes to mutiny, occasioned by information, almost every day meeting us, of formidable reenforcements from the enemy for the defence of this place, and it will not seem unaccountable that it was not till the fifteenth instant we arrived at Bomba. We had now been twenty five days without meat, and fifteen without bread, subsisting on rice. Happily, the next morning, discovered the Argus, to whom I made signals by smoke, which were discovered and answered. The Hornet soon after appeared. Capt. Hull sent off a boat. I went on board, and had the honor and inexpressible satisfaction of receiving your communications of 22d ult. The timely supplies which came forward in these vessels gave animation to our half famished people; and no time was lost in moving forward. On the morning of the 25th, we took post on an eminence in the rear of Derne. Several chiefs came out to meet the Bashaw with assurances of fealty and attachment. By them I learned that the city was divided into three departments; two of which were in the interest of the Bashaw, and one in opposition. This department, though fewest in numbers, was strongest in position and resource, being defended by a battery of eight guns, the blind walls of the houses which are provided in all directions with loop holes for musketry, and by temporary parapets thrown up in several positions not covered by the battery; this department is the nearest the sea and the residence of the Bey. On the morning of the 26th, terms of amity were offered the Bey on condition of allegiance and fidelity. The flag of truce was sent back to me with this laconic answer, "My head or yours!"—at 2, P.M. discovered the Nautilus, and spoke her at six. At 6 in the morning of the 27th, the Argus and Hornet appeared and stood in. I immediately put the army in motion, and advanced towards the city. A favorable land breeze enabled the Nautilus and Hornet to approach the shore, which is a steep and rugged declivity of rocks. With much difficulty we landed, and drew up the precipice one of the field pieces; both were sent in the boat for the purpose, but the apprehension of losing this favorable moment of attack induced me to leave one on board. We advanced to our positions. A fire commenced on the shipping. Lieut. Evans stood in, and, anchoring within one hundred yards of the battery, opened a well directed fire. Lieut. Dant dropped in and anchored in a position to bring his guns to bear on the battery and city. And Capt. Commandant Hull brought the Argus to anchor a little south of the Nautilus, so near as to throw her 24 pound shot quite into the town. A detachment of six American marines, a company of 24 cannoniers, and another of 26 Greeks, including their proper officers, all under the immediate command of Lieut. O'Bannon, together with a few Arabs on foot, had a position on an eminence opposite to a considerable party of the enemy, who had taken post behind their temporary parapets and in a ravine at the S.E. quarter of the town. The Bashaw seized an old castle which overlooked the town on the S.S.W. disposing his cavalry upon the plains in the rear. A little before 2, P.M. the fire became general in all quarters where Tripolitans and Americans were opposed to each other. In three quarters of an hour the battery was silenced, but not abandoned; though most of the enemy withdrew precipitately from that quarter and joined the party opposed to the handful of Christians with me, which appeared our most vulnerable point. Unfortunately the fire of our field piece was relaxed by the rammer being shot away. The fire of the enemy's musketry became too warm, and continually augmenting. Our troops were thrown into confusion; and, undisciplined as they were, it was impossible to reduce them to order. I perceived a charge our dernier and only resort. We rushed forward against a host of savages more than ten to our one. They fled from their coverts irregularly, firing in retreat from every palm tree and partition wall in their way. At this moment I received a ball through my left wrist which deprived me of the use of the hand, and of course of my rifle. Mr. O'Bannon, accompanied by Mr. Mann of Annapolis, urged forward with his marines, Greeks, and such of the cannoniers as were not necessary to the management of the field piece; passed through a shower of musketry from the walls of houses; took possession of the battery; planted the American flag upon its ramparts; and turned its guns upon the enemy; who, being now driven from their out posts, fired only from their houses, from which they were soon dislodged by the whole fire of the vessels, which was suspended during the charge, being directed into them. The Bashaw soon got possession of the Bey's palace; his cavalry flanked the flying enemy; and a little after four o'clock we had compleat possession of the town. . . .

In Flanders Fields
ALEXANDER J. M. TUCK

⫸ After World War I, in which he was twice wounded and was awarded the British Military Cross, Alexander Tuck 1914 had a business career. He was again in uniform in World War II, serving in Italy as an intelligence officer in the United States Air Corps. The following chapter of war experience was published in the December 1915 number of the *Alumni Magazine*.

AT THE OPENING of the war I was at Oxford, taking some lectures to complete my course for the Bachelor of Arts degree which was later given to me by Dartmouth College. In the midst of all the European excitement it did not take me long to decide that I would like to join one of the Allied Armies. I tried at first to join the Foreign Legion in France, with little success or encouragement. After this I joined the University and Public School Battalions, which were known as the 18th to the 21st Royal Fusiliers. These battalions were made up of men from the great public schools and universities of England. It was not long before the mistake of inaugurating these battalions was realized. With the large armies that England would have to raise it soon became apparent that these men should be trained as officers rather than private soldiers, with the result that shortly after the formation of these Battalions men with any military experience whatsoever applied for and received Commissions to the battalions of the new armies. Being an American, I had a great deal of difficulty in taking a Commission, until finally I ran across a Battalion whose senior Officers knew my people when the battalion was stationed in Egypt. This Battalion was the 7th King's Own Scottish Borderers. I was given my Commission in this regiment as a Second Lieutenant in January, 1915. I had learned the rudiments of battalion and company drill while I was in the ranks, which stood me in good stead in this new unit.

Our camp was very near Aldershot, and we spent six weeks doing our musketry course on the most desolate range and in the most awful weather I have ever seen. From here we moved to Winchester, where we went into billets. We enjoyed our stay of six weeks here a great deal. It is one of the prettiest towns imaginable, with its glorious cathedral and the beautiful surrounding country. It was in this country, in the very early spring, that we did most of our field manoeuvres. At the end of six weeks we moved to a camp on Salisbury Plain, which had recently been evacuated by the Canadians. Here we went into tents for the first time, and the life in this bracing air had a beneficial effect on the health of the men. After a month in this camp we moved to Draycott Camp, near Swindon, in Wiltshire. Here we fired our second musketry course. By this time I had been made one of the two Machine-Gun Officers which each Battalion has, and we did our machine-gun training on the same range as the men used for their musketry.

After we had been here about two months, the men were plainly showing signs of staleness, and we were feeling rather discouraged at not having been sent out sooner. Early in July rumours started flying about our departure for the Continent. Shortly after this we were reviewed by the King as a Division, and then we realized that the rumours were no doubt true. Sure enough, on the evening of the 5th we received our mobilization orders, and on the 10th of July we entrained for Folkestone and sailed that same night for Boulogne. An hour after our arrival in this town we were asleep in our tents in a rest camp, so well were all the details of our disembarkation arranged.

The following night, at 2 o'clock, we marched four miles to Pont-les-Briques, where we once more entrained for the Front. We arrived the following morning at Audruicq. A very short march brought us to Ostove, where we spent four days. We found ourselves here in the middle of the cherry season, which was a source of great pleasure to the men as nowhere else are there to be found such wonderful cherries as in this part of the country. The weather all this time continued to be excellent. From here we started a long trek which roughly speaking was parallel to the fighting line. It led us through Zutquerque, Lam-

In Flanders Fields 253

bres, St. Omer, Aire, Lillers, and finally to Allouagne. This was a distance of about 60 miles, accomplished in three and a half days' marching. We had a great deal of trouble with the men's feet, as the ammunition boots with which they had been served out just before leaving England had not been worn long enough. After a few days at Allouagne, Major Gordon Forbes, C.M G., D.S.O., Lieutenant Scott, known in the regiment as "Wee" Scott because his father had been in the regiment with us in England and who was the other machine-gun Officer, and myself were sent up to the trenches on a tour of instruction. These tours were locally known as "Cook's Tours." Unfortunately, on the second day of this trip, Major Forbes, our Second in Command, was killed by a stray shell. When we returned to the regiment we found that the Colonel, who had been working very hard in the last few months, was seriously ill and had been sent off to the base. In addition to this our Brigadier had had a bad fall from his horse and had also been sent down country with concussion. Luckily we had a very efficient Third in Command to take charge of us. In the meantime during these mishaps the Companies had been sent up to the trenches as half companies on tours of instruction.

Soon after this we marched off to take our regular place in the fighting line, or rather fighting trenches. The stays in the trenches varied anywhere from two to eight days, which were usually followed by two or four days in rest billets, and in this way we spent our summer, with very little excitement after the novelty of the life had worn off. And then it was noised about that a great attack was impending. The details came to us, but unfortunately the attack was postponed. Finally we were told that it was to take place on the 25th of September. It was preceded by four days and four nights heavy bombardment. This was to break up the enemy's barbed wire, and was to be followed by a forty-minute gas attack. On the night of the 24th we took our places in the trenches, relieving an outgoing battalion. Our objectives had been given to us as follows: Our Brigade was to attack to the left of Loos, taking a half right wheel and finally to take Hill 70. The next Brigade on our right had the village of Loos itself to invest, and the third Brigade of the Division was to support these two attacks. Of course this is a very small part of the general attack, but it was what concerned us most. One's idea of an attack and an attack itself are two very different things. After a good meal in an interesting restaurant with a good orchestra playing, one often feels very capable. Annihilating a company of Germans seems a very small thing;—at least that is the way I have often felt. But the attack itself is a very different thing.

Let me give you the details. We did not take our places in the trenches until about midnight of the 24th. The rest of that night was spent in dealing out the next morning's rations and in filling the new machine-gun magazines which we had just drawn from the ordnance. All through the night there was a steady drizzle, and then a hopeless grey dawn broke upon us, everyone wet through by this time and feeling like anything but an attack. The scanty breakfast was quickly served out and consumed. For this great attack the breakfast included an ounce and a half of rum for each man. This allowance of rum varies both as to its frequency of issue and amount, and is usually put in the men's tea, to keep them from hoarding it up and making an occasion of its consumption at the end of the month. That morning it was given to us neat, and well we needed it. At 5:40 we started our gas, and huge gusts of this yellowish green vapour started drifting towards the enemy trenches. Our Battalion had been given the honor of leading the attack on Hill 70 and we were to be the first out of the trenches.

No sooner had our gas started than a veritable hail of German machine-gun fire could be heard on the parapet of our trench. By this time the Germans could no longer see our trenches, but having previously fixed their guns on our trench parapets their fire was only too accurate. At the same time their guns started bursting shrapnel over us with equal accuracy. Words of mine could never describe the noise and din of all this firing. All we knew was that at the end of forty minutes we were to leave our trenches and start our attack. Our watches had been synchronized the night before with those of the Engineers who were controlling the gas. Then orders started coming down the trenches. "Fix bayonets" was the first order, and this was hastily and willingly complied with. Then the cry came down: "Remember the 25th," for this was the number of our regiment as it was known in the old days. The next order came: "Put on gas helmets," and then we knew that only a few minutes separated us from the comparative safety of our trench and the veritable sheet of lead outside. The air by this time reeked of a sickening sweet smell of high explosive and shrapnel shells and the atmosphere was even more clouded by the faint smoke of these.

It had been prearranged that as we left our trenches automatically our artillery was to lift its curtain of fire from the German first line trenches to their second, and as we advanced to their third, and so on, time limits being given for these movements. As the 40th minute ticked itself into eternity orders were given and the men climbed up on the fire steps and over the parapet. We threw our heavy tripods over the parapet, passing the guns and magazines after them, and straightened out our line so as to resemble the formation of the infantry as much as possible. I had not advanced more than forty yards when a shell burst over us, the concussion of which as well as the fragments knocked men all around me to the ground. At the same time as I fell I felt a blow in my hand and chest. What followed directly after this is very hazy in my mind, and what concerns the advance of the regiment has been told me since. I found later that I had been shot through the right hand and a flesh wound in the left breast. I got up working more as a machine than myself before I stumbled and fell again thirty yards further on. Our machine-gun team only went on and I learned later that this team was knocked out two minutes afterwards.

I remember vaguely crawling into a shell hole and from there being helped into the head of a sap by a stretcher-bearer. These saps are short trenches that run out from the main trench at right angles and are used as listening posts. Here a stretcher bearer gave me a first field dressing, and later I found my way to Quality Street, which was the name given to a very small mining village which was being used as a small base for the attack of these two Brigades. Here was a scene which none who saw it could ever forget.... The street was covered with men lying on the pavements or just sitting wherever they found room; other men lying on the coal trucks, whose upper frame work had been so changed as to hold three stretchers. Here dressings were being applied to the most serious cases. The street literally ran red with hot fresh blood, and although half a dozen shells would have wiped out the lot the enemy were too busy with our advancing infantry to bother about this place. And so we were passed on in motor ambulances to various casualty clearing stations, until we reached one about five miles behind the lines. Here we remained all afternoon until the large motor ambulance convoy started that night for Lapuygnoir. Here we were put in the Red Cross train, consisting of twenty-eight carriages of sitting and lying cases and we started our trip down country.

When we reached Abbeville, which is very near Boulogne, we were told that our destination was Versailles. This was very much to my liking, because I happened to know that the morning of the attack my people had left England to stay with their friends, Mr. and Mrs. Edward Tuck, on their way through to Egypt, at the Château de Vert-Mont, which was only twenty minutes by motor from Versailles. We reached the hospital at Versailles, which had formerly been the Hotel Trianon, a very comfortable and luxurious sort of place. The next morning I saw my people, a very lucky coincidence as it was more than likely that we should have been sent straight through to England and a few days later my family would have been on their way to Egypt.

It was here that we first learned the price the regiment had paid. The official casualties in officers out of the twenty who went to the attack, were 14 killed or died of wounds, five wounded and one alone came through untouched. Yesterday I went to the funeral of our Colonel who had died of his wounds in the same hospital at Versailles, a very gallant soldier, who had returned to his regiment after having been retired four years and had been given the command of this new Battalion. Out of 1000 peace loving citizens in a few months he had made a perfect machine. After I fell I remember seeing lines of Khaki advancing towards the German trenches which were then invisible on account of the gas, and later I realized how great had been the work of our Colonel and how successful it had all proved. He was buried with full military honors, accompanied by 200 Cuirassiers and a small detachment of English troops from the hospital. I have learned that one of our pipers has been recommended for the V. C. His gallantry consisted in walking up and down the parapet after the hail of bullets had started and piping his men to the attack.

In a few days I return to the base, from which place I will be sent up to what is left of the regiment, which is now refitting behind the line. New draughts of officers and men are arriving shortly. The casualties in the ranks we do not know officially as yet, but they must number well over 500 men out of a thousand, as the casualties in the Brigade, consisting of four Battalions were 2000 out of 3500. The Officer casualties in the Brigade number 72 out of 80. And this was the price a Battalion paid for leading a Brigade, and a Brigade paid for leading an attack which resulted in the capture of Hill 70 and the village of Loos.

The Liberation of Rome

HAROLD L. BOND

❧❧❧ *Return to Cassino* (New York, 1964), Harold Bond's memoirs of wartime experiences in Italy, was published in 1964, twenty years after the Allied entry into Rome that is described in the passages from his book that are reprinted here. A member of the Class of 1942, a professor of English, he has been on the Dartmouth faculty since 1952.

There was no noise in the city except for the rumble of our tanks and the sound of our trucks behind us. Trees with the full green foliage of summer lined the route. The tanks moved slowly, and we had gone almost a full mile without seeing a single person. The air was clean and fresh, and the slanting beams of the rising sun shone orange-yellow on the buildings as we passed. Then, out of nowhere seemingly, people began to appear, Romans in their bathrobes and nightdresses, cautiously, a few at a time, and then more and more. Someone started cheering, and very soon the streets were lined with people, clapping, calling gleefully to one another, shouting. We waved back to them, smiling, but kept moving at the same speed straight on.

Soon the column came down a slight hill and there on our left stood the enormous Colosseum, glowing in the early morning sunshine. There was no one near it, and its empty arches stood out boldly against the sky. Ahead of us was the wide avenue, entirely deserted, while behind our jeep, after we passed, the crowd of Romans grew and grew. On our left was the temple of Venus and Rome, and then the ruins of the Basilica of Constantine at the edge of the Forum. We passed the Imperial Forum on our right and the triumphant column of Trajan, the modern vehicles of war clanking and rumbling over ground trod by the emperors of old. Soon we entered the Piazza Venezia, with the gigantic monument erected by Victor Emmanuel II to the Italian victory in World War I, its white marble looking pink where the sun hit it at the top. The soldiers were soon to dub this "the wedding cake," instinctively recognizing its tasteless extravagance. Down in the square in front of the monument we were still in the shadows, for the sun was only just above the horizon, but we could clearly see the window in the Palazzo Venezia where Mussolini had stood in all his pride, so many times, to harangue his fanatical followers.

This square, too, was deserted as we entered, perhaps the only time in recent history when one could not see a soul at Rome's busiest crossroads. But as we drove ahead through the deserted streets we had the sense of thousands of eyes watching us from behind closed blinds, waiting to see what we would do. Not a shot had been fired, and as soon as we had peacefully passed crowds swarmed into the streets. But at the head of the column we saw empty streets and shuttered windows. There was not a person, a car, a bus, anywhere.

All of my life I had wanted to see Rome but when as a boy I read Caesar and struggled through the orations of Cicero I had never dreamed that I would see Rome for the first time from the back of a jeep, the city waiting in empty silence, expectantly watching as the victors moved through. How different was our steady, measured march this early morning from the riotous pillaging of the Goths, or the cruel and bloody sack of the city by the troops of Charles V! Passing the Forum, just behind the lead tank in an assault column, the general and I [the general's aide de camp] might have felt that nearly three thousand years of history had come together in a moment, but I at that time had not read enough history to realize what those three thousand years had been. I do not know what went through the general's mind, but in mine there was merely excitement, born of my awareness that something significant was happening, something which I did not fully understand. Had I had more knowledge at the time, perhaps the one dominant thought in my mind would have been that people do not really change, and that after three thousand years we were engaged in doing much the same things for very much the same reasons that the first citizens of the ancient Roman Republic had done; and in freeing Rome from Mussolini and Hitler we were helping the city in her eternal fight against barbarism. Rome's great mission has been to civilize the world, and a truth which the Romans understood and passed on to future generations was that barbarism often has to be stamped out by war. Now British and Americans, both of whom had taken so much of their culture and so many of their ideals from the mother city, were slowly marching through the ancient streets, come from thousands of miles away, some to die, others to live to see a kind of victory, so that these ideals could continue to live in the spirits of men. Our methods were different from those of the Roman legions. Instead of swords, pikes, and javelins we had guns and shells and tanks; but our ends were the same as theirs. I did not think of these things that morning, however; instead I kept my eye on the lead tank and the deserted streets in front of it, wondering what would come next.

Soon our column was approaching the Tiber, and there across the river was the Castel Sant' Angelo. The warring angel Michael, holding his sword, gleamed brightly at the top. As we came to the Tiber we were relieved to find that none of the bridges had been blown. The way was clear to cross over and continue our march. We crossed near the castle and, looking up to its great ramparts, I could not see anyone. Here Hadrian had been buried and Benvenuto Cellini had been imprisoned. It had been the residence of many popes; and from these ramparts, so the opera goes, Tosca jumped to her death. Later I was to explore the castle, but this morning we silently passed by its huge bolted doors.

The road led up a wide street which Mussolini had built, tearing down the horrible slums which had for centuries disfigured the west banks of the Tiber. At the end stood the giant Basilica of St. Peter, with Michelangelo's dome towering high above it, delicate in design, yet solid and huge in the early morning light. The two great fountains in St. Peter's Square were not playing, and nobody was in sight. Not even a pigeon moved in the square. Our leading tank clanked across the cobblestones and came to a halt. The long arms of Bernini's enormous porticoes encircled the front of the column. Our medium tanks looked tiny in the face of such grandeur. The Italian guides were talking excitedly to the tank commander, and they seemed to be arguing among themselves as to where they should go now. Behind us, winding for many miles through the city, stretched the column of the entire 36th Division, tanks, troop carriers, jeeps, long regiments of infantrymen, all halted now that the head of the column had stopped.

The general got himself slowly out of the jeep to see what the matter was. He had recognized the Vatican and cried out angrily, "We can't go in here. We'll create an international incident!" He walked up to where the Italian guides were gesticulating heatedly. He understood no Italian, and I had known him long enough now to realize something of his impatience. It looked to him as if the guides did not know what they were doing, as if they had now got us into a mess by leading us into Vatican City. The leading tank was pointed straight at the stairs which led up to St. Peter's.

The general looked at his map briefly, then angrily roared at the tank commander, "Go that way!" and pointed to a street leading out of St. Peter's Square on the right. The tank commander said, "Yes, sir!" and started to turn his bulky vehicle. The Italian guides, who knew that this was the wrong way, started to protest, but the general motioned to them to be quiet. This short scene was the cause of considerable confusion.

The long column turned, and we drove out of St. Peter's Square toward the northeast, following the esplanade which leads along the north banks of the Tiber. The sun was now shining brightly on the streets and houses, and life was appearing all over the city. Crowds were forming along both sides of the road, and there was much shouting and cheering as we rolled along. Very soon we saw ahead of us another long column of American troops, streaming over one of the bridges and cutting directly across the road in front of us. It was all too clear that the general had given the wrong orders. He now had the entire front part of the column lost and on the wrong road. I had known nothing about our orders. The general had not told me, and I had no way of finding out, so I was not in a position to help him. He got out of the jeep when our column had to stop and consulted with the Italian guides, this time quietly and with some humility. We had turned right, out of St. Peter's Square, when we should have turned left. There was nothing to be done but turn around and go back.

There were some trolley tracks in the center of the big highway, and after crossing these we started to lead the column toward the Vatican again; but now, with crowds all over the streets, and with Romans bringing their own cars out, we had slow going, and it looked as if a major traffic jam was building up. The tank in front pushed its way slowly through the crowd, while excited Romans jumped up onto the turret, shouting and waving flags. One blond-haired man with a Luger revolver at his waist, dressed in civilian clothes, jumped aboard our jeep. He shouted to his comrades to follow him. They would all join in our pursuit of the Germans. He spoke broken English with what seemed to me a German accent, and I wondered at the time whether this was not the last arrogant act of some German officer, caught in the city, showing his contempt for us by getting aboard our very vehicles as we rode through. But he may, in fact, have been a legitimate partisan; many of them had been active in the city. The general had trouble enough without having an extra, excited passenger, so I made the man get off.

Meanwhile, confusion was growing in front of us, and our column came to a full halt, hopelessly snarled, it appeared, in a huge traffic jam. MPs arrived to try to straighten out the tangle, and wild crowds of cheering Romans raced around us. The general, completely chagrined, sat quietly in his jeep. Soon the division commander came up in his jeep. He was furious with Stack for having mistaken the turn. The consequences could have been serious. It was of utmost importance to the army to get the troops through the city as quickly and in as orderly a fashion as possible, and out to the other side to make contact with the Germans again. Instead of doing this, our division was in a bad tangle right in the middle of the city. The other American divisions were streaming through on their prescribed routes quickly and efficiently. But gradually the MPs got the troops on the right roads again, and General Stack, who had shown his ability and shrewd military skill at

The Liberation of Rome   263

Velletri by cracking the German lines, weathered the short storm of his commander's wrath over the traffic jam.

Back on the other side of the Tiber, the high-ranking officers of the army command were entering the city. The army commander, the three stars of his rank brightly displayed against a red background on the front of his jeep, was greeted with tremendous cheers as he drove along the streets. Obviously he was enjoying his role as hero of the hour. Not long after, he could be seen posing on Mussolini's balcony on the Palazzo Venezia, while press photographers snapped their flash bulbs.

The Romans were singing and dancing, throwing flowers to the American troops as they marched through. The square in front of the Colosseum was jammed with people, with soldiers, and with army vehicles. Bottles of wine were brought out of their hiding places in cellars and from under floors and freely offered to the Americans. Fruit, which could hardly be spared by the hungry Romans, was generously offered to the tired infantrymen, and everywhere there was rejoicing. So far as we could tell there were no Germans left in the city, and not a shot was fired on this brilliant, happy morning. The gray, weathered stones and broken pillars of the ancient Forum looked down once again on a triumphal procession. But no captives were dragged at the wheels of the conqueror's chariot, and instead of celebrating the final victory, the successful completion of a war, our march through Rome was but one stage on the way to the final victory. There were no bands, either, no blaring of trumpets, and no long-haired barbarians to provide a spectacle for the citizens of Rome. Instead of elephants, huge tanks and the long artillery pieces of modern war lumbered over the ancient cobblestones. Instead of the Roman legions with their polished breastplates and shining helmets, unshaven infantrymen in their dirty clothes, some with camouflage netting still on their helmets, most of them without much sleep for several days, marched slowly along, taking now a drink of precious wine offered by an enthusiastic citizen, offering in return an extra cigarette.

The sun was high in the sky before the 36th finally untangled itself from the jam General Stack had got it into, and the front of the column began to make its way slowly up the Janiculum Hill where, a century before, Garibaldi had fought so bravely for the freedom of Italy. . . .

The division . . . set up its command post at a villa on the Janiculum Hill on the edge of the city. This was a fine Renaissance mansion, elaborately adorned with sculpture and medallions on the walls. Formal gardens, laid out with pools and cypress trees and enclosed with flowering hedges, graced the grounds and gave the place an elegance rarely seen in the modern world. In sharp contrast to this beauty were our olive-drab tents and vehicles which cluttered the garden and grounds. Now the villa was empty of all former inhabitants. The furniture had been removed, and the vacant rooms and halls, beautifully decorated with richly colored murals, this night housed the war room with its maps, and division intelligence and supply officers. The generals' caravans had been placed in the shade in the corner of the garden under some flowering trees, while the generals' mess was backed up against a laurel and rhododendron hedge. All of us were exhausted from the excitement of the day, and my general retired to his caravan immediately after eating. I found that despite my fatigue I could not sleep.

There is a terraced walk on the Janiculum not far from the villa which affords a superb view of the whole city. In the gathering dusk I strolled out there, hoping to fix in my mind the image of Rome on the night of our victory. Even in wartime, city gardeners had been busy tending the beds alongside this walk, and the air was heavy with the scent of many June flowers. The first stars of the evening were coming out. The air was warm. Almost no one but myself was on the terrace. Down in the city, lights were coming on in the many villas and apartments, despite the old, standing orders for a blackout; but the great monuments of the past, the Colosseum, the ruins of the palaces, the columns of Trajan and Marcus Aurelius were slowly lost in the increasing darkness. For nearly three thousand years men had lived on these hills and in the valleys that I now looked out upon. Nor had they been, in their strife and turmoil, their loves and hates, much different from ourselves. Eternal Rome had been and still was the center of our civilization. Pagan, Christian, enlightened, romantic, agnostic, from

The Liberation of Rome   265

youth to ripeness to decadence, to new truth, Rome has always been revitalized and rejuvenated. She still provided, even in her decay, inspiration to successive generations of men. The marble fragments, the ruins of the palaces, the great Renaissance villas, the hundreds of fountains, the aged cypress and cedar trees, all made this a unique city, one of the "quick" spots of the earth. There was life here, insuppressible life, welling up always like the marvelous fountains, which could not be stopped despite conquest, disaster, decline, the loss of empire, the coming of every kind of evil. Tyranny in all of its forms—the latest being Fascism—and even the loss of faith in the meaning of life could not suppress the eternal vitality in this ageless city. So long as men walk this tired earth, Rome will be a center for them . . .

Far below me the Tiber, which looked muddy and dirty in the daytime, reflected the many lights along its bank, soft and shimmering in the night. An occasional sound of music floated up from the celebrating city, and now and again one could hear laughter from the houses stretched out below. Rome was now entirely in the hands of the Allies: Americans, British, New Zealanders, Canadians, Brazilians, French, Indians, North Africans. Soldiers from every continent in the world had participated in her liberation. Officers of the Allied military government were already beginning to take over responsibility for civil services. Colonels and clerks from army headquarters were busily establishing themselves in new comfort, not to say luxury, in the great hotels of the city. The last of the combat units had cleared out on their way north in pursuit of the fleeing Germans. . . . I took one last stroll along the terrace. The moon was rising slowly in the east when I finally turned my back on the city. Tomorrow there would be more fighting, more driving ahead, and for some of my friends in the infantry companies, death in the valleys and passes to the north.

Able Day

DAVID BRADLEY

≫ It was as a medical man that David Bradley 1938 served at the Bikini atomic bomb tests and acquired the material for his well-known *No Place to Hide* (Boston, 1948), from which the selections below are taken. He has been a war correspondent, a teacher and lecturer, a selectman of the town of Hanover and a member of the New Hampshire legislature.

ABLE DAY—MONDAY, JULY 1, 1946

OUR ALARM CLOCKS rang at 3:30. Last-minute reports showed that Able Day had arrived as scheduled. With the remainder of our gear we stumbled through the darkness to Squadron Headquarters, where the crews and pilots were gathering. My plane had been at her mooring all night, and so after digging up a few spare canisters for the gas masks I hiked across the cement apron to the wharf. In the faint light our giant birds were being trundled off to the launching ramp, their engines spitting bursts of fire and thunder in last-minute checks. I felt very small among such birds. . . .

This was Able Day. What would happen when *Dave's Dream* hatched its famous egg? Would the prophecies they had read and heard be fulfilled—would pieces of our venerable Navy be spread all over the Pacific from the Philippines to Panama? Would a tidal wave sweep the islands clean and surge on to inundate Los Angeles? Would, indeed, the very water itself become involved in a chain reaction until the whole Pacific Ocean disappeared in a colossal eruption? Who was to say? Or who, at least, was to say No? . . .

By 5:30 in the first light of dawn we were airborne, climbing slowly to 8000 feet and swinging away to the northwest. Dawn came and passed unnoticed. There was much to do, and the sweet singing of our twin motors, perfectly tuned for their day of work, seemed to warn that they would give me only a minimum of time to prepare. First there were the instruments on the navigation table. Turning them on, I tested each one with a small pocket radium source. Over the Geiger counters the clicks were coming in at their usual hundred or so counts per minute. The cosmic rays were manifesting no particular excitement over the approaching explosion. Next there were the film badges, protective goggles, and gas masks to pass out to all hands....

The live fleet was strung out in several columns under us, and some twenty miles away the target fleet was visible bunched up at one end of the [Bikini] lagoon.... At 3000 feet we were running into a steady sea of fleecy clouds and there was some doubt in our minds whether the drop ship could make out the target. However, we soon picked up the broadcast we had been waiting for. Calmly and slowly the bombardier aboard *Dave's Dream* was saying "This is Skylight One, Skylight One. Ten minutes before first simulated bomb release. Stand by. Mark: ten minutes before first simulated bomb release. First practice run."

It came through clear and sharp and instinctively we looked up even though we knew that Skylight One was too high to be visible. Radio silence had been ordered throughout the fleet so that all planes and ships could hear the big bomber.

"This is Skylight One, Skylight One," came the voice again. "Two minutes before simulated bomb release. Two minutes before simulated bomb release. Stand by. Mark: first practice run."

By this time, Commander Pew had checked in with the control ship and was lazily circling in his prescribed area. Since we were to work together, we fell in behind him about a half mile distant. The sight of another ship suddenly evoked a feeling of the loneliness of our mission. Everything to do with the task force had to be done by remote control. There was the target—twenty miles away to the southwest, barely visible in the hazy sunlight. There was part of the live fleet a good ten miles farther from the target than we. Overhead we knew the sky to be full of planes, some of them five or six miles aloft, and yet none were to be seen. The capricious radio was to be our only contact with the gigantic movement.

The voice from above called the one minute mark—then, "This is Skylight One, Skylight One. Coming up on simulated bomb release. Stand by. Mark: end of first practice run, first practice run." In our minds we could see the slim, silvery B-29 swinging slowly away to begin her next run. Would this be it?

As though in answer the calm voice said: "This is Skylight One, Skylight One. Predicted time of actual bomb release 30 minutes. Predicted time of actual release 30 minutes."

Then our control ship, Sadeyes, came in. "Skylight One, this is Sadeyes. Over."

The answer came at once: "Sadeyes, this is Skylight One. Over."

"Skylight One, this is Sadeyes. Interrogation: will you say how conditions were for bombing on your first practice run? Over."

"Sadeyes, this is Skylight One. Bombing conditions were okay [with a trace of satisfaction in the 'okay']. Over."

"Sadeyes to Skylight One. Roger—out!"

We made another sweep over the fleet.... The ships were strung out in Indian file and barely stirring up a green wake. You could see the people standing motionless at the rail, watching the faint smudge of Bikini Atoll on the horizon line. Even the smoke lazily tailing out from the stacks seemed intent upon the fateful island. For all the roar of our twin engines, everything seemed to be holding a breathless silence. Finally, after twenty minutes had passed and no sound had come from Skylight One, our radioman began to get the jitters. Suppose we shouldn't receive the word of the bomb drop, and were blinded by the flash. He began to spin his dials. What a relief when the words came through, calm as ever: "This is Skylight One, Skylight One. Five minutes before actual bomb release. Mark: five minutes before actual bomb release. Stand by."

Five minutes!

"Skylight One, Skylight One. Two minutes before actual bomb release. Mark: two minutes before actual bomb release. Adjust all goggles. Adjust all goggles. Stand by."

And then at last: "Coming up on actual bomb release. Stand by.... [an eternity]... Bomb away. Bomb away. Bomb away. Bomb away."

Able Day 269

I began to count the seconds to myself. Skylight One would be up on one wing, going into a long curving dive so as to be miles away when its mysterious burden came to life. Meanwhile, our pilot had been fumbling with the controls, and I heard him mutter to his co-pilot: "Now wouldn't that frost you. I forgot to set this crate on automatic pilot. I must be getting to be an old man."

The seconds passed—20—our ship was now righted and flying away from the target under automatic pilot—30—nothing to be seen through the black goggles, and the pounding of one's heart made counting difficult—35—40—I suddenly realized I had been holding my breath since the time of the bomb release—45—50—60—nothing happened.

For us the Bomb went off unannounced. The ball of fire which had fused several acres of the New Mexico desert into glass and turned Hiroshima into a symbol of man's inhumanity burst over the target ships, seared the paint from their decks and melted down their masts, but at twenty miles gave us no sound or flash or shock wave.

Coming out from under we could discern no change in the world. Had it been a dud? Had we miscalculated the time now to be blinded by the flash? The radio was silent.

Then, suddenly we saw it—a huge column of clouds, dense, white, boiling up through the strato-cumulus, looking much like any other thunderhead but climbing as no storm cloud ever could. The evil mushrooming head soon began to blossom out. It climbed rapidly to 30,000 or 40,000 feet, growing a tawny-pink from oxides of nitrogen, and seemed to be reaching out in an expanding umbrella overhead.... For minutes the cloud stood solid and impressive, like some gigantic monument, over Bikini. Then finally the shearing of the winds at different altitudes began to tear it up into a weird zigzag pattern. Winds high up were from the west and so the head tended to move out over us and menace the live fleet, while shreds of the torn column beneath could be seen moving slowly westward above the water....

We turned and made a couple of sweeps over the live fleet just to reassure the senators and admirals, and then climbed to our specified altitude and headed for the tiny atoll. For a long time we could see nothing. Someone ventured to suggest that all the ships had been sunk. But smoke at least was visible, moving slowly downwind. Then our pilot said, and his voice was something to hear: "Say, look, there's the *Sara* . . . still standing . . . beautiful, ain't she? Just like she was getting up steam to move out."

Soon after that we were able to make out the entire target area. Few ships, if any, had been sunk. Many of them were beginning to smoke and new fires seemed to be breaking out by the minute.

We were by now well under the tawny canopy. Nothing, however, had shown up on our instruments. The air was clear of fission products, which, carried aloft by the boiling updraft, would soon be joining those from the three other atomic bombs in the stratosphere. Then we heard Larson break through with the message:

"Leg three completed. Zero dose leg three."

That made us feel a lot better, and we decided to try to make our sweeps without gas masks. Things were hectic. We would fly a leg for a few minutes and then Lieutenant Lower would up-end his ship in a vertical bank, with the lagoon and its ships spinning like a pin wheel on the end of our wing, and we were off on the next leg. Up front the navigator, standing between the pilots, called our orientation points and checked the course for the skipper by the pattern of ships ahead. Back on the navigation table we had our instruments and our charts, where readings were made and plotted, and messages made out for the radioman to send on to Sadeyes.

Lars, transmitting on the same frequency, had found radiation, and we, as we approached the center of the target area, ran into it too. With a nervous sputter my Geiger counters came to life. At first it was patchy, seeming to be highest when we were passing over some ship. Toward dead center the ships were more closely bunched and there our counters really began to sing. Upon our first contact with radiation I had called over the interphone to the skipper to reassure him. Now with radiation a hundred times stronger I called him again: "Skipper, where are you now?"

"Coming in over the main target area."

"Well, we're really in it. Are we halfway through?"

Able Day 271

"Just about. The *Nevada* is just ahead. Want to turn out?"

"No. It's not that bad yet. You could stick around here for several days if you had to."

"Thanks."

The *Nevada*, gaudy red forward and pretty well singed aft, turned out to be some distance from the most intense radiation, so we knew that *Dave's Dream* had not exactly scored a bull's-eye. We were flying low enough so that the ships passed rapidly beneath us and it was impossible to get more than a fleeting glimpse of them. Most of them seemed to be afire but not in critical condition. The apparent damage was surprisingly slight. The *Sara*, of course, had been wiped clear. Some of the cruisers and battleships had had their superstructures twisted and melted into a tangle of junk, and the light carrier *Independence* had been blown into a cocked hat. But otherwise the fleet looked as if it might survive.

Expecting much more dire and dramatic events our crew was disappointed. There was much pooh-poohing of the Bomb over the interphone, and at last the co-pilot growled: "Well, it looks to me like the atom bomb is just about like the Army Air Force—highly overrated."

Our first sweep went very well. There was nothing to be found in the air; the only radiation was coming up from the water and from the ships. Most of this was doubtless due to radiation induced in the central target ships themselves, for each one seemed to catch us in a beam, as though from a searchlight, as we passed overhead. However, up near the northwest corner we suddenly ran headlong into an unexpected jolt of radiation which made the counters sing. We were by that time miles away from the ships. Thinking that we might be running into an invisible streamer from the original cloud I called Lieutenant Lower:

"Monitor to Captain! Skipper I don't know what we just ran into but we're back in the hot stuff. See anything below?"

In a moment: "Nope—not a thing. No oil slick, no ships."

The co-pilot chimed in: "What about that smoke? We're just about downwind from those fires now. See it?"

That caused a spontaneous scramble for gas masks, and so for the next two hours, making surveys at lower altitudes, we huffed and puffed, sweated and cursed, and struggled with communications from the inside of the steamy masks. The radiation got progressively more intense as we came down, and, of course, the smoke got more generalized. However, the fires seemed to be pretty well self-limited, and we were thankful that no ships, loaded with ammo as they were, blew up beneath us. . . .

At last from Sadeyes came the welcome message: "Mission completed. Return to base." We had been in the air nearly twelve hours. Now that the tension was gone, everyone suddenly became tired and starved. No smoking and eating had been permitted during the surveys, lest anyone should thereby pick up dangerous material from the air. So a complete survey of the ship was in order. We discarded everything that had been open, all cigarette packs, bread, fruit, . . . The boys took it pretty well, especially when I okayed a fresh gallon jar of olives and some canned beef. But not to be able to smoke—that was torture. Finally, Lieutenant Lower could stand it no longer:

"Bradley," he barked over the interphone, "how soon will I die if I smoke?"

"How old are you, Skipper?"

"Thirty."

"Oh, probably not for another thirty years."

"Well, hell, I'll die a lot sooner than that if I can't have a smoke."

After that we abandoned all conservative policy. The Captain ordered the ports to be opened to air out the ship, and we began to live like human beings again. Kwajalein looked as sunny and serene as ever as we circled for our approach.

How We Climbed Everest

BARRY C. BISHOP

>>> Barry C. Bishop 1953 was one of five Dartmouth men on the United States Everest Expedition in 1963. The others were J. Barry Corbet 1958, David L. Dingman 1958, Barry W. Prather 1961, and John E. Breitenbach 1957, who lost his life in a sudden icefall. Bishop, who was at Dartmouth for only part of his freshman year, was on the second assault team that reached the summit of Everest on May 22, 1963. His account of the final day's climb is from the *National Geographic Magazine*, October 1963.

"L UTE, I THINK I'm going mad." I speak through clenched teeth to Lute Jerstad, lying beside me in the two-man tent. For several hours I have been fighting a terrifying claustrophobia. We are alone at Camp VI, 27,450 feet up on the Southeast Ridge of Everest. I suppress a wild desire to break out of the cluttered tent.

As all climbers know, lack of oxygen produces weird mental effects. The thin air and the antibiotics I have been taking cause my claustrophobia—and a muddled sense of balance as well. Lying flat I feel as if I am at an absurd and sickening angle. Nausea wrenches my stomach. Breathing is quick and shallow. By bracing myself semi-upright, I maintain some semblance of equilibrium.

Lute tries to make me comfortable, but without success. Finally, I turn the regulator and increase the flow of oxygen into my plastic sleeping mask from one to two liters per minute. The little extra helps. Oxygen is our most precious commodity and our lives depend upon how well we conserve it. . . .

Drifting snows have compressed the sides of the tiny tent, robbing us of a third of our floor space. We are trying to sleep amid a chaos of equipment—clothing, oxygen apparatus, medicines, photographic supplies. Outside, a shrill wind lashes the crest of the ridge.

Tomorrow, May 22, is our big day, our try for the top. We both know that we will need every physical resource we can muster. And we both wonder if my illness will leave me too weak for the summit climb. We say nothing; consciously, we force the thought from our minds. At my urging, Lute takes a sleeping pill. Soon he rolls over in his cramped sector and drifts into uneasy slumber.

For me, braced in my awkward position, the hours pass like a slow nightmare. But the increased oxygen finally takes effect. Almost in command of myself once more, I too close my eyes and sleep.

At five o'clock I awake, feeling much better. Lute is already moving about the tent, melting snow on two butane stoves for some hot soup. Our extremely heavy breathing and the excessively low humidity at this high altitude sap the body of fluids at an alarming rate—sometimes almost a cup an hour.

Fifteen minutes later, Lute attaches a fresh gas cylinder to one of the stoves. A sudden whoosh, and a sheet of orange flame envelops the entire end of the tent. I smell Lute's burning beard. In one blinding second, the fire consumes my plastic mask. My eyebrows and part of my beard go with it. Dirty white smoke fills the tent.

Panic grips us. Lute struggles toward the zippered entrance. I try to smother the flames with a sleeping bag, but my legs are still inside and I can gain no leverage. The fire feeds greedily on the air in the tent, soon exhausting it. Our lungs ache.

I am groping desperately for a knife when Lute tears open the zipper and literally dives outside. His momentum is so great that he almost pitches down the steep slope toward the South Col. I am on his heels. We snatch the flaming stove from the tent, douse it in the snow. The fire soon dies in the thin air.

Choking and gasping, we sag on our hands and knees. Minutes pass before we can breathe with any semblance of normality. As we crawl back inside, we say nothing to each other. But we share the same thought. The omens are bad, all bad.

At five miles above sea level, every movement is laborious and exhausting. Within the smoky, reeking tent, we struggle into layer upon layer of clothing, finally sheathing ourselves in nylon parkas. Slowly we pull on boots and overboots, lash steel crampons into place, and attach our climbing rope. Stuffing two bottles of oxygen into our packs, we attach our regulators, pull on helmets and masks, and begin inhaling oxygen at the rate of three liters a minute.

Four liters a minute is regarded as the best flow for activity above 27,000 feet. But such a rate exhausts a cylinder in four hours. At three liters, a cylinder will last more than five hours; at two liters, eight.

Since each bottle weighs 13 pounds—and since weight is critical—the summit teams restrict themselves to two per man. Throughout the expedition, seldom do we enjoy the luxury of four liters.

The bad night and disastrous morning have thrown us two hours behind schedule. Not until 8 o'clock, still with no breakfast, do we slog upward at that monotonous, dreary pace mountaineers find necessary at such elevations. The weather is magnificent—windy but clear. Fluffy cumulus clouds cling to the sides of the surrounding mountains. . . .

With Lute at the head of the rope that joins us, we pick our way for 500 yards across shattered, unstable rock flecked with snow and ice. Then we turn directly up a long snow slope. Our progress is slow, and I know that the night has taken a heavy toll. I am having an off day. And to have it now, of all times! Every climber has such days, but you always hope to be hot for the big ones.

Just before 11 o'clock, we attain the crest of the Southeast Ridge. From here we look down the 10,000-foot drop of the Kangshung face into Tibet. I take the lead from Lute and for another three or four hundred yards we follow a knife edge of hard snow.

The wind picks up and I feel like a novice tightrope walker as I fight to keep my balance. The fearful Kangshung face drops precipitously on my right; on my left, a steep half-mile below, lies the South Col.

Lute resumes the lead. Dead ahead we spy our first goal, the South Summit. It towers some 500 vertical feet above us. In an exhausting two and a half hours, we gain only 200 of those forbidding feet. At a rocky outcrop, we pause for the only food we take that day—a quarter of a candy bar apiece.

Ten minutes later we continue the aching upward plod. We inch along the line of contact between steep snow on our right and rock outcrops on our left. The slope tilts at a dangerous 40 to 45 degrees. We generally keep to the snow, but when it becomes difficult, we gingerly tread upon the bare rock, enjoying the best of two very tricky worlds.

At 28,500 feet my first cylinder of oxygen runs dry. Lute checks his and finds it almost empty. So we halt on a small sloping ledge to change bottles. Discarding the old cylinders, we lean back against the mountain.

Suddenly I trip over one of the empty bottles at my feet and fly out into space. Instinctively, I twist in mid-air. Hitting the slope face-down, I claw at the snow with hands and feet. I manage to stop.

I glance to my left and see Lute beside me, holding me with his right hand. He has jumped out after me, flipped on his belly, and grabbed. We crawl back up to the ledge, and lie there for a long moment.

"That could have been serious," Lute says.

I nod. Both of us have narrowly missed falling all the way into Tibet.

We continue, our packs lighter because of the discarded oxygen bottles. I feel spent, dull. One step . . . six long breaths . . . another step . . . again six breaths. Each pace requires almost half a minute. My entire body aches.

We cross hard, steep snow. Lute, in the lead, chops steps. We mount toward the South Summit, slowly, slowly.

An hour passes . . . another thirty minutes. I wonder if we will ever reach the summit.

Upward. Always upward. Foot by painful foot. Gradually, I become convinced that we will indeed go all the way. And at 2 o'clock, beneath a piercingly blue sky, we stand at 28,750 feet on the South Summit of Everest—our first way station. We lean into the heavy wind that buffets us with gusts of 60 to 70 miles per hour. . . .

Atop the South Summit, Lute and I peer at the awesome route to the true peak. It rises above us in craggy, snow-scarred grandeur. Long ago we memorized this view from a photograph taken by Sir Ed-

How We Climbed Everest 277

mund Hillary. We know it as well as we know the streets we live on. But somehow it looms steeper, closer, more forbidding than in the picture.

While on the mountain, all of us in the summit teams think of ourselves as intelligent and lucid. Only afterwards, in reconstructing our actions, do we discover how irrational we really were.

So it is that Lute looks down with dismay at a 30-foot vertical wall of rotten snow—our jumping-off-point for the North Summit. Unaccountably, he starts walking due west, down a small slope.

Later Lute explains: "I was a little bit spooked by this 30-foot vertical pitch. I thought that this couldn't possibly be the way. And I don't know whatever possessed me, but I suddenly took off down to the left.

"I walked 75 feet down the South Summit and saw some rocks, and I apparently thought I saw some footprints down there, and Barry all this time thought I was completely crazy. He just looked at me and shook his head and threw up his hands and didn't know where on earth I was going. I think he thought I was going to end it all right there.

"I got to the end of the rope and I realized that I had made a very foolish mistake, and I had to grind my way back up this 75 feet—which, at this elevation, is kind of tough."

With Lute back on the South Summit, we gird for the crucial assault. He leads the way down the nasty wall. With our goal so close, we move more rapidly now. Lute negotiates Hillary's Chimney—an upward cleft in the rock face—in beautiful style by climbing out halfway up and flanking it from the left. Finally we emerge above all the rock outcrops onto the final summit cornice ridge. Here we trudge over bump after bump of hard snow. The intense winds force us constantly toward the unsafe overhanging edge of the cornice on our right; we concentrate on staying to the left.

I plod along with my head down. Seven full, gasping breaths now punctuate each step. I focus on my feet ... lifting ... placing ... lifting ... placing.

Suddenly the rope that ties me to Lute, 75 feet in front, goes slack. I look up as Lute raises his right arm. I know he has at last sighted the top.

A few more agonizing steps and I too see the American flag held taut by the wind on the summit. How the sight of it affected us is vividly expressed by Lute in an account he dictated after the climb:

"Just then we came over the last rise and there was that American flag—and what a fantastic sight! The great big flag just whipping in the breeze, and the ends were tattered. It kind of reminded me of the pictures I'd seen of this thing on Iwo Jima—the flag raising and everything. It was quite a sight." . . .

Lute coils in the rope as I come up to him. Arm in arm we then begin to trudge the last hundred feet to the summit. We are bone weary; our lungs suck wildly for air; thinking is a torment. But, if necessary, we would crawl to that flag.

What do we do when we finally reach the summit and flop down? We weep. All inhibitions stripped away, we cry like babies. With joy for having scaled the mightiest of mountains; with relief that the long torture of the climb has ended.

It is 3:30 p.m. The wind whips and tears at us as we perch precariously on earth's highest pinnacle. The American flag . . . chatters in the gusts.

We cut off our oxygen—already low—and set about our tasks. Lute strikes his ice ax into the hard snow, anchors a motion-picture camera to its head, and shoots the first movies ever made from the top of the world. The ax shudders in the wind. Lute's silk-gloved fingers begin to freeze—quite literally—as he turns the camera's metal crank.

I take a series of still photographs. Movements are sluggish at 29,028 feet, and the pictures take a long time. Too long. My fingers too freeze badly.

The view is spectacular. To the north stretch the rolling brown hills of the Tibetan Plateau, crowned by range upon range of snow-capped peaks. Cloud banks some 10,000 feet below mask the east, but looming above them in the distance we see the Kanchenjunga Massif. India, to the south, lies veiled beneath a solid mass of clouds. The 22,494-foot summit of Ama Dablam that I had climbed two years before seems insignificant from the lofty eminence of Everest.

I reflect for a moment on the climbers who had pioneered the Himalayan peaks only a generation or two before. They had reached—or almost reached—these heights without oxygen, without any of the complex equipment we now deem indispensable.

In my mind's eye, I see them: Mallory, Irvine, the others who struggled so valiantly on these slopes. In puttees, Norfolk jackets, and jaunty felt hats, trudging doggedly into the thin, high, freezing air.

For 45 minutes we stay on the summit—seated in deference to the powerful wind that threatens to blast us back down the mountain... Lute brought pictures of his family to leave, but he forgets to dig them out of his pocket. He also brought a New Testament given him by his parents that he had planned to place at the summit. But now he decides it is too good to leave on this desolate peak.

About 4:15, short of oxygen, we begin the descent. Life-giving gas hisses once more into our masks, but we allow ourselves a barely perceptible one liter a minute. The wind, blowing strongly still, stretches the rope between us into a taut crescent that arcs over emptiness beyond the crest.

Lute goes first as we traverse a section of the corniced ridge. He disappears around a bend in the undulating snow. The rope, stiffened by the wind, catches the edge of the cornice, cuts itself a groove, hooks the edge. Danger!

I shout into the 70-mile gusts, but Lute hears nothing. The fouled rope draws me inexorably toward the edge. I dive onto the snow and wriggle out on the cornice, attempting to free the rope. My face is just above the snow. But my weight is too much; a section of the cornice at my chest gives way. I have a sudden, hair-raising view of Tibet's Kangshung Glacier 10,000 feet below.

Scrambling back, I notice that Lute's continued forward movement causes the rope to cut ever deeper into the snow. I undo the knot that secures it to my waist. It whips up and away across the whiteness. Unroped, I parallel its route. I wait until the end of the rope, like a frozen snake, slithers free of the cornice. Then I re-tie it to my waist. Elapsed time: less than a minute. Not until I tell him back in Katmandu does Lute know of this tight moment.

We negotiate the chimneys, but barely. At the bottom of the last one, we both collapse onto the crumbly rock for a breather. When we push on, I notice that Lute is staggering. He halts, checks his oxygen equipment. He tears away a string that has been fouling the bladder. No gas at all has been flowing into his mask.

We allow ourselves a generous two liters to ascend the steep, perilous pitch angling back up to the South Summit. We thank God that it is the last climb of the day.

Cautiously we ease down the sharp southeast slope. Our oxygen again cut back, our bodies drugged with fatigue, we stumble and fall. But we move steadily down. . . .

Everest is a harsh and hostile immensity. Whoever challenges it declares war. He must mount his assault with the skill and ruthlessness of a military operation. And when the battle ends, the mountain remains unvanquished. There are no true victors, only survivors.

Vietnam
JOHN MARTIN MECKLIN

≫ A son of John Moffatt Mecklin (see page 200), John Mecklin grew up in Hanover, was graduated from Dartmouth in 1939. His vocation was journalism: he was a war correspondent in North Africa and Western Europe, and for years at home and abroad he represented Time Inc. before becoming an editor of Fortune. *Mission in Torment* (Garden City, N.Y., 1965), which he wrote after serving as public affairs officer with the United States Embassy in Saigon, is the source for the following personal impressions of Vietnam.

Vietnam is an intensely tragic land. It might be called the Poland of Asia. The Vietnamese, like the Poles, are racially and culturally related to a mighty, predatory neighbor, and this has produced a proud, intelligent, hardy breed. Like the Poles the Vietnamese have been victims of aggression for centuries, occupied and reoccupied by foreign armies, yet they have never lost their courage, nor their determination to be free. Like the Poles the Vietnamese deserve better than history, to date, has granted. It is a country that often gets under an American's skin.

This was the case with me when I worked there as a newsman in 1953–55. It was there that I first began thinking seriously of government service, after more than a decade as a foreign correspondent. I wanted to try to do something myself about such problems, rather than simply writing about them from the outside looking in. My chance came in 1961, midst the bright promise of the New Frontier, when I was invited to become a foreign service reserve officer of the U. S. Information Agency. A British friend in Germany, where I was working at the time, neatly pinpointed the troubles to come with my former colleagues of the press by remarking with a huge guffaw that I was "a poacher turned gamekeeper."

On leave of absence from my employers, Time Inc., I was first assigned to Paris as public affairs advisor to the U. S. Mission to the Organization for Economic Cooperation and Development (OECD). After a few months, by a remarkable quirk of fate, the Agency asked me to transfer to Saigon.

I was aware of the truth later articulated by the New York *Times* (June 28, 1963) that Vietnam is "a graveyard for the reputations of American diplomats and soldiers." The pull of that tortured country nevertheless was still there, and I was eager to go. Twenty-one months later, the assignment ended in despair—and no doubt another headstone in the graveyard. In March 1964 I resigned from USIA....

* * *

Deep in the night over Pakistan and India, Burma and Thailand, moonlight glinted on the tapered wing outside, and flickered occasionally on the water of a paddy far below. I talked with a friend about the work ahead. He was returning to his post in the American Embassy in Saigon. I was reporting for duty as Public Affairs Officer in Saigon, returning to Vietnam after seven years' absence.

He was a big, gentle man, slouched in his seat, his fingers nervously tightening and then relaxing around a drink in which the ice had long melted. "I think we are making progress," he said, "but it is slow, very, very slow."

As he talked on, dwelling on a score of problems and frustrations with which he had learned to live, I tried to think how it would be this time. It had been my fortune as a news correspondent to witness the agonized collapse of French colonialism in Vietnam in 1954, and the subsequent intervention of U.S. power to shore up the beleaguered, newly independent government of Ngo Dinh Diem. Now this commitment was being put to arduous trial by renewed Communist guerrilla warfare against the Diem regime, the same stealthy, ugly warfare in the jungles and hip-deep slime of the paddies that I recalled so well. Could we succeed, where the French had failed?

It was midday, May 1, 1962, when the pilot cut the engines of the weary DC-3 of Air Vietnam that had brought us from Bangkok, the last leg of the journey, and I stepped out into the searing glare of the

Saigon airport. In an instant the confident, bureaucratically tidy briefings I had received in Washington were forgotten. It took only a glance around the airport to sense something of what it meant for my own country now to be so inextricably involved in this foul and bitter struggle.

It was like a time machine. The airport was cluttered with military aircraft. An armed policeman stood at the foot of the landing gangway, still more at various points around the terminal. There was a heavy leavening of men in uniform in the airport crowds. Nothing had changed. Except the markings on the aircraft. Instead of the French tricolors, there were the black and white symbols of the United States Air Force and the United States Army. And the men in uniform. Instead of crew-cut Frenchmen, or black Moroccans, or lean German Foreign Legionnaires, there were lean, crew-cut, and sometimes black Americans.

Memories flooded back . . .

The futile, murderous battles I had witnessed between the French and the swarming, elusive Vietminh (Communist guerillas), an enemy of "termites" as Jean Lartéguy was later to call them in his superb novel *The Centurions*. A column of two thousand men in tanks, armored cars and armored halftracks, stalled on a road along a dike between the paddies in the Red River Delta by Vietminh mines, and hidden snipers. The reply of the sweating, sun-tanned French colonel when I asked how the operation was going: "*Comme toujours, Viets partout*" (As always, Vietminh everywhere) . . .

The night I circled for hours in a command plane high over the doomed garrison of Dienbienphu, the lonely pinpoint of a shielded navigation light in the inky depths below, and the intermittent slow-motion blossoms of garish red flames from Vietminh mortars falling among the paratroopers we were dropping into the pitifully small French perimeter. The steady young voice on the garrison's radio link to our plane, advising that the paratroopers had landed, and concluding "*rien à signaler*" (nothing to report) . . .

The arrogant French motorcycle courier I watched one day near Hanoi as he playfully crowded a trudging column of heavily laden peasants into the ditch—an eloquent glimpse of why the French were hated, and why they lost...

The French forces evacuating Hanoi in 1955 in their throbbing tanks and halftracks and six-by-six trucks, towing their useless artillery (all American aid), to be replaced by silent, expressionless Vietminh troops on foot, wearing sneakers. Western technological genius, Western industrial might, outflanked and routed by Asian peasants...

General René Cogny, the defeated French commander in North Vietnam, standing on the beach at Haiphong one day in 1955 for the departure of his last rearguard troops on a waiting LST. His towering frame guidon-straight, his voice loud and steady, but a telltale glistening in his eye. "France is proud of you," he cried. "You have fought well. *Vive la France!*" He saluted as the Tricolor was lowered for the last time. Quickly he then boarded a helicopter. A storm of swirling dust and he was gone, ending French power north of the 17th Parallel...

In Saigon, later that year, cynical French plotting with a Vietnamese gangster mob called the Binh Xuyen to destroy Ngo Dinh Diem because he had refused to take orders. Diem's lonely courage. Some twenty blocks of Cholon, the Chinese quarter of Saigon, swathed in black smoke and flames from Binh Xuyen mortars. The French journalist watching, sipping his Pernod at a sidewalk café, sneering that Diem's troops were "cowards" as they filed stolidly into the inferno to wipe out the Binh Xuyen in less than forty-eight hours. The frail American hope that Diem might be the leader so desperately needed...

French despair, mixed with petulant, insensate arrogance as the reality of defeat settled upon them. Their vindictive resentment of American support for Diem. "Children leading children" sneered a French businessman who had made a fortune selling French textiles to Vietnamese peasants at exorbitant prices fixed by colonial authorities. Threats against American newsmen for reporting the sordid spectacle of French maneuvering against Diem. My hurt dismay when my friend M. Boyer, proprietor of l'Amiral, my favorite restaurant, refused to serve me.

It was no homecoming to return to Vietnam. But few Americans have ever worked there without finding themselves emotionally involved, as I had been, with the land and with its sturdy, tormented people. As we drove into the city, along the broad, tree-lined boulevards left by the French, I was pleased to be back, yet also fearful, for I knew something of the elusive dangers of this contested nation. In Vietnam I had known France at her finest, and her shabbiest. In many ways Vietnam was now to provide a similar glimpse of the United States.

THE VOICE OF A NATIVE

North of Boston

PARKER MERROW

>>> Parker Merrow 1925 was a man of the North Country. He was editor and publisher of a weekly newspaper, the *Carroll County Independent and Granite State News*. He was a judge of the Ossipee, N.H., municipal court. He was in the lumber business. For several years he contributed to the *Dartmouth Alumni Magazine* a column, "North of Boston," in which he wrote of the way of life he lived and loved.

THEY AINT much happened sence the last riting. Leaves is down and dead and the country buttoned up for winter. Paid my taxes and it didn't hurt much more than having a tooth pulled with no anesthetic.

The Dreadnaught said it was time to start planning for Christmas. Not being no fool, I give her a check and told her to do the shopping for the various relayshuns.

Next evening, when I was awl alone in the house, I set down to make my own personal private Christmas list. First uv awl, a big bone with lots uv meat on same for our new Labrador. Then a cupple uv cases uv ale for the boys down to the jail. Some of them fellers is there on my say so.

For my son, a flash gun and case uv bulbs for his camera. For the Dreadnaught and our long-legged red-headed dotter, a big flask uv perfume and a Dartmouth scarf each. When you give a female perfume plus a lovely scarf you never do no wrong.

As for me, if truth was known they aint really nothing money can buy that I really need. Uv course they is lots uv things I want, but do not really need. Them things I need, money just cant buy, like taking the wear and tear uv twenty-five years uv day and night work offen the body and the forgiveness of God for the sins uv commission and the waste uv the precious hours and abilities He gives me.

I had a very wise uncle which used to send me a jack knife every Christmas. He sed "When you dont get that knife no more, why I'll be gone and you'll be the head uv the family. They wont be nobody older than you in the family to give you nothing and you wont be young no more."

He was right. I let the fire die on the hearth and went out and walked the Labrador and watched the hills under the stars and so to bed. It was a moment that stays with a feller a long time. Them of you as has turned that corner know just what I mean, and them of you as aint, never can know until you do.

* * *

Few weeks ago an extra rugged character what runs a saw mill come to see me. He looks and talks just like he was a actor in a movie about logging, but this guy he aint acting. He wants to buy sum extra big hard pine to saw some barn sills on a rush job.

Driv to a timber lot and put the jeep into low low frunt wheel drive and went down an old road. Then we lit and trod around for half an hour. We see plenty of big pine. This character allowed as how they was just what he wanted.

We come to a big clearing and slumped down onto the moss and pine needles and lit up. Very nice and poetic with the setting sun slanting in and the usuwil liquid note of the usuwil hermit thrush in the quiet air.

I ast him what he would give. He shakes his head "Deals off. Dont want 'em."

I started to get mad. He shhhes me and points around in a circle.

"See them yung pine. You never notissed them at awl and I never see them till just now. For every big tree we drop we'll smash ten of them little fellers. You got a boy. I got a boy. Mebbe your boy will sell them to my boy thirty years from now when you and me is gone."

I know awl this sounds just too pat to be true. But that is exactly what that character sed. We went back to the jeep, fired it up and went elsewhere.

I wisht sum of you fellers could of ben along. You might of liked it.

***

More'n a month ago I drove over to see a friend to order my maple syrup. They want no one in his sap house when I got there. A good fire was going, the place was full of steam and the sap was boiling lively. Pretty soon a crawler tractor comes grunting down over the hill, pulling a big tank of sap. The owner gets off, hooks up the hose and starts to siphon the sap.

I give him my order. Then he asts, "How about you and me getting a real old-fashioned bellyache?" I tell him that I'm his huckleberry and will go right over town and get the donuts and sour pickles.

When I get back he has the coffee brewing on the back of the evaporator and a big pan of thick syrup stewing on the frunt. A tub of snow is parked in frunt of the sap house steps.

He took a big serving spoon and poured the hot syrup onto the snow. It made a patch of clear brown candy, supple and warm. When he twisted it onto a fork and wadded it into his mouth, a few snow crystals was blended in, shining real pretty. Then I done likewise. We set on the steps and et till our mouths cloyed. Then we had half a donut each, half a pickle and a half a cup of black coffee. That put our taste back in business.

We set and et and settled the affairs of this world while the sap boiled away and the sun worked down. We cleaned up everything. He loosened his belt and grinned "Its good to sneak back and be a boy again, even if its only for an hour—thanks for helping me." You cant get mad at a guy like that....

***

Long last January I driv to Concord to get sworn in to the Governor's Council, representing the northern part of the state. Father, he done the same thing in 1909.

Lane Dwinnell '28, who lives in Lebanon, he got sworn in as Governor. They was the usual treading around and flashing brass and lunches and popping flash bulbs. The Dreadnaught she went with me and wore the remains of deceased animils around her neck and looked real nice if I do say so.

The next morning at ten, Lane he blowed the whistle. They is five of us on his Council. We work with him and argue with him on all major appointments, taking of land, highway layouts, payment of bills, pardons and some departmental policies.

The Council Chamber is laid out real impressive. I trod in and dumped the brief case and put on my nigh-to glasses. The other four Councillors done likewise. I had the same place at the table my Father had. Behind me was the clock that his Governor, Quimby, gave the State when he and his Council finished their term. It set there, ticking time away very quiet and persistent. Outside the wind rumbled the windows and the snow was white lines against the old buildings.

Picked up the first item on the agenda and thot "This is it. Poli Sci under Big Jim Richardson and English with Doc White. Doc Griggs trying to make us see the sweep and cycle of life. Prexy Hopkins hammering away at the open mind and the search for truth and what is man's duty to society. Thousands of miles of the long roads and the work of the years to sharpen a fellow's ability—and now, are we as good men as our Fathers were—can we do as good a job as they done?"

Then it was half past twelve and Lane stood up at the head of the long table and like our Governors have done for over 150 years, closed the meeting.

A quick bite to eat while we laid out our work and run a quick postmortem. Then home through the snow and the wind. . . .

* * *

I am toasting the body at the fireplace when a Trooper Dangerous Dan McGrews through the door and bats the snow out of his fur hat.

He asts will I chaperone him while he lugs two runaway girls to the County Home. The female Deputy Sheriff is out of town, so he picks on me.

We start off with two very scared, cold and wet 17-year-olds out of Maine crying quietly in the back seat. Their particular little world has come apart on them like a cheap alarm clock. I try to extend some words of comfort and advice but get nowhere.

The road is a white carpet and the wind-driven snow laces back into the headlights. The radio talks about a three-car pile up around Portsmouth.

Then they is a tense whispering in back. The Trooper yells "Watch it," snaps on the big center light and we go into a skidding stop.

One of the girls has a big white pill going into her mouth. Dont stop to ask if it is an act with aspirin or the real McCoy. I reach back and handle her just like I would my Labrador when separating him from suthing he should not eat, only much faster.

We unload them at the County home. The matron says she will fit them to a warm bath, supper and bed.

On the way back, the Trooper talks to Concord. Pretty soon Concord says parents of said subjects have been contacted and will call for same tomorrow.

Stop at the mill pond and clean back seat and throw half a dozen pills onto the ice. So we never knowed if it was the real thing or just an act.

Ast the Trooper in and make coffee and sandwiches. The thermometer is two clapboards below zero and the wind and snow building up.

He thanks me as he buttons his jacket and sets the fur cap just so. "Funny thing—those girls are off the cold road and safe from some fellers that would give them as much chance as a fox gives a rabbit—and they hate us for it."

"If they got the brains the Good Lord give a goose they'll be thankful some day," I tell him. He grins and his tail lights wink out in the storm.... It was an affair that sticks quite a while in a man's mind.

* * *

I am driving between Augusta and Lewiston and much to my surprise find myself in a gun shop and ast what is new. The owner of the dead fall says "Dewey Bryant of Gray—he's got a wonderful cased Patterson Colt—practically stole it. Just refused $1600."

I learn that this Dewey Bryant is a highly skilled machinist. In his spare time he collects and restores old arms. He even builds muzzle loading rifles and shoots same in competition.

Drive to Dewey's small house. He is a State of Mainer just as foolish as two dens full of foxes. Roll my eyes around his living room and come up with a snap inventory of $5,000 in beautiful old rifles.

Presently he produces the Patterson. I tell him that I aint no Colt collector, but have got a friend who can and will lay the old pluribus unum right on the line.

"I can't afford to keep this pistol" says Dewey "for I got a girl to educate. And I earn my living with my hands. What I want is a thousand in cash to put away for her and the balance in fine old guns to sort of take the place of the Patterson."

He fumbles a cigarette out of his overalls. "I'm just a little guy. What I have in this room I got the hard way. Done it nights. I love what's rare and built beautiful. Them old time gun smiths done work such as we'll never see again. I can do real fine work but I cant come up to what they done."

Light reflected off the Patterson's case. "You know I can't afford to keep that pistol. But I want to hold onto it just a little longer. All my life I dreamed about finding one. I found it. So don't bring your buyer too soon."

Dewey walked out to the car with me. "You see what I'm driving at?"

I just nodded. They aint much you can say to a guy like that.

Just as winter set in good I driv down into Maine on a matter of worldly business. Swung along the coast seeing various characters. About an hour after dark, shot the brakes and slid into Rick Jackson's long driveway. He is '27.

Spent a short evening going over his old cars and guns. Turned in early and got up early, for it was a business day coming.

Just starting to warm up the car and say so long when he ast me to take a short ride. I done so. The road come out onto a high hill. He swung off through a bar way in a stone wall and stopped short.

It was a picnic spot with outdoor fireplaces and tables and a view that stopped your breath quick. And there stood a brand new Episcopal Chapel. They had dug and blasted into the side of the young mountain for the foundations. The building was set so that folks meeting in the parish house, which was the basement, had the whole view at a glance.

We stood side by side in the deep cold, dragging at our cigarettes. Rick told, in short words, how they had worked for three years to get the land, the material, the labor and the money to put it up.

I looked over the valley with the long ice-locked lake, the snow-patched fields, the black woods and the far off houses with the breakfast smoke coming straight up. The East was red behind a snow cloud bank.

"You and I," I sed, "have kidded each other ever since we first met at Horace Hurlburt's gun rack in Hanover in the fall of '23.

"Let's get serious for a moment. What you've done here—in helping raise this House of God on this hilltop—justifies your having lived. I'm proud to call you my friend of most a third of a century." Then I run out of words.

Rick give me that level Maine stare, "Well," he flipped his cigarette, "probably no great harm will come out of it all. Now let's roll." ...

SOME FICTION

The Plastic Age
PERCY MARKS

❧❧❧ When *The Plastic Age* was published in 1924, every student in Hanover who read it, and most did, not only identified with it but took for granted that the story was about Dartmouth. Percy Marks, the author, had been briefly an instructor in English at Dartmouth, and rumor ran that he had written a good deal of his novel of college life while in Hanover.

ENGLISH 53 had only a dozen men in it; so Henley conducted the course in a very informal fashion. The men felt free to bring up for discussion any topic that interested them.

Nobody was surprised, therefore, when George Winsor asked Henley to express his opinion of the value of a college education. He reminded Henley of what he had said two years before, and rapidly gave a résumé of the discussion that resulted in the question he was asking. "We'd like to know, too," he concluded, grinning wickedly, "just whom you consider the cream of the earth. You remember you said that if we were you felt sorry for the skimmed milk."

Henley leaned back in his chair and laughed. "Yes," he said, "I remember saying that. I didn't think, though, that you would remember most of what I said. I am truly astonished." He grinned back at Winsor. "The swine seem to have eaten the pearls."

The class laughed, but Winsor was not one to refuse the gambit. "They were very indigestible," he said quickly.

"Good!" Henley exclaimed. "I wanted them to give you a bellyache, and I am delighted that you still suffer."

"We do," Pudge Jamieson admitted, "but we'd like to have a little mercy shown to us now. We've spent four years here, and while we've enjoyed them, we've just about made up our minds that they have been all in all wasted years."

"No." Henley was decisive. His playful manner entirely disappeared. "No, not wasted. You have enjoyed them, you say. Splendid justification. You will continue to enjoy them as the years grow between you and your college days. All men are sentimental about college, and in that sentimentality there is continuous pleasure.

"Your doubt delights me. Your feeling that you haven't learned anything delights me, too. It proves that you have learned a great deal. It is only the ignoramus who thinks he is wise; the wise man knows that he is an ignoramus. That's a platitude, but it is none the less true. I have cold comfort for you: the more you learn, the less confident you will be of your own learning, the more utterly ignorant you will feel. I have never known so much as the day I graduated from high school. I held my diploma and the knowledge of the ages in my hand. I had never heard of Socrates, but I would have challenged him to a debate without the slightest fear.

"Since then I have grown more humble, so humble that there are times when I am ashamed to come into the class-room. What right have I to teach anybody anything? I mean that quite sincerely. Then I remember that, ignorant as I am, the undergraduates are more ignorant. I take heart and mount the rostrum ready to speak with the authority of a pundit."

He realized that he was sliding off on a tangent and paused to find a new attack. Pudge Jamieson helped him.

"I suppose that's all true," he said, "but it doesn't explain why college is really worth while. The fact remains that most of us don't learn anything, that we are coarsened by college, and that we—well, we worship false gods."

Henley nodded in agreement. "It would be hard to deny your assertions," he acknowledged, "and I don't think that I am going to try to deny them. Of course, men grow coarser while they are in college, but that doesn't mean that they wouldn't grow coarser if they weren't in college. It isn't college that coarsens a man and destroys his illusions; it is life. Don't think that you can grow to manhood and retain your pretty dreams. You have become disillusioned about college. In the next few years you will suffer further disillusionment. That is the price of living.

"Every intelligent man with ideals eventually becomes a cynic. It is inevitable. He has standards, and, granted that he is intelligent, he cannot fail to see how far mankind falls below those standards. The result is cynicism, and if he is truly intelligent, the cynicism is kindly. Having learned that man is frail, he expects little of him; therefore, if he judges at all, his judgment is tempered either with humor or with mercy."

The dozen boys were sprawled lazily in their chairs, their feet resting on the rungs of the chairs before them, but their eyes were fastened keenly on Henley. All that he was saying was of the greatest importance to them. They found comfort in his words, but the comfort raised new doubts, new problems.

"How does that affect college?" Winsor asked.

"It affects it very decidedly," Henley replied. "You haven't become true cynics yet; you expect too much of college. You forget that the men who run the college and the men who attend it are at best human beings, and that means that very much cannot be expected of them. You do worship false gods. I find hope in the fact that you recognize the stuff of which your gods are made. I have great hopes for the American colleges, not because I have any reason to believe that the faculties will become wiser or that the administrations will lead the students to true gods; not at all, but I do think that the students themselves will find a way. They have already abandoned Mammon; at least, the most intelligent have, and I begin to see signs of less adoration for athletics. Athletics, of course, have their place, and some of the students are beginning to find that place. Certainly the alumni haven't, and I don't believe that the administrative officers have, either. Just so long as athletes advertise the college, the administrations will coddle them. The undergraduates, however, show signs of frowning on professionalism, and the stupid athlete is rapidly losing his prestige. An athlete has to show something more than brawn to be a hero among his fellows nowadays."

He paused, and Pudge spoke up. "Perhaps you are right," he said, "but I doubt it. Athletics are certainly far more important to us than anything else, and the captain of the football team is always the biggest man in college. But I don't care particularly about that. What I want to know is how the colleges justify their existence. I don't see that you have proved that they do."

"No, I haven't," Henley admitted, "and I don't know that I can prove it. Of course, the colleges aren't perfect, not by a long way, but as human institutions go, I think they justify their existence. The four years spent at college by an intelligent boy—please notice that I say intelligent—are well spent indeed. They are gloriously worth while. You said that you have had a wonderful time. Not so wonderful as you think. It is a strange feeling that we have about our college years. We all believe that they are years of unalloyed happiness, and the further we leave them behind the more perfect they seem. As a matter of fact, few undergraduates are truly happy. They are going through a period of storm and stress; they are torn by *Weltschmerz*. Show me a nineteen-year-old boy who is perfectly happy and you show me an idiot. I rarely get a cheerful theme except from freshmen. Nine tenths of them are expressions of deep concern and distress. A boy's college years are the years when he finds out that life isn't what he thought it, and the finding out is a painful experience. He discovers that he and his fellows are made of very brittle clay: usually he loathes himself; often he loathes his fellows.

"College isn't the Elysium that it is painted in stories and novels, but I feel sorry for any intelligent man who didn't have the opportunity to go to college. There is something beautiful about one's college days, something that one treasures all his life. As we grow older, we forget the hours of storm and stress, the class-room humiliations, the terror of examinations, the awful periods of doubt of God and man—we forget everything but athletic victories, long discussions with friends, campus sings, fraternity life, moonlight on the campus, and everything that is romantic. The sting dies, and the beauty remains.

"Why do men give large sums of money to their colleges when asked? Because they want to help society? Not at all. The average man doesn't even take that into consideration. He gives the money because he loves his alma mater, because he has beautiful and tender memories of her. No, colleges are far from perfect, tragically far from it, but any institution that commands loyalty and love as colleges do cannot be wholly imperfect. There is a virtue in a college that uninspired administrative officers, stupid professors, and alumni with false ideals cannot kill. At times I tremble for Sanford College; there are times when I swear at it, but I never cease to love it."

"If you feel that way about college, why did you say those things to us two years ago?" Hugh asked.

"Because they were true, all true. I was talking about the undergraduates then, and I could have said much more cutting things and still been on the safe side of the truth. There is, however, another side, and that is what I am trying to give you now—rather incoherently, I know."

Hugh thought of Cynthia. "I suppose all that you say is true," he admitted dubiously, "but I can't feel that college does what it should for us. We are told that we are taught to think, but the minute we bump up against a problem in living we are stumped just as badly as we were when we are freshmen."

"Oh, no, not at all. You solve problems every day that would have stumped you hopelessly as a freshman. You think better than you did four years ago, but no college, however perfect, can teach you all the solutions of life. There are no nostrums or cure-alls that the colleges can give for all the ills and sicknesses of life. You, I am afraid, will have to doctor those yourself."

"I see." Hugh didn't altogether see. Both college and life seemed more complicated than he had thought them. "I am curious to know," he added, "just whom you consider the cream of the earth. That expression has stuck in my mind. I don't know why—but it has."

Henley smiled. "Probably because it is such a very badly mixed metaphor. Well, I consider the college man the cream of the earth."

"What?" four of the men exclaimed, and all of them sat suddenly upright.

"Yes—but let me explain. If I remember rightly, I said that if you were the cream of the earth, I hoped that God would pity the skimmed milk. Well, everything taken into consideration, I do think that you are the cream of the earth; and I have no hope for the skimmed milk. Perhaps it isn't wise for me to give public expression to my pessimism, but you ought to be old enough to stand it.

"The average college graduate is a pretty poor specimen, but all in all he is just about the best we have. Please remember that I am talking in averages. I know perfectly well that a great many brilliant men do not come to college, and that a great many stupid men do come, but the colleges get a very fair percentage of the intelligent ones and a comparatively small percentage of the stupid ones. In other words, to play with my mixed metaphor a bit, the cream is very thin in places and the skimmed milk has some very thick clots of cream, but in the end the cream remains the cream and the milk the milk. Everything taken into consideration, we get in the colleges the young men with the highest ideals, the loftiest purpose.

"You want to tell me that those ideals are low and the purpose materialistic and selfish. I know it, but the average college graduate, I repeat, has loftier ideals and is less materialistic than the average man who has not gone to college. I wish that I could believe that the college gives him those ideals. I can't, however. The colleges draw the best that society has to offer; therefore, they graduate the best."

"Oh, I don't know," a student interrupted. "How about Edison and Ford and—"

"And Shakspere and Sophocles," Henley concluded for him. "Edison is an inventive genius, and Ford is a business genius. Genius hasn't anything to do with schools. The colleges, however, could have made both Ford and Edison bigger men, though they couldn't have made them lesser geniuses.

"No, we must not take the exceptional man as a standard; we've got to talk about the average. The hand of the Potter shook badly when he made man. It was at best a careless job. But He made some better than others, some a little less weak, a little more intelligent. All in all, those are the men that come to college. The colleges ought to do a thousand times more for those men than they do do; but, after all, they do something for them, and I am optimistic enough to believe that the time will come when they will do more.

"Some day, perhaps," he concluded very seriously, "our administrative officers will be true educators; some day perhaps our faculties will be wise men really fitted to teach; some day perhaps our students will be really students, eager to learn, honest searchers after beauty and truth. That day will be the millennium. I look for the undergraduates to lead us to it."

The Professor's Wife

BRAVIG IMBS

⇛ After two years at Dartmouth, Bravig Imbs 1927 went to France where he became acquainted with Gertrude Stein and her circle. It was under their influence that he wrote *The Professor's Wife* (New York, 1928), his semi-fictional account of his undergraduate experiences as a butler in the household of Professor David Lambuth. In the latter days of World War II he became a popular broadcaster for the OWI in France, where he was killed in a jeep accident in 1946.

IT WAS a great honor to be invited to dine with the Ramsons, but to be invited to a Sunday morning breakfast was a special mark of favor. In the summer, breakfasts were held in the Garden Room, but in the winter, in the dining room, where Mrs. Ramson said it was summer all the year. The walls were paneled with vivid wall paper they had bought in Alsace depicting a tropical scene. There were castor-oil plants and orchids and hibiscus and a blue bay and a blue sky, and the ceiling was made to resemble the sky too, light blue plaster with swirls of white and cream. Mrs. Ramson called them "skirls" because they turned around like music. She was very proud of the Scotch blood in the family and used to sing Scotch songs very off key in the drawing room with Scarot on her lap, and after the second verse he would always join in, wailing in a most unearthly manner. Then Scarot would be extremely proud for the rest of the evening.

Nobody could even touch him after that except perhaps James Stephens. Stephens had a wonderful way with animals; Scarot lost all his dignity before this little man and rolled around the Chinese carpet just to get his attention. Mrs. Ramson had her heart in her mouth all the time Stephens was there because she was afraid Scarot would bite "the precious hands" that had written "The Crock of Gold." The more she warned the author, the more daring he became, tickling Scarot and

The Professor's Wife 307

turning him over, and Scarot squealed and barked till all the guests were thoroughly frightened. You know the way James Stephens is in a drawing room; he's such a tiny man and he is never happy till he is sitting on the floor. He begins at first by sitting properly on the sofa, and then little by little he leans forward and everybody is hypnotized by his Dublin accent—the way he says, "Hooves, the t'umping hooves"—and he leans more and more forward, and gradually he slips farther and farther off the sofa down the sofa leg, and the first thing you know, he is on the floor telling that story about James Joyce. He said that Joyce had invited him into a pub to drink just to tell him that he thought that he was the worst Irish writer that ever was, and then Stephen told Joyce that he thought *he* was the worst Irish writer in the world, and Mrs. Ramson got very flushed and excited and said "Bravo!" clapping her hands and missing the point of the story altogether, saying that she was sure that that Joyce was not a gentleman, he couldn't be after that terrible bore of "Ulysses."

Stephens stayed three days, talking to all the sparrows around the place in the morning; he was the first great man to visit Otterby, and Robert Frost, who came later, said he had bewitched it, that was what made the house so lovely. Professor Ramson always called Frost "the good gray poet," and the Ramsons were both very fond of him too....

Miss Rebecca West . . . was the first, last, and only woman celebrity to be received in Otterby while I was there, for Mrs. Ramson was extremely wary of creatures of that *genre*. "I can't understand how men are so fond of these glittering, brilliant women," she said. Besides, Mrs. Ramson felt a woman's place was in the home at housewifely pursuits. "I can understand how a gentlewoman could write a charming book or paint china or even dabble in water colors, but to write a troubling, serious book like 'The Return of the Soldier' . . . and besides," she whispered to me in the pantry while I was preparing the caviar *canapés* (Miss West's invitation was Myron's doing), "what kind of woman is it that would take for a *nom de plume* the name of that wretched character of Ibsen's? Oh, no, Eric, it's for men to write books and women to feed them and be charming," and she felt more than ever justified in her opinion when she caught rumors of Fannie Hurst's famous party in New York for the English authoress.

The dinner proceeded at a brilliant pace, for Miss West felt Mrs. Ramson's enmity and was extremely sweet and disarming and haughty with her, which set Mrs. Ramson's teeth on edge, as she did not know how to attack politely then; and Miss West, in her simple white gown, which she wore totally without *chic*—"English women always wear evening gowns like sport costumes," said Delia, who had given up *chic* years ago but could still detect the lack of it unerringly in others—kept on directing her attention to Myron, retailing vividly all the gossip of literary London, which so entranced him that he kept on putting more and more of an English accent in his responses, making me feel like a butler more than ever.

"The Grand Concourse of New York," said Miss West, "thrilled me much more than the Champs-Élysées, though I was taken aback at first by the presumption of the name."

"Oh, New York . . . !" said Myron with repressed ecstasy.

"It is certainly one of the architectural wonders of the world," broke in Professor Wadman heavily, "but I shouldn't care to live there. Now, Constantinople . . ."

"Oh, tell us your wonderful 'droshky' story again!" exclaimed Delia brightly to Professor Wadman. Mrs. Ramson used the word "droshky" because she said the story—an adventurous ride in a Turkish carriage—gave her "a Russian feeling," but Professor Wadman was too slow getting under way and Miss West had already launched into the subject of American advertising.

"Advertising," said Myron impressively, "just fails being an art. It employs all the literary effects of a fine poem—I mean it is highly suggestive; it is composed, it has form, construction often more rigid than a sonnet, but inasmuch as it is not an expression of man's spiritual life it fails as an art."

"Some of the phrases are marvelously ingenious," said Miss West, "for instance, one I saw advertising for advertising: 'Tell it to Sweeney; the Stuyvesants will understand.'"

At this point in the dinner Miss West dropped her handkerchief on the floor, but only I saw it and, of course, I immediately picked it up, and she took it so mechanically and so under cover that I felt she might have dropped it on purpose to pull off that very American line from a current musical comedy: "And it still works, it still works . . ." but she said nothing, not even "Thank you."

When I came back into the room with the sherbet, conversation had turned to winter sports.

"Skiing always seemed to me to be a spectacular way of committing suicide," said Myron, "though it rarely happens that we have accidents even on the big jump."

"Our whole family," said Delia, "is very fond of skiing. Of course, I am an invalid"—Miss West looked particularly solicitous—"and never stir from the house in the winter, but Myron is ardent for the sport."

"Not the jumping, my dear," said Myron. "Cross-country, however, is rather agreeable."

As a matter of fact, Myron did very little skiing; indeed, his skiing might be called an annual affair, for it was rarely more than once in the season that he ventured forth, usually on the day of the big ski jumps, when everyone would be on the paths. Myron knew that an interest in sports inspired student respect, but he really did like football and never missed a game in the season. . . .

Miss West left the same night—or rather on the early morning train. . . . As the subject of Rebecca West always had a ragged edge, Mrs. Ramson refused to read her new novel, "The Judge," on the ground that it "would surely be too grim for pleasant reading," and when it was announced that Edna St. Vincent Millay was coming, Mrs. Ramson was strangely deaf to the hints of the president of the Arts Club about the entertainment of Miss Millay while she was in the town, and did not even go to hear the lecture.

Jane, who had returned from a visit in Virginia, and Myron went, . . . like hordes of others, for the poet at that time was enjoying a tremendous collegiate vogue, members of the more esoteric coteries lisping her numbers on every possible occasion, but they went only to be disappointed, for neither the poet nor her husband turned up until late that night, claiming they had pushed the Ford farther than the Ford had carried them, and the whole town was agog the next morning at the story that Edna—everyone called her Edna then—had not eaten at the fashionable hotel but in the lowest of the student hashhouses and there, surrounded by a group of wide-eyed lads, talked so much that her husband at length set his back resolutely to the most audacious listeners and addressed his wife: "For God's sake, Edna, shut up and eat!"

The lecture was held in the Little Theater the next afternoon at four, and it was packed with an impatient and curious crowd. Suddenly, after a long wait, she appeared magically in the aisle, following Bob Merlton, the Arts Club president. She was dressed in a dark blue serge dress, with the skirt heavily embroidered in flowers of the same color, and over her shoulders, in a romantic gesture, was thrown a violently yellow Spanish scarf.

On the platform she looked extremely timid and frail, which impression was augmented by a slight cough in the beginning of her reading. The cave-man protective instinct of every man in the audience was roused, and they were all sympathetically inclined to her anyway.

Before she began speaking she took off her shawl and nonchalantly threw it over the high-backed Italian Renaissance speaker's chair, making an immediate and vivid stage setting for her little play, "Two Slatterns and a King."

Old Mrs. Finckner, on hearing the word "slattern," felt all her suspicions concerning Edna were realized, and did not wait to hear any more, and caused a great deal of disturbance leaving, as she had been seated in the middle of a row rather far front. Miss Millay looked after her with some wonderment, and then, putting her head on one side slightly, her large pale eyes carefully adjusted to be just over the heads of the audience, she began reading in a low, restrained voice. There was no applause when she finished, only a holy silence and a wind of gentle smiles and nods.

The high point of the lecture was reached, however, near the end—the boy who wrote sonnets with Greek titles nearly swooned, while some of the ladies followed after her, whispering the lines to themselves—when her voice began rising and falling in augmented thirds to the tune of

> We were very tired, we were very merry,
> We had been riding back and forth all night on the ferry.

The thrill in the audience, however, was due to the fact that the poem was supposed to be telling a true story: of arriving too late before the closed, disapproving gates of Vassar and so spending the night by aimlessly crossing and recrossing the river.

I remember when Louis Untermeyer came, one of the first questions flung to him was: "What about all these myths attached to Edna St. Vincent Millay?"

"Oh, but they aren't myths," said Untermeyer, with an arch of his eyebrows. "That's just the trouble; they're all true."

At the close of the lecture, of course, the poet was enthusiastically applauded, and she had a hard time escaping the autograph hunters who came with fountain pens in hand and opened books, pleading with her at every step.

Myron was not very well pleased with the lecture. "I cannot help thinking," he said, "that there was more of the afflatus in 'Renascence': 'All I could see from where I stood Were three long mountains and a wood.' She has lost that *naïveté* which was her chief charm, and she has gained nothing by the loss except a shallow, fashionable cleverness."

Mrs. Ramson was even stronger in her denouncement: "Her poems do not read to me as though they were written by a gentlewoman. Perhaps I am mistaking impertinence for candor, but I do know there is a deplorable lack of discretion. When I read that sonnet, 'Oh, World, I cannot hold thee close enough,' I positively blushed, for it is far too intimate a revelation of the soul to be put into such bold words on paper."

The collegiate vogue of Edna held on for a long while nevertheless, until one Sunday the Rev. Dr. Fosdick arrived. He spoke in the late afternoon, a winter vespers service, and the green walls of the chapel were as sour-colored as the skies outside. The chapel was an ugly place, Romanesque Mansard style, with a useless tower all bevels and niches and arrow slits, containing three of the loudest, most jangling, and ill-tuned bells in America. The president thought that part of the lack of religious interest among the students was due to the forbidding aspect of the chapel and its lack of comfort. The seats were of wood and wicker, and on each one was placed a doleful ticket which had to be signed in order to register attendance. Chapel was compulsory, and the only pleasant thing about it was the organ, which Hampden played that day, a beautiful Bach *toccata*. Fosdick spoke, and what he said was conservative enough, but his manner was that of a man of the world, which deceived one to listen. And finally, to give a modern fillip to his discourse, he quoted:

> The world stands out on either side
> No wider than the heart is wide;
> Above the world is stretched the sky,—
> No higher than the soul is high.
> The heart can push the sea and land
> Farther away on either hand;
> The soul can split the sky in two,
> And let the face of God shine through.

The æsthetes shuddered with horror at these lines without knowing who had written them, for they sounded very strange removed from their context, and then, when it dawned that the poet was the beloved Edna, dark suspicions as to her poetry began to rise, for the quotation was far more apt for a sermon than to be used lightly over the teacups.

The Dartmouth Murders
CLIFFORD B. ORR

➢➢➢ Clifford (Kip) Orr 1922 was all his life concerned with the written word, the printed word. He was on the old Boston *Transcript*, he had a spell in book publishing, and longest of all he served on the staff of *The New Yorker*. The following recapture of the Dartmouth atmosphere in the 1920s is taken from his novel, *The Dartmouth Murders* (New York, 1929).

BYRON COATES and I were seniors together at Dartmouth, and roommates. We were roommates by chance as freshmen and by choice the rest of the time. We were good companions, careless friends, and happy enemies when anything small enough arose to fight about. His claim to undergraduate fame lay in his really excellent baritone voice. Mine lay in a facility with the piano and an ability, after a fashion, to write dancy tunes for the annual musical shows. He was more of an athlete than I and dabbled a bit as a sophomore in both track and swimming, and he was also more studious, though his grades almost always fell slightly short of mine. Mine was the quicker wit, his the greater doggedness. We took to each other's friends as easily as we did to each other's clothes. He was apt to be moody and go into fits of silence in which there was no ill nature nor (I thought) any particular depression, and for which, as far as I could see, there was no particular cause.

One of these moods struck him right after the football game that cold Saturday afternoon. And although it was the last game we should see Dartmouth play as undergraduates, and although we were badly beaten in a ragged, dull game in weather which was far from inspiring, he was not football enthusiast enough to let the afternoon's performance throw him very far into the dumps. Yet, as we walked back from the field he begged Professor Bostwick to excuse him from the tea we had planned at the Bostwick house, nodded good-bye to the rest of us, and plodded across the campus to North Massachusetts Hall, our dormitory.

Jean Coates, Byron's sister, was with me. She had come from Vassar for the game and week-end at her own invitation and with Byron's grudging consent, and was handed to me as a companion. I was neither pleased nor displeased. She was, I thought, a nice girl, quite good-looking in a dark, slim way, but a little strange. And she had brought with her the angular Miss Case, some sort of part-time companion and secretary to Jean's mother, as week-end chaperon—a needless procedure which she said her mother demanded. With us, too, at the game and at the tea was Charlie Penlon, who lived two floors below Byron and me in North Mass. and had recently become one of my intimates.

And as for Professor Bostwick, Byron and I had long ago selected him as by far our favourite among the faculty. Tall, slightly stooped, and blondly bearded, he had arrived at college when we were freshmen. He was in the Department of Music, and besides teaching the rudiments of its appreciation and composition, he puttered on the side with glee-club-training, oratorio presentation, and my musical comedies. The same musical bond that held Byron and me together drew us to Bossy, as we called him, and we found him excellent company. He was a bachelor and had the epicurean taste that so often accompanies bachelorhood so that the innumerable meals that By and I had eaten at his house stood out as quite exciting milestones in our college course. Three evenings a week, at the very least, saw us playing his piano, pawing over his scores, eating the steaming dishes his housekeeper delighted in preparing for us, burning his fireplace wood, listening to his tales of Munich, Fontainebleau, the Sorbonne, and the Quartier, and drinking his wine. By the time I was a senior I should no more have omitted Bossy from a social gathering of any size than I should Byron. He was host, guest, companion, and father confessor.

But at the tea that afternoon I was somehow uncomfortable. Byron's leaving it seemed so unnecessary it vaguely troubled me. Bossy played his part as elder all too well and devoted practically all his attention to Miss Case, while Jean and Charlie bantered with each other over the teacups, ignoring the rest of us entirely. And when, as was seldom, the conversation did become general for a moment or two, it was merely to recall a particularly poor try for a field goal that Dartmouth had made, or a certainly unnecessary appreciation of how good the fire felt after the chill of the stadium. And it was somehow with relief, though with great surprise, that I heard myself summoned by Bossy's housekeeper to the telephone.

"Long distance," she said, "for you, Mr. Harris."

I was completely surprised to hear my father's voice: "Is that you, Kenneth?"

"Father!" I cried. "Where are you?"

"In Barre, Vermont. I had to come yesterday on that corporation case and I'm through earlier than I expected. How's the car? Is it in condition? Can you run over and get me? I'll spend the week-end with you."

"To-night?" I asked.

"If it's at all convenient. I've got to have dinner with a man, but if you can get over here in the middle of the evening, everything will be fine. How far is it?"

"I don't know exactly," I said. "Somewhere between fifty and sixty miles, I think. Good two hours run, anyway. . . Oh, Father, it's fall house party, you know, and I've got a girl up—Byron's sister. I may have to bring her along."

"Oh! Sure you want to? Hadn't you rather dance? I can hire a car."

"Not at all. Don't think of it. I'll be there sometime, somehow. At the hotel?"

"At the hotel. Bundle up warm; it's cold as Greenland."

"Right. See you soon."

"Good-bye, Ken."

I broached the subject as soon as I got back to the living room. "Father's over in Barre, Jean, and wants me to come and get him. Had you rather have me find you someone to take you to the dance, or do you want to come along with me? We'd start after dinner, probably about eight."

Jean showed more interest and animation than I'd seen her show the entire week-end. "Oh, Barre by all means! By says it's a beautiful drive, and there's a full moon to-night. Can Miss Case come along?"

"I'm afraid," I said, "that the car'll only hold three, and bring Father back—"

"Don't mind about me," said Miss Case. "I trust you two implicitly."

Shortly afterward we said our thanks and farewells to Bossy and started toward the Inn where Jean was staying. On the way we dropped Charlie at North Mass., and while he was giving his final whispers to Jean I called from the portico up to Byron, suggesting that he come to dinner with us. He leaned out of the window and begged to be excused, saying he'd snatch a bite somewhere and go to bed early. I recognized his mood and didn't press the matter, told him I'd see him later, spoke too brusquely to Charlie, and piloted the women toward the Inn.

All the way, and all through dinner, Miss Case chatted incessantly, trying to draw me out on the subject of music, of which I found she knew practically nothing. Jean sat silent, eating busily for a few moments and then staring ahead of her with a curious, far-off expression. Every now and then she shook her head as if to get rid of a disturbing thought and for a moment or two seemed to take an interest in our conversation. I remember thinking, "Queer family."

It was nearly eight when we were through, and as we rose I said, "Put on something warm, Jean. We've got four hours of cold ahead of us."

She put her hand on my arm. "Ken," she said, "would you mind awfully if I didn't go with you?"

"Why—no," I began, "but—"

"I think I've started a sore throat or something sitting on those damp seats. I'll talk with Miss Case for a while and then go to bed."

"Why, just as you say," I told her. "Only hadn't you rather I'd get someone—Charlie or someone—and let him take you to the dance? It seems a pity—"

"No, Ken, really. I'd much rather not. You run off, and I'll meet you for breakfast. About ten?"

And after further remonstrance I left her standing in the lobby, adamant to the last, but looking after me, her hand clutching the skirt of her dress. And it was at that moment that I thought, "Gosh, if she were only more human, I'm afraid I'd fall for her."

The drive to Barre was lonesome, I'll admit, but I had the rising full moon behind me to make fascinating if bewildering shadows on the rocks and fields, and the Vermont roads twist and turn enough so that no driving upon them is ever really dull. But it was cold and there were mists in the hollows and I was glad when the first lights of Barre shone ahead.

I found Father in the hotel lobby, deep in conversation with a gray-moustached gentleman. Father greeted me affectionately and told me he'd be through in ten minutes. But while I waited, still in my overcoat and gloves, the conversation continued, and it was after eleven when Father rose, made his good-byes, and dispatched a bellboy for his bags.

"Sorry," he said, "but it couldn't be helped," and told me no more.

"Where's the girl?" he asked almost at once.

I told him.

"H'm," he grunted. "Like her brother, isn't she?"

I flared a bit. "What do you mean by that?"

"Why, moody—strange."

"By's not moody," I exclaimed, lying, as usual, in his defense.

"Well, strange then," said Father. "I never liked him, what little I've seen of him. Strange bringing up, I think's the matter with him. What do you know of his father?"

"Nothing," I confessed. "He died when By was very young and Jean was only a baby. I don't think I ever knew what he did, but he left plenty of money."

"And his mother?" asked Father. "In Boston, isn't she, and yet you've never been asked there, even though you've had Byron to Detroit a couple of times."

"Well," I confessed again, "I guess she *is* sort of queer. Likes to keep to herself anyway. But By's all right. And I'm sure Jean is, once you give her a chance."

Conversation lapsed then, and save for Father's inquiry about the health of Bossy, whom he had met several times, and his remark about the Hunter's Moon, which I have recorded before, we spoke very little all the way back to Hanover. Father has always been difficult to me. He is clever, I know, and extremely observant and canny. There are those who say that if he had taken up criminology as a profession instead of as a hobby he would have made a remarkable success. But sons can't judge, and certainly his corporate and contract law failed to interest me. When, in a group, he told of some famous criminal case in which he had assisted as an unofficial expert, I was always fascinated, but between us the common barrier of father and son was almost always reared when we were alone.

However, a Dartmouth man himself, he loved Hanover and came as often as he could. Moreover, he almost always put up with me, sleeping on the couch that By and I kept for guests in our study, and so it was directly to North Mass. that I drove him.

"Go right in, Father," I said, "and go to bed. I'll skip the car down to the garage. You know the room. Top floor, number 39. By'll probably be asleep, but the door is always unlocked. I'll be up in ten minutes."

But I wasn't. After I'd put the car away I dropped into one of the restaurants for a cup of coffee to take the chill out of my bones, and there joined several who were eating after the dance, chatted with them for half an hour, and then walked with them to the Psi U House for another half hour before the fireplace. And the clock on Dartmouth Hall was just striking three across the campus when I reached the dormitory.

I found the door to the room locked. Strange! By and I never locked the door except when we were both away on week-ends. I rattled the knob, and fished for the key I knew I didn't have. Damn Father for locking the door! I knelt and called in a whisper through the letter slot. "Father! Father!"

No answer.

"Father! It's Ken!"

Still no answer.

And then I peered through the slot. The moon was high, and shone

The Dartmouth Murders 319

through the south window directly on the couch, and it was empty, and the room, save for the white rays, was dark.

So now I banged louder and called, "By! By!" But still no answer came, and I suspected that the door from the study into the bedroom was shut and By in his usual sound sleep. Then I cursed the fact that we lived on the top floor, else I could have gone into the room above us and tossed out the rope fire escape with which each college room is supplied, and clambered down it into our bedroom. It was often done, though the coiling of the rope again was a nuisance.

I rattled the knob again, and thought. . . . Jay Corey, Charlie Penlon's roommate, was away for the week-end, I knew. If his door was unlocked, I'd swipe his bed for the night. They lived directly underneath us, two floors below, and—thank heaven!—I found the door unlocked and the room dark. But I swear that as I opened the door I saw the light in Charlie's bedroom suddenly switched off, and I heard the click. But when I tiptoed in, and whispered, "Charlie! Oh, Charlie, are you awake?" I got no response, and saw Jay's bed empty and Charlie's sleeping form in the other bed, his head turned to the wall and the bedclothes pulled tight around his neck.

I threw off all but my underwear and climbed into the empty bed, shivering in the wind which whirled in through the window until I had closed the door to the study. For half an hour, perhaps, I lay awake, wondering about Father and watching the tops of the trees waving in the wind above the old, old cemetery that lies almost below the rear walls of North Mass.

I suppose I slept. I know I slept, but it couldn't have been long, or the light thump on the window would not have awakened me. But it came, a decided thump—muffled, uncanny.

I opened my eyes and stared at the window. The moon was already nearing the west, and I could see as plain as day. The window was open at the bottom, and the shade was pulled down some ten inches from the top, but there was nothing there. And yet—

Thump! Muffled. Dull.

Two stories up. What could knock, even softly, on the window?

What the hell!

I slept again.

And again I woke. It was faintly dawn, and I could see and feel that the clear cold night had given way to a damp, foggy, chilly morning. I lay, for some reason, wide awake, cursing the unusual luck that stopped my sleep so early on a Sunday. And the Dartmouth Hall clock struck a cold, damp six.

Thump!

It came again, muffled as before, but clearly something rapping at the window.

I jumped from the bed, grabbed the string of the window shade, and ran it up.

And there, against the dawn, swaying so that even as I watched they came against the window with a dull impact, were two bare feet!

I think I made a guttural noise. I'm not sure. I know that in a moment my head was out of the open lower sash and I was looking up. And from our room, hanging on the rope fire escape, with his wet pajamas sticking to his skin, was Byron.

The Disenchanted
BUDD SCHULBERG

⋙ For Manley Halliday, read F. Scott Fitzgerald. For Shep, read Budd Schulberg 1936. For Victor Milgrim, read Walter Wanger 1915. For Webster, read Dartmouth. The disastrous scene at The Inn, and there is little fiction in it, is taken from the Schulberg novel, *The Disenchanted* (New York, 1950), which concerns in part a trip to Hanover by Schulberg and the broken Fitzgerald, who were collaborating on a movie script, "Winter Carnival," that was being filmed on campus.

AT BOTH ENDS of the long table in the inner lounge were large cut-glass bowls filled with a timid concoction popularly known as Faculty Punch, an unsuccessful compromise between teetotal beverage and alcoholic fillip. Although at least a hundred academicians had gathered to welcome these strange birds descended on them from Hollywood, there was such an emphasis on decorum that it did not sound like a social gathering at all but more like an assembly of lip readers standing around murmuring to themselves.

The entrance of Manley Halliday was a sly joke, passing swiftly from one end of the gathering to the other. These cool, clean, sober, respectable people were duly shocked, but in a way that pleased them. They began to share the delectable piece of gossip, *Halliday is positively plastered*, that murmured and snickered discreetly through the lounge.

The humor of it did not escape Manley Halliday as he stood on the landing looking in at this gathering of the courteous and proper. He had a reasonably clear appreciation of the spectacle he was making of himself but he was neither embarrassed nor otherwise disturbed. There was his basic independence, his old enjoyment of shocking staid gatherings and, working just below the level of consciousness, his superiority to all those who had lived less fully and with far less accomplishment. What also carried him into the room was a dim but overwhelming sense of inevitability, a sense of being borne on through darkness, through strange corridors, unfamiliar rooms, as on one of those boats gliding through an amusement pier's tunnel-of-love, except that those had a clearly identified beginning and end and offered a journey for the light-headed who had parted with a specific amount of small change to immerse themselves in a routine experience with darkness, while this journey was through a tunnel whose end no one could foretell, that grew darker and darker and for which he had not had to pay anything in the beginning (on the contrary they were paying *him*) but for which a terrible price might be exacted before he could exit.

Shep was helplessly aware of the grotesque figure slumped beside him, a bloodless face behind a three-day beard, a crumpled body in a stained and crumpled suit that had become so baggy as to suggest the soiled classé elegance of Charlie Chaplin. The comparison, thought Shep, was more than casual, for Manley Halliday in his humiliating contrast to the orderly people gathered to honor him had something of Charlie's innate dignity, his laugh-provoking, absurd, yet somehow impressive superiority to the self-possessed assembly.

When Victor Milgrim [the film's producer] saw them his face lost its assurance. For a moment it actually could not seem to find any expression at all and remained blank. Then, when the Secretary to the President said, "Ah, Mr. Halliday," and came forward to intercept him, Milgrim muttered something about "how hard he's been working, hasn't even had time to clean up" and decided on the desperate measure of passing Halliday off as a colorful eccentric—the traditional mad genius of the arts.

Manley Halliday started forward and—perhaps through accident, perhaps through buckling of the knees—stumbled and might have fallen if Shep had not in quick reflex caught his elbow.

The Dean, who had made excellent grades for an athlete at Webster, made a remark Shep couldn't quite hear, yet got the pith of it—something about this beginning to look like a real Hollywood cocktail party, complete with drunks who got two thousand a week. Shep sensed the hostility this outlandish income aroused in educated people having their troubles being middle class on three to six thousand dollars a year.

The Secretary threaded them smoothly through the assembly, introducing them to the more important of the campus hierarchy who acknowledged Halliday with conscious good manners. "Well, you must be having quite an *adventure*, Stearns," said Prof. Blodgett, an owlish, apple-cheeked bachelor of fifty known for the catty quality of his wit. Loyally, Shep felt he had to say, "Yes, I'm learning a lot from Mr. Halliday." "I'm sure you are," said Prof. Blodgett with an emphasis that stung. "Now tell me, is this going to be one of those super-colossal productions, or merely colossal?"

Another English professor, Bridgman, a young man who had never known youth, said to Manley Halliday with unconscious cruelty, "I had occasion to reread *Friends and Foes* last summer. It holds up surprisingly well."

"Well, don't we all?" Manley Halliday said.

Farther down the table they met Prof. Crofts, the Emersonian who had had such hopes for Shep as an undergraduate and who could not pretend to be pleased that Shep was "doing movies." With the characteristic directness that bordered on rudeness, Crofts asked, "Will you be able to get anything of your own into this film?" Shep answered uncomfortably, "Not this one. Maybe eventually—I hope." Then Prof. Crofts had turned to Halliday. "Did Shep tell you he chose your work for his final paper in my course? He admired you very much. Although he saw you as the classic decline of the middle-class artist."

Manley Halliday lowered the punch glass someone had handed him. "Well, I admire him as the clashic decline of the young Marxist critic, so we're even. Maybe the reashon we admire each other so mush is becaush we've been declining together so mush."

"He's a total wreck, isn't he?" Prof. Crofts managed to say to Shep in an undertone as the Secretary steered Halliday along. Shep said, "Well, he does have another book he's working on." "Then what is he doing up here on the movie?" Prof. Crofts wanted to know. "Needs money," Shep said. "Huh!" snorted Prof. Crofts, transcendental as Emerson.

At last they reached Milgrim who was cornered by Prof. Connolly, the head of the Drama Department, a worldly monk of a man. Prof. Connolly was springing on Victor Milgrim a cherished idea. Ever since he had been brought to Hollywood as technical adviser for *Twelfth Night* and had had pictures taken with Bette Davis, Paul Muni and George Arliss (the one with his arm around Joan Crawford he had decided not to hang with the others in his office), he had been movie struck. It long had been his plan to establish a movie course with a library of actual scenarios and perhaps with Hollywood notables as guest lecturers. "I thought perhaps we might have a special wing in the library," Prof. Connolly was saying. "With your permission, the 'Victor Milgrim Room,' with bound movie scripts and a collection of all the books and magazines on the films."

"If a thousand dollars will start the ball rolling," Milgrim replied. "I'm sure I can get Academy co-operation on old scripts."

"Most gratifying," Prof. Connolly purred. "And perhaps—I know how busy you are—you could deliver the opening lecture on The Art of the Cinema."

"I'm delighted you recognize that it is an art," Milgrim said modestly.

"Oh, my, yes. Before you leave perhaps you'll have time to look over an article I'm doing. I call it 'The Eighth and Liveliest Art.'"

"This summer you should come out as my guest and study film production at first-hand," Milgrim said, confident he was picking up the scent of his honorary degree. "You can use one of our executive offices. I'll be glad to loan you a secretary."

"That would be elegant," Prof. Connolly beamed.

All through this buttery exchange, Manley Halliday had been standing by with his eyes practically closed, his head bent forward as if too heavy for his neck, his legs strategically apart to afford better balance for his swaying. Milgrim and the professor had been ignoring him politely when suddenly he interrupted with a blurt:

"Scrip's no good."

The two men looked up warily. Like a man talking in his sleep, Manley Halliday continued.

" 'S like reading a book about plumbing. On'y way t' learn how to fit th' pipes t'gether is t' get some pipes 'n try it. Let 'im send you the pipes, movie camera, sound equipment, a movieola, study a picture on y'r movieola, take it apart 'n put it t'gether again. Learn more that way 'n memorizing Eisenstein."

"Yes, yes, I quite see your point, Mr. Halliday," Prof. Connolly promptly agreed. "Of course if Mr. Milgrim could spare us some movie equipment..." He did everything but rub his palms together.

People were coming up and wanting to be introduced to Halliday, a few with genuine admiration, the rest merely sightseers eager to get back to their friends with a vivid story of Manley Halliday's debacle. —"I saw him at a party in New York years and years ago," Shep heard someone saying behind him. "God, what a beautiful man! He's gone completely to pieces."

Then Shep knew what it was that had been angering him. Manley *was* drunk and he was a spectacle. But they seemed *glad* this had happened to him. That is what galled.

"Shep!"

"Hello, Hank."

Shep had been strong for Prof. Osborne from the time they had worked together in the League Against War and Fascism, in the years when most of the faculty hesitated even to sign a petition against the Nazis for fear of forfeiting their precious and precarious objectivity. But at this particular moment, knowing Osborne's friendship for Halliday, Shep welcomed him like a fellow-countryman in a strange land.

"Shep, I think we ought to get Manley upstairs."

"Have you seen him yet?"

"I'm afraid so. But I don't think he's seen me. Or maybe he doesn't want to see me."

"He's—he's in pretty tough shape."

"How long has he been drinking?"

"Let's see—'bout three days."

"Damn. I read somewhere, I thought he was all through with his drinking."

"He was. Hank, it was my fault. I started him drinking on the plane. I didn't know."

"Aw he's been doing it for years. I love him but damn it makes me mad, a man like that, well, anyway, the big talent of our crowd, deliberately destroying himself."

Near them Manley Halliday was fortifying himself with punch while holding off a group that could best be described as fawning tormentors. "What makes you think you know enough to cri'size *Shadow Ball*? Bet you anything you don' even understan' *Shadow Ball*. C'n see it in y'r face. Jus' because you grew up without a sense o' humor—prol'ly a Presbyterian minister's son—you mistook it for intelligence."

"Man can still see in the dark," Osborne said. "Bridgie is a small-town New England minister's son. But we better get him out of here before he swings on the Dean. I know the symptoms."

"Come on, Man, let's go up to your room. I haven't had a chance to talk to you," Osborne said, taking Halliday's arm firmly.

Manley Halliday thought he heard, imagined he saw Hank Osborne as one of the phantom figures looming up in this dark labyrinth where the past twisted with terrible confusion into the present. Remembering the arm of Hank Osborne as having guided him many times along the edge of the precipice, he went along peacefully. He didn't even bother with *hellos*, for this was not a meeting in time and place but more like the resumption of a memory. . . .

COMMENCEMENT 1955

A Graduation Address

ROBERT FROST

≫ Commencement day in June 1955 dawned gray and drear. There was rain, there was more rain, until any thought of outdoor exercises had been washed away. Graduation was held that year in the Alumni Gymnasium, overcrowded, overheated, humid from all the wet clothes of the assembled. It was in this atmosphere that Robert Frost 1896 delivered the graduation address, one hard to hear because of the hall's poor acoustics. It was an address that was typical of the poet; in fact, he had said almost the same things many times before, and that is partly why it deserves reprinting. This was Robert Frost, complete with variations in the spoken verse.

THIS IS a rounding out for you, and a rounding out is the main part of it. You're rounding out four years. I'm rounding out something like 63, isn't it? But it is a real rounding out for me. I'm one of the original members of the Outing Club—me and Ledyard. You don't know it, and I shouldn't tell it perhaps, but I go every year, once a year, to touch Ledyard's monument down there, as the patron saint of freshmen who run away. And I ran away because I was more interested in education than anybody in the College at the time.

I thought I'd say to you just a few words about that, and so as to lead up to two or three poems of my own. I usually am permitted to say a poem or two—am expected to. I'll make them short and easy for you to listen to.

But you came to college bringing with you something to go on with—that was the idea from my point of view: something to go on with. And you brought it with an instinct, I hope, to keep it—not to have it taken away from you, not to be bamboozled out of it or scared out of it by any fancy teachers. I've known teachers with a real hanker for ravishing innocence. They like to tell you things that will disturb you.

Now, I think the College itself has given you one thing of importance I'd like to speak of. It's given you, slowly, gradually, the means to deal with that sort of thing, not only in college but the rest of your life. The formula would be something like this: always politely accept the other man's premises. Don't contradict anybody. It's contentious and ill natured. Accept the premises—take it up where it's given you, and then show 'em what you can make of it. You've been broadened and enlarged to where you can listen to almost anything without losing your temper or your self-confidence.

You came from the "Bible belt," say. You are confronted with the fact of evolution. It was supposed to disturb you about your God. But you found a way to say—either with presence of mind, wittily, or slowly with meditation—you found the way to say, "Sure, God probably didn't make man out of mud. But He made him out of *prepared mud.*" You still had your God, you see.

You were a Bostonian and you had been brought up to worship the cod. To you the cod was sacred and her eggs precious. You were confronted with facts of waste in nature. One cod egg is all that survives of a million. And you said—what did you say? You found something to say, surely. You said, "Perhaps those other eggs were necessary in order to make the ocean a proper broth for the one to grow up in. No waste; just expense." And so on.

I myself have been bothered by certain things. I've been bothered by rapid reading. All my teaching days I've heard rapid reading advocated as if it were something to attain to. Yes, sure; accept the premises, always, as a gentleman. Rapid reading—I'm one of the rapidest of readers. I look on all the reading you do in college—ten times as much a year as I do in ten years, and I'm a reader—I look on it as simply *scansion*. You're simply looking the books over to see whether you want to read 'em, later. It comes to that; and accepting it that way. The word's gone forth, you happen to know probably, that the rapid reading is going to be played down in the educational world. But it can be regarded as simple scansion.

What you're doing as a rapid reader is saying, per paragraph, per paragraph, "Yeah, I know" (two words you see in it)—"Yeah, that's about 'togetherness.'" "Yeah." And, paragraph by paragraph you say, "Yes, I know." It doesn't take long to know that that's what it would say if you read it all. And you can do that by the chapter—the chapter titles. You say, "Yeah," you know, "I know what that chapter would be." You can go further than that: "I can tell by the spine of the book." Very rapid reader.

Always fall in with what you're asked to accept, you know; fall in with it—and turn it your way. Expression like "divine right."—Divine right? yes,—if you let me make what I want of it: the answerability of the ruler, of the leader; the first answerability to himself. That's his divine right. First answerability to his highest in himself, to his God.

Then one more that I'd just like to speak of—you run on to these things all the time. I live on them. I'm going to tell you that every single one of my poems is probably one of these adaptions that I've made. I've taken whatever you give me and made it what I want it to be. That's what every one of the poems is. I look over them. They are not arguments. I've never contradicted anybody. My object in life has been to hold my own *with* whatever's going—not *against*, but *with*—to hold my own. To come through college holding my own so that I won't be made over beyond recognition by my family and my home town, if I ever go back to it. It's a poor sort of person, it seems to me, that delights in thinking, "I have had four years that have transformed me into somebody my own mother won't know." Saint Paul had one conversion. Let's leave it to Saint Paul. Don't get converted. Stay.

This one turns up, too—another expression. They say, "If eventually, why not now?" I say, "Yeah," but also, "If eventually, why now?"

You've got to handle these things. You've got to have something to say to the Sphinx. You see, that's all. And you've been, I'm pretty sure —you've come more and more to value yourself on being able to handle whatever turns up.

What would you say to this one? (You probably haven't encountered it. I have lately.) We hired a Swede to come over here and pass an expert's opinion on our form of government. And after he passed his judgment on it, we invited him back and gave him another honorary degree, just like this. (Never mind his name—we won't go into names—maybe I've forgotten it.) But, anyway, did you hear what his judgment was? That our form of government is a conspiracy against the common man.

You've been enlarged and broadened to where you can listen to anything without getting mad. So have I. But I have to have something to say to that, sooner or later—on the spur of the moment, to show my wit, or at leisure, you know, to show my ability at reasoning, my reasoning powers. Well, the answer to that is that that's what it was intended to be. It was intended to be a conspiracy against the common man. Let him make himself *uncommon*. He wasn't to be put in the saddle. And so on. Now I conclude that.

This is an emotional occasion to me. Mr. Dickey has made it an emotional occasion, very much of an emotion, such as has seldom happened to me in my life. I've been in and out of Dartmouth all these many years and known the presidents—no one so intimately as I've known Mr. Dickey. Part of what I'm saying to you springs from what he's been saying. He spoke very sternly to you; splendidly, with splendid sternness.

What I ask of you is the same: Have you got enlarged a little bit? Have you broadened a little bit in these years, as you might have outside? (I don't know, maybe more so in college than out.) Have you got where you can take care of yourself in the conflicts of thought—in the stresses of thought, not conflicts, stresses. I'd rather say hold my own *with* anybody than hold my own *against* anybody—with him. That makes a polite evening—and polite class, a better class than any other.

Shall I say you a poem or two? And you can maybe guess what I was doing in the poems, after what I've said. Suppose I say to you one called "Mending Wall"—countrified poem. And shall I tell you beforehand what I was dealing with in it? I'd heard that life was cellular, in the body and outside the body. Nobody'd ever put it in so many words, but I kept hearing something that made me see that life was cellular. (Even the Communists have cells.) All life is cellular, that's all the poem says. It didn't say that when I was writing it; it didn't say it until long afterward. It's of the nature of mythology to be wiser than philosophy, because it says things in stories before it says them in abstractions. All mythology's like that. The Greeks' mythology covered everything we've ever thought in philosophy, but covered it in stories. And the abstraction emerges even with the man that makes the stories.

> Something there is that doesn't love a wall,
> That sends the frozen-ground-swell under it,
> And spills the upper boulders in the sun;
> And makes gaps even two can pass abreast.
> The work of hunters is another thing:
> I have come after them and made repair
> Where they have left not one stone on a stone,
> But they would have the rabbit out of hiding,
> To please the yelping dogs. The gaps I mean,
> No one has seen them made or heard them made,
> But at spring mending-time we find them there.
> I let my neighbor know beyond the hill;
> And on a day we meet to walk the line
> And set the wall between us once again.
> We keep the wall between us as we work.
> To each the boulders that have fallen to each.
> And some are loaves and some so nearly balls
> We have to use a spell to make them balance:
> 'Stay where you are until our backs are turned!'
> We wear our fingers rough with handling them.
> Oh, just another kind of out-door game,
> One on a side. It comes to little more:
> There where it is we do not need the wall:
> He is all pine and I am apple orchard.
> My apple trees will never get across
> And eat the cones under his pines, I tell him.
> He only says, 'Good fences make good neighbors.'
> Spring is the mischief in me, and I wonder
> If I could put a notion in his head:
> '*Why* do they make good neighbors? Isn't it
> Where there are cows? But here there are no cows.
> Before I built a wall I'd ask to know
> What I was walling in or walling out,

And to whom I was like to give offense.
Something there is that doesn't love a wall,
That wants it down.' I could say 'Elves' to him,
But it's not elves exactly, and I'd rather
He said it for himself. I see him there
Bringing a stone grasped firmly by the top
In each hand, like an old-stone savage armed.
He moves in darkness as it seems to me,
Not of woods only and the shade of trees.
He will not go behind his father's saying,
And he likes having thought of it so much
He says again, 'Good fences make good neighbors.'

See, that's all about life being cellular. I didn't think of that 'til years after I wrote it. And you may be sure it is—walls going down and walls coming up, between nations and inside your own body. In seven years, you know, you're a different person, though you don't notice it.

Then, little one—two more—little one, again. This is called "Stopping by Woods on a Snowy Evening."

Whose woods these are I think I know.
His house is in the village though;
He will not see me stopping here
To watch his woods fill up with snow.

My little horse must think it queer
To stop without a farmhouse near
Between the woods and frozen lake
The darkest evening of the year.

He gives his harness bells a shake
To ask if there is some mistake.
The only other sound's the sweep
Of easy wind and downy flake.

The woods are lovely, dark and deep.
But I have promises to keep,
And miles to go before I sleep,
And miles to go before I sleep.

A Graduation Address

Now everybody suspected there was something in that line, "But I have promises to keep." You see. And they pursued me about that, and so I've decided to have a meaning for it. Finally, a committee waited on me about it. I said, "Promises may be divided into two kinds: those I make for myself, and those my ancestors made for me known as the social contract." See, that's a way out of that.

Then, two more—one another little one. I'd like to say one to you that I wrote when I was about your age—just about the time ('95 or 6 along there) just when I should have been graduating, you know, instead of now.

I saw you all I suppose, pretty much—'tis but yesterday, isn't it, we were in the G.I.—had you all where I could talk to you—about Tom Paine I talked about to you there. I didn't get any great answer out of you. You didn't get angry enough.

This one is called—it's better without the name. It's about our American Revolution. I've met *many* who thought the British were to blame, and I've met a *few* Americans who thought the Americans were to blame. Well, it doesn't matter. Accept the premises. Anybody's premise is all right. Nobody was to blame. All it was was the beginning of the end of colonialism. No animus on my part.

> The land was ours before we were the land's.

It's all summed up in that, you see—

> The land was ours before we were the land's.
> She was our land more than a hundred years
> Before we were her people. She was ours
> In Massachusetts, in Virginia,
> But we were England's, still colonials,
> Possessing what we still were unpossessed by,
> Possessed by what we now no more possessed.
> Something we were withholding made us weak
> Until we found out that it was ourselves
> We were withholding from our land of living,
> And forthwith found salvation in surrender.
> Such as we were we gave ourselves outright
> (The deed of gift was many deeds of war)

> To the land vaguely realizing westward,
> But still unstoried, artless, unenhanced,
> Such as she was, such as she would become.

That poem's twenty-five or thirty or forty years old. It isn't just got up for the occasion of all this talk about the end of colonialism. Ours was the beginning of the end of colonialism, and that poem makes the point that ours was the beginning of the end of colonialism.

Then, one more. You know you hear about retreat and you hear about escape. When people talk about escape, I want to talk about retreat. Just that way it's pretty near the same thing, but just my shade of difference. This is the last one. This is called "Birches."

> When I see birches bend to left and right
> Across the lines of straighter, darker trees,
> I like to think some boy's been swinging them.
> But swinging doesn't bend them down to stay
> As ice storms do. Often you must have seen them
> Loaded with ice a sunny winter morning
> After a rain. They click upon themselves
> As the breeze rises, and turn many-colored
> As the stir cracks and crazes their enamel.
> Soon the sun's warmth makes them shed crystal shells
> Shattering and avalanching on the snow-crust—
> Such heaps of broken glass to sweep away
> You'd think the inner dome of heaven had fallen.
> They are dragged to the withered bracken by the load,
> And they seem not to break; though once they are bowed
> So low for long, they never right themselves:
> You may see their trunks arching in the woods
> Years afterwards, trailing their leaves on the ground
> Like girls on hands and knees that throw their hair
> Before them over their heads to dry in the sun.
> But I was going to say when Truth broke in
> With all her matter-of-fact about the ice-storm
> I should prefer to have had some boy bend them
> As he went out or in to fetch the cows—
> Some boy too far from town to learn baseball,
> Whose only play was what he found himself,
> Summer or winter, and could play alone.

One by one he subdued his father's trees
By riding them down over and over again
Until he took the stiffness out of them,
And not one but hung limp. He learned all there was
To learn about not launching out too soon
And so not carrying the tree away
Clear to the ground. He always kept his poise
To the top branches, climbing carefully
With the same pains you use to fill a cup
Up to the brim, and even above the brim.
Then he flung outward, feet first with a swish,
Kicking his way down through the air to the ground.
So was I once myself a swinger of birches.
And so I dream of going back to be.
It's when I'm weary of considerations,
And life is too much like a pathless wood
Where your face burns and tickles with the cobwebs
Broken across it, and one eye is weeping
From a twig's having lashed across it open.
I'd like to get away from earth awhile
And then come back to it and begin over.
May no fate wilfully misunderstand me
And half grant what I wish and snatch me away
Not to return. Earth's the right place for love:
I don't know where it's likely to go better.
I'd like to go by climbing a birch tree,
And climb black branches up a snow white trunk
Toward heaven, till the tree could bear no more,
But dipped its top and set me down again.
One could do worse than be a swinger of birches.

Shall I say one absurd one in parting? Somebody congratulated me the other night on getting through an occasion without ever reciting this one. It's hard—it's a sort of temptation to sort of break it up, you know, break up the meeting. One of the things that you suspect the academic world of is overpowering, overwhelming departmentalism, you know—passing-the-buckism, whatever you call it. But now I've never suffered from that at all. That's why I ran away and all that. I've just kept dodging round—just the same as I ran away, I dodged—and

I've never got caught at the departmentalism, never suffered from it. But you'd think I had from this poem. This is an agony. Shows where agonies come from, you know, from nowhere. The less there is to them, the stronger they can be.

I'll emphasize the rhyme and meter in this for the fun of it. Of course you've heard me do it, some of you have. This is about an ant I met in Key West. It's not a New England poem at all, I like to say that disclaimer. It's got nothing to do with college or my having suffered from departmentalism, but it's just *very objective*.

>   An ant on the tablecloth
>   Ran into a dormant moth

See, cloth-moth, that's the way it's made—

>   An ant on the tablecloth
>   Ran into a dormant moth
>   Of many times his size.
>   He showed not the least surprise.
>   His business wasn't with such.
>   He gave it scarcely a touch,
>   And was off on his duty run.
>   But if he encountered one
>   Of the hive's enquiry squad
>   Whose work is to find out God
>   And the nature of time and space,
>   He would put him onto the case.

Philosophy department—

>   Ants are a curious race;
>   One crossing with hurried tread
>   The body of one of their dead
>   Isn't given a moment's arrest—
>   Seems not even impressed.
>   But he no doubt reports to any
>   With whom he crosses antennae,
>   And they no doubt report
>   To the higher up at court.
>   Then word goes forth in Formic:

That's that acid language the critics use—

> Then word goes forth in Formic:
> 'Death's come to Jerry McCormic,
> Our selfless forager Jerry.

See, that's socialism in a line—

> Our selfless forager Jerry.
> Will the special Janizary
> Whose office it is to bury
> The dead of the commissary
> Go bring him home to his people.
> Lay him in state on a sepal.
> Wrap him for shroud in a petal.
> Embalm him with ichor of nettle.
> This is the word of your Queen.'
> And presently on the scene
> Appears a solemn mortician;
> And taking formal position
> With feelers calmly atwiddle,
> Seizes the dead by the middle,
> And heaving him high in air,
> Carries him out of there.
> No one stands round to stare.
> It is nobody else's affair.
>
> It couldn't be called ungentle.
> But how thoroughly departmental.

And remember for me, will you, the one thing, that you've reached the place where you can listen to what anybody says and, you know, just pull it your way with one little, nice pull. That's what makes life.

DARTMOUTH, there is no music for our singing,
No words to bear the burden of our praise;
Yet how can we be silent and remember
The splendor and the fullness of her days?
Who can forget her soft September sunsets?
Who can forget those hours that passed like dreams?
The long cool shadows floating on the campus,
The drifting beauty where the twilight streams?

Who can forget her sharp and misty mornings,
The clanging bells, the crunch of feet on snow,
Her sparkling noons, the crowding into Commons,
The long white afternoons, the twilight glow?
See! by the light of many thousand sunsets,
Dartmouth undying, like a vision starts.
Dartmouth, the gleaming, dreaming walls of Dartmouth,
Miraculously builded in our hearts!

—from "Dartmouth Undying"
Franklin McDuffee 1921

PRINTED AT THE STINEHOUR PRESS
LUNENBURG · VERMONT

www.ingramcontent.com/pod-product-compliance
Lightning Source LLC
Chambersburg PA
CBHW030302080526
44584CB00012B/413